The World of Flora
Thompson Revisited

The World of Flora Thompson Revisited

CHRISTINE BLOXHAM

TEMPUS

Frontispiece: Flora Thompson. (Henry Westbury)

First published 2007

Tempus Publishing Limited
The Mill, Brimscombe Port,
Stroud, Gloucestershire, GL5 2QG
www.tempus-publishing.com

British Library Cataloguing in Publication Data.
A catalogue record for this book is available from the British Library.

ISBN 978 0 7524 4348 5

Typesetting and origination by Tempus Publishing Limited
Printed in Great Britain

Contents

The road leading from Cottisford to the hamlet of Juniper Hill, which can be seen in the distance. Flora and her brother Edwin walked along this road to school at Cottisford in the 1880s. (David Watts)

Acknowledgements

It is impossible to thank enough, the many people who have kindly given me items of local and family information and given me access to material and photographs, without which this would have been a slim and vastly inferior book. My thanks go above all to David Watts, a leading expert on the history of the Bicester area – without whom this book would have been a great deal slimmer – who has generously not only offered his vast expertise and information on the Oxfordshire area, done additional research and generously contributed much on the Wallington family and collated most of the family trees, but has lent many wonderful local photographs. His father, the late John Watts, generously gave me access to unpublished material and photographs, James and Audrey Lambert gave information on the Waine family history, William and Beryl Plumb and Miss Agnes Plumb gave fascinating information about the forge at Fringford and lent photographs. Henry Westbury very generously let me have access to family photographs and to unpublished letters written by Flora Thompson to her nephew, Leslie Castle. David Morris and his wife, who kept the Fox Inn at Juniper Hill for many years, have generously allowed me access to unpublished information about Juniper Hill and the use of photographs. Baroness von Maltzahn and Doris Lown also kindly let me use photographs. The late Patrick Kirkby gave me access to his researches and much encouragement. Peter Barrington wrote an article about my research for the *Bicester Advertiser*, from which I gleaned help from many people. William Hunwick gave me his photograph of Flora's moving tombstone.

Gillian Lindsay, author of *Flora Thompson: The Story of the 'Lark Rise' Writer*, generously shared her expertise, particularly her fascinating research into Flora's adult life, and Anne Mallinson gave invaluable help about Flora's time in the Liphook area. Jo Smith gave advice on Grayshott and let me read his fascinating plays about Flora's life in Grayshott and Liphook and lent photographs.

Tony Webster has kindly lent photographs of Buckingham and he and other committee members of the Old Gaol Museum, Buckingham have generously shared information and permitted me to use photographs. Kathleen Hunt gave much interesting local information and access to family photographs, while Madeleine Bennett gave valuable information about and checked the chapter on Ardley and Fewcott. Mrs Watkins gave information about the Baines family and Mr P.E. Morrall provided information about and photographs of the Mansfield's grocery shop in Fringford. Mr Norman Whitton added information about the Whitton and Kirby families. Many local people gave information, including Flora's nephew Bernard Lane, Revd Ricky Yates, Mr and Mrs Winnington Ingram, Gordon Allan, Mr and Mrs Bell and Simon and Vanda Emery (who are descended from Uncle Tom and revealed his real identity). Susanne Shatford introduced me to genealogy (which has now become my obsession) and helped with work on the Timms and Lapper family trees. Peter Hoare has painstakingly copied and touched up photographs. Gordon Crossley, Archivist of the Fort Garry Horse Regiment, Winnipeg, supplied the information about Edwin Timms' army career. Carol Knight kindly provided information about the Thompson family.

My thanks go also to Oxford University Press, the librarians in Oxford and Winchester and at the Harry Ransom Humanities Research Centre at the University of Texas at Austin. I am infinitely grateful to my late father, John Bloxham, for drawing a diagram, to my husband, Norman Blanks, who has taken on many extra tasks while I have been writing the book, providing invaluable help with all my computer problems and proofreading, and our sons, Richard and Peter, and to Hugo Brunner, my first publisher who has let me expand the book way beyond the original brief and been very patient with me. My thanks also go to Tempus and to my patient editor Nicola Guy who had enough faith in the book to let me produce a revised edition, and gave me the space to do it.

Introduction

Flora Thompson once met an ancient gipsy woman when she was wandering in the woods and was rewarded for helping her find medicinal wood-sage by having her fortune read:

> ... to thank me she promised me all the delightful happenings she could lay tongue to. No, not quite all; there was no dark or fair stranger. Neither did she promise me riches: she passed such things over disdainfully, as stock properties kept for the commonalty who crossed her hand with a shilling. She even confided that she did not go by the hand at all, that it was only a formality to secure the shilling.
>
> 'It's the face,' she said, 'not the hand. It's all writ in the face what a person is. And if I know what you are, I can tell pretty well how things'll go with you!'
>
> She was certainly able to read the secret desire, for she promised me love and praise and friendship!
>
> 'You are goin' to be loved,' she said, 'loved by a lot o' folks – strangers shall become friends – people all over –' and she waved her bundle of wood-sage to include the entire horizon.
>
> Nonsense, of course. Yet after I parted from her, I trod more lightly, and strange to say, when I reached home I found a letter awaiting me from a complete stranger praising some trifle I had written.

Flora Thompson, from *The Peverel Papers* quoted in *A Country Calendar*, Oxford University Press 1979, p. 131

The gipsy's prophecy was made to Flora Thompson at a time long before the publication of her famous trilogy *Lark Rise to Candleford*, when she can have had no inkling of how popular her work was to become, indeed she died just as her work was beginning to become known. That her trilogy was written at all came as a great surprise to many who had known her. When the villagers of Juniper Hill heard that their Flora Timms had published a book, they were dumbfounded and racked their brains to recall the stonemason's daughter they had known as a child, (she had not lived in Juniper since she was fourteen, and had seldom visited it as an adult) and the only thing that came to mind about her was that she was good at skipping! Flora Thompson, born Flora Jane Timms on 5 December 1876, was the daughter of Albert Timms, a stonemason, and his wife Emma who had been a nursemaid, who brought her up in the tiny village of Juniper Hill in North Oxfordshire. She was a quiet child, an observer rather than participator from a very early age, always noticeably different from the boisterous village children, who carefully noted in her mind details of the people and places around her. Most of the girls who were contemporary with her at school left to become servants, whereas she was lucky enough to find work in a Post Office and, by dint of reading as much as she could, succeeded in becoming a poet and author, writing material as diverse as romantic short stories, nature notes and ghost writing for a big-game hunter. She even had the confidence in her own abilities and the desire to help others in her own position, to found and successfully run the Peverel Society to encourage poets and give writing lessons. However she will be best remembered for her *pièces de résistance,* the trilogy *Lark Rise to Candleford* and *Still Glides the Stream*, books written in her later years, as she began to realise that people were interested in Victorian rural life, based very much on her memories of her childhood. A tribute to her quality as a writer is that these were published by the Oxford University Press, which had to describe *Lark Rise to Candleford* as autobiography as the Press did not publish fiction, but were so impressed by Flora's writing that they were determined to publish it. Not only did they publish it, but Sir Humphrey Milford, the publisher, gave her a great accolade when he wrote in the *Periodical*, the house magazine of the Oxford University Press, that he considered that the two most important books he had published during his twenty-two years at the Press were Arnold Toynbee's *A Study of History* and Flora Thompson's *Lark Rise to Candleford*.

Although her first publication, a slim volume of poetry entitled *Bog Myrtle and Peat* has long been out of print we are fortunate that a wide variety of Flora's work has been published since her death. Margaret Lane wrote a short biography of Flora and has edited various pieces including some of the nature notes she wrote for *The Catholic Fireside*: *Heatherley* (a continuation of her autobiography which covered her time at the Post Office in Grayshott) and some of her poems for a book entitled *The Country Calendar*. Julian Shuckburgh edited a longer version of her nature notes in *The Peverel Papers*, and Gillian Lindsay has skilfully researched her biography: *Flora Thompson: The Story of the 'Lark Rise' Writer*, which reveals much about her hitherto unknown adult life. John Owen Smith has republished *Heatherley* and followed up Flora's life in Surrey and Hampshire in *On the Trail of Flora Thompson Beyond Candleford Green* and in two plays based on her life, *Flora's Heatherley* and *Flora's Peverel*. Keith Dewhurst's plays *Lark Rise* and *Candleford* are still frequently performed.

It was a great personal achievement for Flora to become such an accomplished writer as she came from an ordinary, relatively uneducated country background, which seldom bred writers. Books about the working classes have generally been written by people of middle or even upper-class status, who have not experienced the actual way of life themselves, but Flora was, almost uniquely, able to write from her own experience, giving an authoritative account of some of the hardships and pleasures of rural life at the end of the nineteenth century. Many books about the Victorians tend to romanticise, painting a rosy haze round the harshness of life, but throughout Flora's work one finds little asides, pointing out that for many it was a struggle to survive. She drew largely from her own rather restricted experience of life in small Oxfordshire villages in her writing, and because of this the same characters, such as her family and her neighbours 'Sally' and 'Queenie', are found in several guises in different stories and articles, often written many years apart. The quality and detail of Flora's writing has made it a rich source for historians of Victorian rural life.

However, the material when used for this purpose, has to be treated with caution, because although *Lark Rise to Candleford* is a thinly veiled autobiography – for example, Flora has changed the name of her heroine to 'Laura', and her brother Edwin's name to 'Edmund' – it must be remembered that she was writing many years later, and has used a certain amount of artistic licence, taking the basic characters and working her magic as a creative writer upon them. In some cases she has deliberately disguised the names of people and places, perhaps to spare her family and her friends' embarrassment. Little information has come to light to identify many of the people she described. For example while she was writing *Still Glides the Stream*, a novel about retired school teacher Charity Finch recalling her rural childhood, she was sent a traditional rhyme about local church spires by her nephew Leslie Castle: 'Adderbury for length, Bloxham for strength and Kings Sutton for beauty'. She commented, 'I want to use it to draw a red herring over the trail in the new book I am writing' (quoted from a letter written to Leslie Castle in July 1946). However, careful detective work looking at parish registers, census returns, maps and local documents and consulting surviving members of the family, has helped to identify some people and places and enough pieces of the jigsaw can be found to fill out the background to the story.

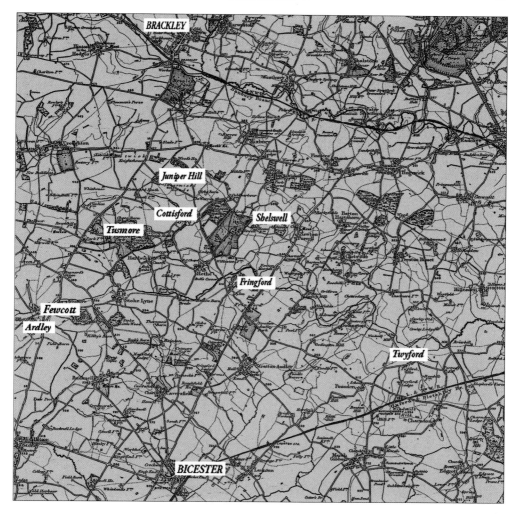

A map reproduced from an Ordnance Survey map printed from an electrotype taken in 1881, showing the area where Flora was brought up. Banbury, one of the towns she visited, is about ten miles to the west of Brackley. Piddington, where her grandmother Martha Wallington was born, is south-east of Bicester. (David Watts)

Flora Thompson was deeply influenced by her background and the people and places she knew, and the aim of this book is to discover more about them, to reveal more about Flora and her work by setting it in its context. The book will concentrate on her Oxfordshire background which most touched her and was the main inspiration for all her writing apart from her nature notes.

Flora's world as a child was a very small, circumscribed one. She was born in the tiny hamlet of Juniper Hill on the Oxfordshire/Northamptonshire border and went to school in its mother village of Cottisford. Her first job was only a few miles away, working in the Post Office at Fringford. She visited relations in Buckingham and Twyford, and shopped in Brackley, where her father worked. She later wrote that she visited Banbury in the carrier's cart, and must have visited Bicester from Fringford. Although she loved the area, she knew little about the places beyond her immediate area, apparently never even visiting Ardley where her mother was born:

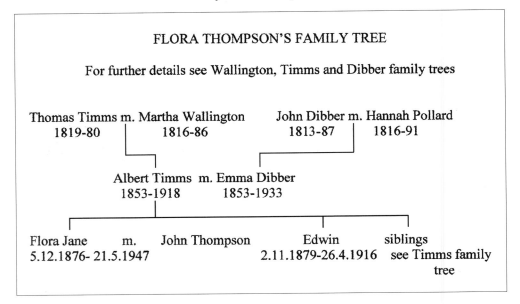

FLORA THOMPSON'S FAMILY TREE

For further details see Wallington, Timms and Dibber family trees

Thomas Timms m. Martha Wallington   John Dibber m. Hannah Pollard
        1819-80   1816-86   1813-87   1816-91

Albert Timms m. Emma Dibber
    1853-1918   1853-1933

Flora Jane   m.   John Thompson   Edwin   siblings
5.12.1876- 21.5.1947   2.11.1879-26.4.1916   see Timms family
                                                                          tree

Flora's family tree.

I … have always wanted to go also to Ardley, where your Grandmother was born. I can imagine how lovely in its quiet way that part of the country is now looking with the elder and the dog-roses out in the hedges and the crops coming on in the fields.

Extract from a letter written to her nephew Leslie Castle in July 1946

In her later years she evinced a great interest in her family background, being conscious that on her father's side she had ancestors, the Wallingtons of Piddington, who had been of higher social status than her immediate family. She herself knew little about them, sending her nephew off on a wild goose chase to visit the Heyfords to see if he could find any family tombstones, when in fact the family did not come from there at all. She would have been fascinated to know about the real history of the Wallington family, which has recently come to light, and from which her paternal grandmother came.

It is a great achievement that *Lark Rise to Candleford* is still in print sixty years after Flora's death, and that she is still so well loved and remembered. This will be further encouraged by the new exhibition about her which opened in Buckingham Museum in May 2007, and by the Flora Thompson study centre which is being established there. How accurate the gipsy's prediction that she would be loved by many people she would never meet has proved.

Piddington: The Wallington Connection

Flora scarcely mentions her paternal grandmother Martha Wallington in her books, although she visited her regularly in Buckingham until she was about ten, and was evidently a little in awe of her. She was, however, very significant to Flora in that it was through Martha that she could claim ancestry of higher standing than her own. Flora was not ashamed of her upbringing, but evidently felt it put her at a disadvantage in her writing; as a stonemason's daughter brought up in a small village she had not had a good education. In her early writing days she believed that if people knew who she really was they would not be interested in reading what she had to say, so she invented an imaginary persona as a doctor's daughter. She recalled her grandmother when writing to her nephew Leslie Castle in 1943:

> My grandmother ... on my father's side, belonged to a good family described in my childhood as gentleman farmers and Aunt Jane ... told me that when she was a child she was once taken on a visit to some branch of the family when she saw paintings and poems painted and written by one of the sons ... I remember my grandmother distinctly as she did not die until I was eleven and we went every year to Buckingham to visit her. She was a woman of refinement and must have been recognised as such as her chief friend was a doctor in the town named King. She brought the brown eyes into the Timms family, so you can see something of her in your mother any day. She had some beautiful old china and other family things which, quite properly, went to the daughter who gave her a home and nursed her through her last illness. My father had some miniatures as part of his share of the family treasure after his mother died, but, unfortunately, there was nobody to appreciate them and they were destroyed by the children.

The daughter referred to here was Ann, who married Thomas Whiting, the shoemaker referred to in *Lark Rise to Candleford* as 'Uncle Tom'. Flora would have talked to her father Albert Timms about her grandmother, as he was the one who instilled in her the pride in their connection with the Wallington family. Some of the details he remembered about the Wallingtons were mythical, including the suggestion that they were related to General Sir John Wallington and his son who was secretary to Queen Mary, wife of King George V.

According to the family legend Martha had been 'a lady by birth', an heiress, and had made a runaway match with Flora's grandfather Thomas Timms. One of the favourite family stories was that of 'Granny's golden footstool':

> Their father's parents had at one time kept a public house and livery stables in Oxford and the story ran that, either going to, or coming from, the 'Horse and Rider', their grandfather had handed their grandmother into the carriage and placed a box containing a thousand pounds at her feet, saying, 'It's not every lady who can ride in her own carriage with a golden footstool'.

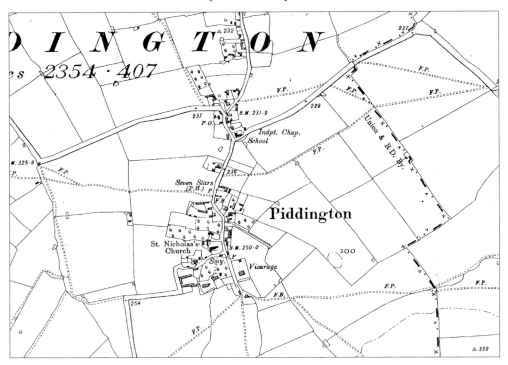

Reproduced from a late-nineteenth century Ordnance Survey map of Piddington. (David Watts)

They must have been on their way there with the purchase money, for they can have brought no golden footstool away with them. Before that adventure, made possible by a legacy left to the grandmother by one of her relatives, the grandfather had been a builder in a small way, and, after it, he went back to building again, in a still smaller way, presumably, for by the time Laura was born the family business had disappeared and her father was working for wages.

Lark Rise to Candleford, p. 274

The real story was far more fascinating than Flora realised. Certainly Martha was of higher birth – but more of yeoman stock than of the aristocracy, and, although the great fortune was a family myth, Martha had a traumatic childhood, details about which do not appear to have been common knowledge by Flora's time.

Martha Wallington was baptised on 2 June 1816 in the small village of Piddington, about five miles south-east of Bicester, which had only 427 inhabitants in 1841. John Drinkwater described the village as it was in the nineteenth century, when the Wallingtons lived there:

It is a plain, grey little village, neutral in design, ambling from cottage to cottage with no apparent sense of direction, its half dozen larger houses of red brick sitting discreetly here and there at the roadside ... When I knew it a stranger was seen only when one passed through in the carrier's cart, or when the Irish labourers came over for harvest, a talkative, thirsty lot, sleeping in the lofts and barns. In the winter, when icicles were on the thatch eaves, the village would lie for days as if it were asleep.

John Drinkwater, *Inheritance, being the first book of an autobiography*, p. 46

The village school (on the left) and an icicle-hung cottage in Piddington, *c.* 1900. (David Watts)

She was one of the children of Martha Shaw, who was born in 1784, daughter of John Shaw, a yeoman of Piddington, whose family had been in the village since about 1690. Martha married Edward Wallington in 1805. Edward, born in 1781, belonged to a family that had farmed in Ludgershall, Buckinghamshire since the late sixteenth century, but he came to Piddington to run his wife's farm on their marriage.

Their farmhouse, now known as Brown's Piece, was in the centre of the village at the road junction with Arncott Road, opposite the bakehouse. The house, which still stands today, is basically eighteenth century. It was built by John Shaw (1718-97), Martha's great-grandfather, whose initials IS are carved on the datestone, though it incorporates earlier elements. He purchased much of the farm from Sir John Aubrey, 4th Baronet of Llantrithyd. His son, John Shaw the younger (1755-1800), died, leaving the farmhouse and farm in trust for his second wife Sarah Toms of Kidlington, and his only daughter, Martha (by his first marriage), who five years later married Edward Wallington. Their farm consisted of house and garden, orchard, barn, stables and yard, rickyard, cow house and yard, paddock, pasture and arable land.

Either the farm was not a very profitable one, or Edward was not very careful with money, because in 1805 Martha and Edward had to borrow £700 from her aunt, Elizabeth Shaw (1751-1820) to buy farm stock, putting up their farm as security. It seems that the farm still did not prosper, as by 1815 the Wallingtons owed Elizabeth Shaw the vast sum of £1,647 10s, so by indenture made on 3 November the ownership of the farm passed to her in payment of the debt, with the proviso that the Wallingtons could have it back on repayment of the money and interest owing. When Elizabeth Shaw died in 1820 she left the farm to her niece Martha for her lifetime, and it was then to be equally shared among the Wallington children. She obviously had no time or respect for Edward Wallington, considering him a spendthrift, as he was to be kept from any responsibility in running the farm and was to have no further personal interest in it should his wife die before him.

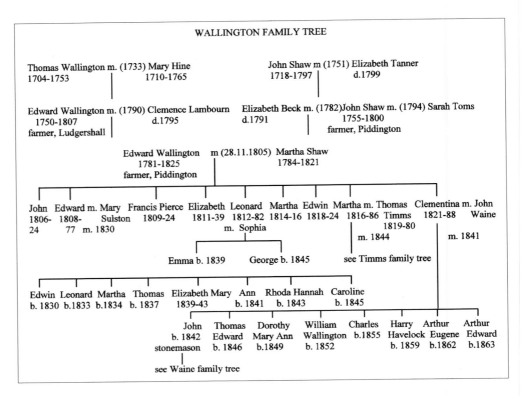

The Wallington family tree.

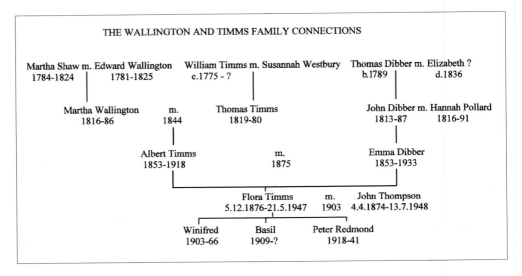

The Wallington and Timms family connections.

In 1824 tragedy struck the Wallington family when some illness, possibly plague, according to family tradition, killed several of them within a few weeks: first the children Francis, aged fourteen, buried on 8 March, then Edwin aged six, buried on 21 March and then their mother Martha herself, aged forty, buried on 30 March. Then, when the family must have felt that everything was improving, John, aged seventeen, died and was buried on 17 May.

A year later Martha's husband Edward died aged only forty-four and was buried on 6 March 1825. The five remaining children were left orphans: Edward, the eldest, who was aged only sixteen, Elizabeth aged thirteen, Leonard aged twelve, Martha aged eight and little Clementina aged three. None of their near relatives seem to have wanted to take on responsibility for them, their two uncles claiming that they could not do so, being in 'indifferent circumstances' themselves. It is not clear what happened then, except that their father seems not to have left any money of his own, certainly not enough to pay off the debt he owed to the late Elizabeth Shaw to redeem the farm, but the provisions of Elizabeth's will to sell the farm and divide the money between the children were not carried out. The children seem to have gone on living in the house, when they were not at boarding school, but evidently the farm did not bring in enough money to keep them, so they ran up extensive bills with local tradesmen. Something had to be done to raise money, and the legal position was uncertain.

This parlous situation carried on for five years, but in 1829 Edward, the eldest surviving child, had reached his majority and needed money to marry Mary Sulston, so it was decided that the situation must be clarified. On 2 May the case was taken to the Court of Chancery where it was claimed that on Martha's death the provisions of Elizabeth Shaw's will had not been carried out, and the farm had been left in the possession of her husband Edward. On his death the surviving children continued living there but 'there being no fund whatever out of which provision can be made for their advancement in the world' it was hoped the court would give permission for the farm to be sold to pay off debts and give the children each their shares.

To complicate matters, other lands which were not mortgaged to Elizabeth Shaw had been settled on Martha Shaw and Edward Wallington at their marriage, which increased the size of the farm, and it would be detrimental to both to sell one without the other, but Edward's brother John refused to sell them unless told to do so by the court. The children also needed a guardian to care for their interests.

After long and convoluted arguments the judge decided that Edward Wallington (the son of Martha and Edward) must pay off the principal and interest on the loan given by Elizabeth Shaw to free the farm from the provisions of her will, or else it must be sold, together with the disputed properties settled on Martha and Edward Wallington at their marriage, and the money could then be used to pay off the debt to Elizabeth if possible, otherwise to pay the bills of the tradesmen and then be divided equally between the surviving children. The case came back to Chancery on 4 August 1830 by which time the Master of the Court had sold the farm to the highest bidder, the Revd John Cleobury of Piddington, who paid £900 for it. Thomas Stevens, a yeoman of Piddington, was made formal guardian of the children, as he had been acting for them since they were orphaned.

The Master reported that the money Elizabeth Shaw had lent Edward and Martha Wallington had never been repaid nor had interest been paid on it so that the grand total owed to her estate was £2,859 19s 10½d. The costs amounted to £189 9s 9d. A suitable occupational rent for the property would be £42 a year from November 1816 to July 1830, totalling £576 16s.

Although the children had been receiving shares in the produce of the farm amounting to £73 16s a year and rents on four small cottages of £8 12s they were otherwise destitute and owed money to a number of local tradespeople for provisions, meat, malt and beer, flour, clothing, linen and hosiery, shoes, mercery and drapery, coals, carpenter's work, barley and a cow. Money was owed to Hannah Smith schoolmistress and Abraham Chapman schoolmaster, both of Islip, for board and education for the children. (For details see Appendix One).

Brown's Piece, Piddington, the farmhouse built by Martha Wallington's great-grandfather, John Shaw, where she lived as a child. (David Watts)

The carrier formed a vital link between villages and their market towns. Flora herself travelled to Banbury on the carrier's cart from Juniper Hill. Here William Humphries, the Greatworth carrier who travelled to Banbury and Brackley is seen outside Mr Chester's bakery in Piddington, *c.* 1900. (David Watts)

Thomas Stevens was given money to pay off all the debts and told that any money left over was to be invested in 3 per cent Consolidated Birminghams and the income used for the future maintenance of the children in case the money allocated from the case should prove insufficient. There cannot have been much left over as the sale of the farm brought in so much less than the money owed.

It was decided that the cost of completing the children's education should be taken from their shares, so after all the debts had been paid off the children received the following shares:

Elizabeth Wallington: £143 9s 11 ¾d less £37 15s 9 ¾d for education,
                        total £105 14s 2d
Martha Wallington: £143 9s 11 ¾d less £64 5s 5 ¾d for education,
                        total £79 4s 6 ¾d
Clements Wallington: £143 9s 11 ¾d less £48 8s 3 ¾d for education,
                        total £95 1s 8 ¾d

Edward Wallington received £109 2s after his debts had been paid. Leonard Wallington had to pay his debts and apprenticeship out of his share and was left with only £7 16s 6d.

Leonard wanted to be apprenticed to Frederick Indermance of Union Street, Southwark, London, as a cabinet maker and needed £70 to cover the cost of the apprenticeship, meat, drink and lodging until he came of age. Although Leonard did become a cabinet maker eventually, in 1841 he was living in lodgings in Westminster working as a horse keeper. Ten years later he was living with his wife Sophia, daughter Emma and son George, this time described as a cabinet maker. Emma became an author, describing herself in the 1881 census as a writer of prose articles.

Edward married Mary Sulston and they had five children. In 1841 he was farming at Chillingplace in Piddington, with his wife Mary and children: Martha (aged six), Thomas (four), Elizabeth (two) and Ann who was just one month. Sarah Kirby worked for them as a domestic servant. However ten years later Mary had died and Edward was a gardener in Hadley near Enfield with Thomas, Elizabeth, Ann and another daughter, Caroline, who was five. His daughter Martha was working as a domestic servant in Hadley. In 1861 he was working as a milkman in Highgate, London, living with a housekeeper. He died in 1877, back in the Bicester area.

Elizabeth moved to 1 Swinton Street, Grays Inn in London where she worked as a dressmaker until her death in 1839. Clementina lived with her, also working as a dressmaker for a while. When she died in 1839 she left her writing desk to Martha and most of the remainder of her estate to Clementina.

In 1841 Clementina married John Waine, who was described as being of independent means in the 1841 census, when the pair were living in Ambrosden. They moved to Launton and in later censuses he is described as being an agricultural labourer, while Clementina was described as a milliner and dressmaker in the 1871 census. Their children were John, Thomas, Dorothy, William, Charles, Henry and Arthur. Clementina died in 1888 aged sixty-seven. Their son John became a successful stonemason in Buckingham and may be the cousin Flora christened 'James Dowland'.

This Chancery case seems to have been the origin of the family legend that Martha had inherited £1,000. In fact she eventually received less than one tenth of that amount. It is possible that she inherited money from elsewhere, but this does not seem likely in view of the penurious situation revealed in the Chancery case and lack of relatives offering to help the children. It is not known where Martha lived after the sale of the farm, although she probably stayed with Elizabeth in London for a time, but she married Thomas Timms at Ambrosden by special licence on 18 November 1844, aged twenty-eight. Presumably as she had achieved her majority she would not have had to make the runaway match of family legend, even though her husband Thomas Timms was younger than she was, being twenty-five and, as he worked as a mason, might have been considered below her in status.

Piddington village scene, *c.* 1900. (David Watts)

Thomas' father William Timms had been born in Bicester around 1775 and served in the Oxfordshire Militia in 1814. He married Susannah Westbury 1802, and they had five children, of whom Thomas, born on 25 September 1819, was the youngest.

It is not known definitely whether or not Thomas and Martha did own the hotel and livery stables in Oxford, which Flora called the Horse and Rider, but considering their finances it seems unlikely. Unfortunately licensing records do not survive from that period, and there is no trace of Thomas Timms in the electoral register for that date, but it may never be possible to know for certain. They were living in St Albans when their first child Ann Elizabeth was born in 1846, two years after their marriage, so if they did have premises in Oxford they did not stay there long. By 1851 Thomas Timms was working as a mason and the family were living in North End, Buckingham, where Ann was baptised with her younger sister Jane in that year. Flora's father Albert was baptised in Buckingham on 23 July 1853 and the youngest son, Edwin was born on 19 July 1855.

Martha seems to have worked to supplement the family income, being described as a dressmaker of 120 Gawcott Road, Buckingham, in the census returns of 1861 and 1871, although the ages given there are totally wrong: in 1861 Thomas' age is given as forty-six when he was forty-two and Martha's as thirty-five, although she was forty-six, and in 1871 Thomas is said to be forty-nine instead of fifty-two and Martha has lost years to become twenty-eight instead of fifty-six! The 1871 census records that not only Thomas but his sons Albert and Edwin, aged sixteen and fourteen respectively, were working as masons and living at the same address. Although little is known about what happened to her Uncle Edwin, Flora suggested in *Lark Rise* that he joined the Royal Engineers and served in Nova Scotia.

Flora remembered meeting her Aunt Jane, as a small child. She had apparently married a master builder who lived in Yorkshire, and seldom visited the family. Her display of wealth seems to have made Emma Timms, her sister-in-law, rather uncomfortable:

Jane was too dressy and 'set up' for her taste, she said. That morning, her luggage being still at the railway station, she was wearing the clothes she had travelled in, a long pleated dove-

The family of Andrew Sulston (1821–1906) and his wife Sarah of Lower Farm, Cowleys, Piddington. Andrew's sister Mary married Edward Wallington so Andrew was brother-in-law of Martha Timms. (David Watts)

The nineteenth-century village school and school teacher's house in Piddington. (David Watts)

coloured gown with an apron arrangement drawn round and up and puffed over a bustle at the back, and, on her head, a tiny toque made entirely of purple velvet pansies...

Lark Rise to Candleford, p. 37

Flora later wrote that at the outbreak of the Boer War, her brother Edwin was staying with relatives in Yorkshire, and immediately joined the West Yorkshire Regiment. It is likely that these relatives would have been Aunt Jane and her husband. Unfortunately Jane did not marry in Buckingham, and her husband's identity has not so far been traced.

Thomas Timms died in the workhouse in Buckingham and was buried on 10 November 1881 aged seventy-one. Perhaps he was ill at the end and needed treatment in the workhouse hospital, as Martha did not have to move into the workhouse with him and after she was widowed continued to live in Mitre Street in Buckingham, where she was described in the 1881 census as being a former dressmaker. Later she went to live in Twyford, Buckinghamshire, with her daughter Ann and her husband Thomas Whiting. Martha was buried in Twyford on 10 August 1886, aged sixty-nine.

Although Flora could not truly claim kinship with the more aristocratic branch of the Wallington family, she would have been delighted to learn that through the Wallingtons and their Delafield ancestry she could claim kinship with Thomas and Matthew Arnold and the aristocracy. Her distant cousin Martha Delafield (1750-89) married William Arnold, a collector of customs from the Isle of Wight. Their son Thomas (1795-1842) was the headmaster of Rugby School immortalised in *Tom Brown's Schooldays*, and his son Matthew became a famous poet, so Flora can legitimately claim to have literary figures in her family. Martha and William Delafield's daughter Lydia married Richard Ford William Lambart, 7th Earl of Cavan.

Ardley and Fewcott: The Dibber Family

Flora Thompson's mother, Emma Dibber, born in 1853, was brought up in Ardley, now known as Ardley with Fewcott, a small village north-west of Bicester. She later worked as nursemaid for the curate at Fewcott, then a separate village, part of the parish of Stoke Lyne. Emma's father John Dibber was recorded as living in Ardley in the 1851 census, having been baptised there on 26 September 1813 although his parents were living in Stoke Lyne. Their surname confusingly appears in several different forms in different documents – in the parish registers as Dibber, in several of the census returns and on Emma's marriage certificate as Dipper and on Flora's birth certificate as Lapper.

John Dibber, Flora's beloved grandfather, was the son of Thomas Dibber, an agricultural labourer born in Tackley, and his first wife Elizabeth who went on to have six other children, two of whom, James and Harriet, died in infancy, and another, Ellen, who died aged nineteen. His brother William, born in 1815, became a servant and in 1851 was living in Stockton, Warwickshire, with his wife Mary and children Emma (twelve) and John (ten) who had been born in Southmoor and Henry (eight) and Ellen (four), born in Stockton. Thomas, who was born in 1823 became a general labourer, navvy and coal dealer and was working in Chatham, Kent in 1891. He had moved to Rugby by 1901.

Thomas Dibber's wife Elizabeth died aged forty-two, shortly after her youngest daughter Harriet was born and five years later Thomas married Hannah Andrews of Ardley. Their two daughters, Sarah and Eliza were born in 1833 and 1836. Hannah was recorded in the 1861 census as being a lacemaker.

John Dibber, Flora's grandfather, married another Hannah on 5 October 1835 when he was twenty-one and his bride nineteen. Hannah Pollard, the daughter of John and Mary, came from Hornton, north of Banbury, where John was an agricultural labourer, but it is not known whether, as Flora suggested, he was also a gamekeeper. Hannah was evidently considered a local beauty, nicknamed 'the Belle of Hornton', with luxuriant waist-length blonde hair. She always considered that one of her chief claims to fame was that she had once attracted the notice of a 'real lord', the son of her father's employer, who had seen her at his coming-of-age celebrations and singled her out to dance with him, preferring her to the more aristocratic young ladies there. He had told her that she was the prettiest girl in the county – a compliment she treasured for the rest of her life, but in those days there was no chance of any lasting romance between people of such differing classes. Flora wrote:

> It was difficult for Laura to connect the long, yellow hair and the white frock with blue ribbons worn at the coming-of-age fête with her grandmother, for she saw her only as a thin, frail old woman who wore her grey hair parted like curtains and looped at the ears with little combs. Still, there was something which made her worth looking at. Laura's mother said it was because her features were good. 'My mother', she would say, 'will look handsome in her coffin. Colour goes and the hair turns grey, but the framework lasts'.

Lark Rise to Candleford, p. 94

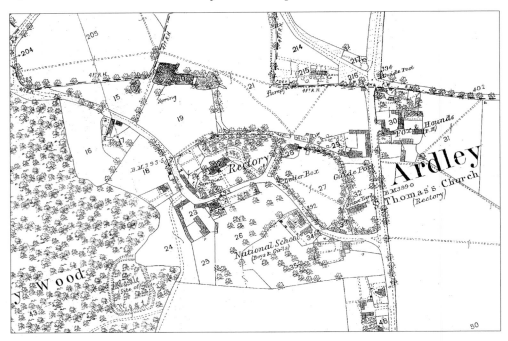

Reproduced from a late nineteenth-century Ordnance Survey map of Ardley. (Oxfordshire Studio)

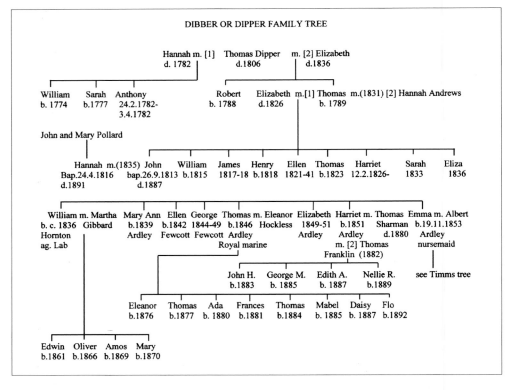

The family tree of the Dibber family.

Hannah was a rather self-centred woman who expected to be cherished. She loved good clothes and wanted pretty things around her, decorating her bedroom with pictures and ornaments and making it comfortable with feather cushions and a silk patchwork quilt. She spent hours reading romantic novelettes which she exchanged with her friends. When she visited the Timms family in Juniper Hill she was always allocated the best chair by the fire and Emma gave her the best tea she could provide.

Flora obviously adored her grandfather, John Dibber, remembering him as a man in his seventies with white hair and beard setting off his bright blue eyes, although he could be strict and demanded high standards of behaviour from her. Although he was described merely as an agricultural labourer in the census returns (a term that can cover a wide variety of occupations), Flora wrote that he worked as an eggler, travelling round the area in a horse and trap to buy eggs from cottagers and farmers which he resold to shops and at markets.

John Dibber was a religious man, attending every service in the church and often going to the church at other times to pray. He later became a local Methodist preacher, walking to other villages to preach in cottage meeting houses, and had a reputation for inspired preaching. As an old man he attended Church of England services again, enjoying the music he could no longer play; he had played the violin with the village musicians in Ardley church and the choir and musicians came to practise in their cottage in the evenings. His skills as a violinist were also in demand for weddings and feasts and at other local gatherings in neighbours' houses.

When Flora asked what had happened to his violin she was told by her mother that he had sold it to raise money when her grandmother had been ill. She seems to have been the only one to realise what a sacrifice it must have been for him. He also had to give up smoking when he retired, because they had little to live on, even though Thomas, his coal-merchant brother, sent them a small allowance. What he hated most was that he no longer had money for presents for his family. By this time he and his wife had moved to a little round house in Cottisford near the Timms family so he managed to visit the end house each day, bringing with him something in season from the garden, such as a marrow, peas or raspberries.

He was badly afflicted with rheumatism in old age, which constricted his movements, so that as his health declined he could no longer walk to church. Then even the journey to Flora's house became too much for him. Eventually, Flora wrote, he was confined to his bed in the attic bedroom he had considerately chosen to sleep in so that Hannah would not be disturbed by his tossing and turning, or woken up when he rose early to read the *Bible*:

> Gradually his limbs became so locked he could not turn over in bed without help. Giving to and doing for others was over for him. He would lie upon his back for hours, his tired old blue eyes fixed upon the picture nailed on the wall at the foot of his bed. It was the only coloured thing in the room; the rest was bare whiteness. It was of the Crucifixion, and, printed above the crown of thorns were the words:
> This have I done for thee.
> And underneath the pierced and bleeding feet:
> What hast thou done for me?
> His two years' uncomplaining endurance of excruciating pain answered for him.

Lark Rise to Candleford, pp. 93-4

John Dibber was buried in Cottisford on 30 March 1887 and his widow Hannah left Juniper to live with her son William in Daventry, where she died in 1891 and their abandoned house gradually disintegrated. Flora commented that Hannah was too full of her own concerns to appreciate the sacrifices her husband had made for her.

The village band playing for the feast of the Stoke Lyne Friendly Society outside the Peyton Arms. Flora's grandfather, John Dibber, played at similar feasts and gatherings. (David Watts)

The seventeenth-century rectory where John Lowe, rector of Ardley from 1815-73 lived, now known as Ardley House. Emma Dibber, Flora's mother, often visited here as a child for singing and writing lessons. (Oxfordshire Photographic Archive)

John and Hannah's eldest son William was born in Hornton. Then the family moved to Ardley, where Mary Ann was born in 1839. Their changes of residence are marked by the places where the children were born: Ellen and George, were born in the adjacent village of Fewcott in 1842 and 1844 respectively while their other children were all born in Ardley: Thomas in 1846, Elizabeth (who only lived for two years) in 1849, Harriet in 1851 and Emma in 1853. The Dibber family can be found in the census returns for Fewcott in 1841 and Ardley in 1861 and 1871, retiring to Cottisford before 1881.

Their son William married Martha Gibbard, and in 1861 aged twenty-three, was working as an agricultural labourer and living with his mother-in-law Hannah Gibbard in Ardley. He and Martha moved to their own home in Ardley and in 1871 had three sons and a daughter. Thomas was a Private in the Royal Marines in 1881, and later became a general labourer and a navvy. He married Eleanor Hockless and they had a son and five daughters. Harriet married Thomas Sharman in 1873 and moved to Juniper Hill, but Thomas died in 1880 aged thirty-two. Harriet remarried Thomas Franklin in 1882 and moved to Oxford. By 1891 they had four children: John H. (eight), George M. (six), Edith A. (four) and Nellie R. (two).

John and Hannah lived for some years in Ardley, which had never been a large village, although it had a small twelfth-century castle built by the Norman, Hugh of Avranches. The village was in decline when John Dibber knew it, with a population in 1821 of 191. For much of the century it boasted a wonderful rector in John Lowe, who was mentioned by Flora in *Lark Rise to Candleford*. Her mother Emma must have told her enough about him to leave a vivid impression. He was born at Brotherton in Yorkshire and became Rector of Ardley in 1815 as a young man of about twenty-four, remaining as the incumbent until 1873 when he was in his eighties. He fell in love at first sight with Susannah, the daughter of his predecessor Thomas Hind, and they married after a short engagement. He also had parishes in Yorkshire, so did not become resident in Ardley until 1833, using curates to run the parish until then. After his wife's death her sister Anne Hind lived for a while at the Rectory and became a great benefactor to the parish.

He became much loved in the parish and revived interest in the church and in one year preached about ninety-five sermons. He attracted congregations of between fifty and sixty in the mornings and seventy to eighty at evening services. He commented on his parishioners that his only problems were 'unbelief and hardness of heart. These are my great hindrances, and, in a few cases, the love of drinking' (from *Wilberforce's Visitations*, quoted in the Victoria *History of the County of Oxfordshire, Vol. VI*, 1959 p.13). He offered to take on the oversight of the residents of nearby Fewcott in 1840, as many of them preferred to attend Ardley church rather than make the longer journey to their parish church at Stoke Lyne but the patron Dr Marcham refused his offer.

The Old Rectory where he lived was a seventeenth-century house, taxed on four hearths in 1665, much enlarged and altered over the centuries, with major alterations made in 1860 and again in 1874. It is now called Ardley House. Anne Hind was living there in 1861 and their staff were coachman John Witham (thirty-five) from Wentworth, Yorkshire, his wife Elizabeth (thirty-five) was cook, Alfred Pine (fifteen) from Radway, Warwickshire, was the footman and Harriet Goodall (thirty-seven) was the housemaid.

In 1871 John Lowe, then aged eighty, had also taken on the role of Justice of the Peace. He lived, after Anne Hind's death, with his niece Mary Ann Willoughby, aged forty-two, Eliza Wilkins, a lady's maid from London, aged forty-seven, Lydia Archer, the fifty-year-old cook from Goddington, Oxfordshire, Sarah Gulliver the housemaid from Launton aged twenty-eight and twenty-five-year-old George Surridge from Ardley, who acted as footman and domestic servant.

John Lowe and the Vicar of Stoke Lyne together supported a small day school in the village by 1854, for which the thirty pupils paid 1d a week. Emma Dibber would have attended this as a child. In 1861 a larger school for sixty children was built by the Duke of Marlborough, subsequently enlarged with money from Miss Anne Hind, which became affiliated to the

Group outside Ardley School, which Emma Dibber attended. (Oxfordshire Photographic Archive)

Ardley church, attended by Flora's grandparents, John and Hannah Dibber, and her mother Emma, where John Dibber played the violin for the church band. (Oxfordshire Photographic Archive)

National Society in 1862. The school closed in 1914 and the actual building was physically moved to Sandford St Martin in the 1920s.

The Dibbers lived in a cottage near the church, so the school would have been opposite. Flora wrote that Emma had caught the eye of the rector's sister, who had taken her under her wing:

> Yet she had brains of her own and her education had been above the average for her station in life ... At the time when she was a small girl ... the incumbent of the parish had been an old man and with him had lived his still more aged sister. This lady, whose name was Miss Lowe, had become very fond of the pretty, fair-haired little girl at the churchyard cottage and had had her at the Rectory every day out of school hours. Little Emma had a sweet voice and she was supposed to go there for singing lessons; but she had learned other things, too, including old world manners and to write a beautiful antique hand with delicate open-looped pointed letters and long 's's such as her instructress and other young ladies had been taught in the last quarter of the eighteenth century.
>
> Miss Lowe was then nearly eighty, and had long been dead when Laura, at two and a half years old, had been taken by her mother to see the by then very aged Rector. The visit was one of her earliest memories, which survived as an indistinct impression of twilight in a room with dark green walls and the branch of a tree against the outside of the window; and, more distinctly, a pair of trembling, veiny hands putting something smooth and cold and round into her own ... The old gentleman, it appeared, had given her a china mug which had been his sister's in her nursery days. It had stood on the mantelpiece at the end house for years, a beautiful old piece with a design of heavy green foliage on a ground of translucent whiteness. Afterwards it got broken, which was strange in that careful house; but Laura carried the design in her mind's eye for the rest of her life and would sometimes wonder if it accounted for her lifelong love of green and white in conjunction.

Lark Rise to Candleford, p. 39

It is likely that 'Miss Lowe' was in fact Anne Hind, John Lowe's sister-in-law rather than sister, who was younger than Flora suggested, being sixty-six in 1861. Her encouragement does seem to have given Emma Dibber a much better education than an agricultural labourer's daughter would otherwise have obtained, so she may in turn have passed this on to her daughter Flora, indirectly helping her to achieve her potential. The story of Flora's visit to the Rectory and the gift of the cup are apocryphal as John Lowe died in March 1874, two years before she was born.

After leaving school Emma became a nursemaid, and went to work in Fewcott Rectory, just down the road. The Rectory has been renamed Weavers and is situated next to the nineteenth-century schoolhouse. Enclosure had taken place in the village in 1794, which increased the value of the land, but the population dropped from 220 in 1841 to 160 twenty years later, and continued to decline.

The Fewcott parishioners were expected to go to Stoke Lyne church but some residents preferred to go to Ardley which was much nearer, so Miss Anne Hind, sister-in-law of the Rector of Ardley, left £2,000 in her will when she died in 1870 to provide a curacy for Fewcott and a further £1,000 for the vicarage of Stoke Lyne. She had written to the Rural Dean in 1865 expressing her intentions:

> I, Anne Hind, having purchased nearly four acres of land with a cottage, a barn, and some small outbuildings in the hamlet of Fewcote, near Ardley, amounting in value to £630 (and when the necessary alterations now begun in the cottage, etc., are completed, the value may be safely stated at £700) do declare that it is my desire and intention to bequeath the land and cottage, etc., etc., to Queen Anne's Bounty in trust for the benefit of the Church of

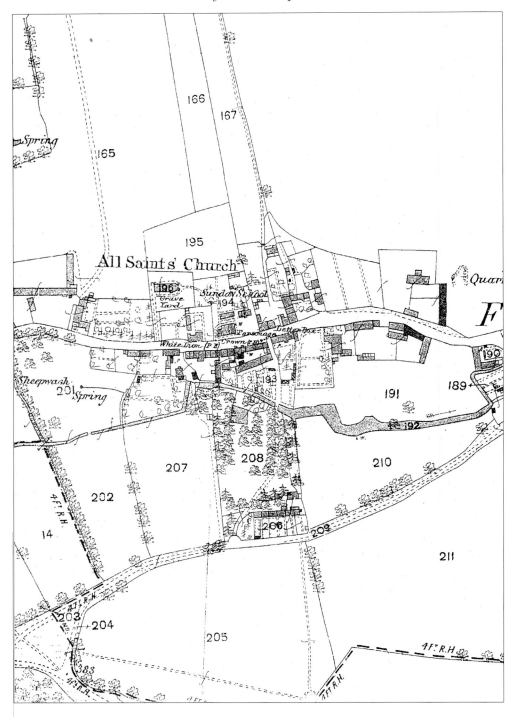

Reproduced from a late nineteenth–century Ordnance Survey map of Fewcott. (Oxfordshire Studies)

England, and of the parishes of Ardley and Stoke Lyne to which the hamlet of Fewcote is now annexed. If the hamlet of Fewcote should be hereafter annexed to the Parish of Ardley, it would then be my desire that the four acres of land with the cottage and outbuildings which I have purchased in Fewcote should become an augmentation of the living of Ardley for the benefit of that living, and of the poor parishioners of Fewcote; if on the contrary, the hamlet of Fewcote should remain as it is, a part of the parish of Stoke Lyne, then it would be my desire that the said portion of land at Fewcote and the cottage aforesaid and the adjoining buildings should be annexed to the living of Stoke Lyne in order to secure the residence of a curate in the hamlet of Fewcote ...

Quoted in J.C. Blomfield, *History of the Present Deanery of Bicester*, 1887

Miss Hind had a schoolroom built in 1865 and assigned the cottage as a residence for the Curate of Ardley, Revd H.J. Joscelyne, on condition he held services on Sunday evenings in the schoolroom. He was the first curate to use the new church which was built in Fewcott, consecrated to All Saints in 1871, which operated as a chapel of Stoke Lyne. It cost £900 to build and was designed by H. Woodyer, comprising a simple nave with apsidal chancel and an open bell turret.

Emma obviously enjoyed working for Revd Joscelyne and his family, and seems to have been treated more as a member of the family than as a servant. The 1871 census shows the residents of Fewcott Parsonage as being the curate, Henry Joscelyne, aged forty-four, his wife Mary Louise, aged thirty-six, their children Louise Elizabeth, aged fourteen, Henry Maurice, aged eleven, Herbert Cathcart, aged seven, Alice Emma, aged six, Arthur Edwin aged four, Ethel aged two and Edward Walter, aged three months, together with their servants, Emma Dipper aged seventeen and Susan Hayward aged sixteen from Chesterton. Flora described how her mother used to tell her about life on Fewcott Rectory, disguising the name of the family as Johnstone:

The living was small and the rectory was poor, but three maids had been possible in those days, a cook-general, a young housemaid, and Nurse Emma. They must have been needed in that large, rambling old house, in which lived the Rector and his wife, their nine children, three maids, and often three or four young men pupils. They all had such jolly, happy times she said, all of them, family and maids and pupils, singing glees and part songs in the drawing-room in the evening.

Lark Rise to Candleford, pp. 39-40

Emma held up the parsonage children as paragons of virtue to her own children, but in that perhaps she was exaggerating, as Flora recalled that when she was taken to visit them the boys pulled her hair and one of them dressed up as a priest, using the cook's apron as a surplice, and proceeded to bury Flora's doll in the orchard!

Emma was a bright, attractive girl, much appreciated by the family, and also influenced by them:

She was a slight, graceful girl with a wild-rose complexion and hair the colour of a new penny which she parted in the middle and drew down to a knot at the back of her head because a gentleman of the family, where she had been nurse to the children before her marriage, had told her she ought always to do it like that.

'A pocket Venus,' she said he had called her. 'But quite nicely,' she hastened to assure her listener, 'for he was a married gentleman with no nonsense about him.'

Lark Rise to Candleford, p. 272, 1973

The former Rectory at Fewcott next to the old village school where Emma Dibber lived when she was employed as nursemaid by the curate, Revd Henry Joscelyne. The house is now known as Weavers.

When Mr Joscelyne moved to Fingest-cum-Ibstone in Buckinghamshire in 1879 his parishioners presented him with farewell gifts of a tea and coffee service and a purse of sovereigns. Emma remained friendly with the eldest daughter Louise Elizabeth, renamed Lily in *Lark Rise*, who must have been twenty-two rather than seventeen when Emma took her family to visit the Rectory in 1879 before they left the parish. Flora recalled that as she accompanied them for some of the walk home she chatted to Emma about her admirers. She must have retained a great affection for Emma and her family as she sent regular parcels of books and toys at Christmas and carried on corresponding with Emma into the 1920s.

The 1871 census records only seven children rather than the nine Flora mentions, so perhaps an older boy was away at school. Another son was born in 1874 and perhaps an additional servant was employed after 1871. Emma probably remained with the family until her marriage in July 1875 when she moved to Juniper Hill.

Juniper Hill: Flora's Lark Rise

The hamlet stood on a gentle rise in the flat, wheat-growing north-east corner of Oxfordshire. We will call it Lark Rise because of the great number of skylarks which made the surrounding fields their springboards and nested on the bare earth between the rows of green corn ... Old men could remember when the Rise, covered with juniper bushes, stood in the midst of a furzy heath – common land, which had come under the plough after the passing of the Enclosure Acts. Some of the ancients still occupied cottages on land which had been ceded to their fathers as 'squatters' rights', and probably all the small plots upon which the houses stood had originally been so ceded. In the eighteen-eighties the hamlet consisted of about thirty cottages and an inn, not built in rows, but dotted down anywhere within a more or less circular group. A deeply rutted cart track surrounded the whole, and separate houses or groups of houses were connected by a network of pathways. Going from one part of the hamlet to another was called 'going round the Rise', and the plural of 'house' was not 'houses', but 'housen'. The only shop was a small general one kept in the back kitchen of the inn. The church and school were in the mother village, a mile and a half away.

A road flattened the circle at one point. It had been cut when the heath was enclosed for convenience in fieldwork and to connect the main Oxford road with the mother village and a series of other villages beyond. From the hamlet it led on the one hand to church and school, and on the other to the main road, or the turnpike, as it was still called, and so to the market town where the Saturday shopping was done.

Lark Rise to Candleford, pp. 17-18

Flora's evocative description of her village is one of the most memorable passages of *Lark Rise* and is still apt today, although several of the houses Flora knew have been demolished or disintegrated and been replaced by new ones. Thanks to the fame of *Lark Rise to Candleford* the little village of Juniper Hill, which Flora re-christened 'Lark Rise' is now part of a conservation area. Yet anyone visiting in 1753 would have seen nothing there except bleak empty heathland.

The first houses were built on the heathland that is now Juniper Hill in 1754, paid for by a poor rate, as recorded in the Cottisford parish records:

MEMORANDUM: Two Cottages erected in the Year of our Lord 1754 on Juniper Hill in the Parish of Cotsford in the County of Oxon for the use of the poor of the sd parish. Expenses of which Houses or Cottages amounted to the sum of £28 7s 6d.
Built by a rate charged on the landholders, viz. Richd Eyre Esq., the Revd Jas Smith, Rector, Mr John Westcar, Henry Sansom, John Tebby, Thos. Jarvis, Robt. Day, landholders.

Recorded in J.C. Blomfield, *History of the Present Deanery of Bicester*, 1887

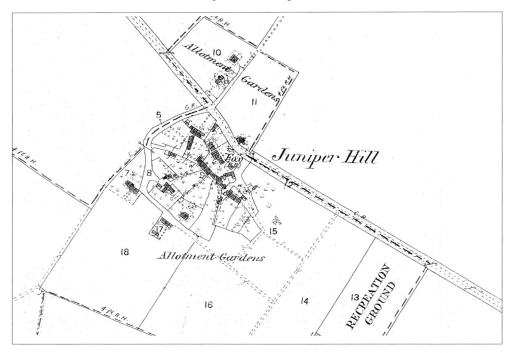

Reproduced from the 1882 Ordnance Survey map of Juniper Hill showing the main road through the village which leads to the turnpike, and the curved road which Flora called The Rise. The Timms' cottage was situated close to the No. 17 marked on the map, set away from the path, with Queenie's cottage in front of it. Flora renamed the Fox public house the Wagon and Horses. (Oxfordshire Studies)

Blomfield explained why it acquired the name of Juniper Hill:

> On some ground to the NE of the village, the low evergreen bushy shrub, known as the Common Juniper, grew in abundance. Its hard wood was useful fuel, and its spicy berries may have been beneficial as medicines. Hence this spot came to be known in recent times as Juniper Hill.

Op. cit. p.37

It seems extraordinary to our eyes to build two houses in the middle of nowhere, but Cottisford, the mother village, which Flora calls 'Fordlow', came under the tight control of Eton College, so the type of resident could be severely restricted, and the college evidently did not want to have the poor people living too close. Two more cottages were built soon afterwards, then little happened until the nineteenth century. Some of those built then were the work of squatters, who built a hearth and a chimney and lit a fire in it between dawn and dusk which was thought to give them a claim to the piece of land, although the claim had a dubious legal basis. Such people would have a measure of independence as they 'owned' their own houses. Some cottages may have been built specifically for letting to agricultural labourers – at enclosure several cottages were owned by the Fermor trustees of Tusmore Park. When the enclosure of Cottisford Heath was first authorised in 1848 Juniper labourers became notorious because of their violent opposition to it over several years, tearing down the notices about enclosure and attacking surveyors. They were rightly concerned that enclosure would deprive them of their right to graze animals on waste ground, cut wood for fires and sedge for the livestock, which supplemented their wages as agricultural labourers.

The local magistrate, J.B. Parry of Cottisford House, wrote a letter in 1853 which indicated that he had little sympathy with these independent-minded, possibly lawless, labourers:

> My object in reference to the Juniper cottagers is to have them put ... on the usual terms on which cottages are let, viz. liable to eviction after a week's notice, with a view to secure their good behaviour, or to get rid of any who shall be guilty of poaching, or other misconduct, and my idea is that the best way to bring about that state of things would be to propose allowing them to remain in their cottages as weekly tenants at some small rent, say 6d a week, with a good-size plot of garden ground included, and to let it be understood that they should not be disturbed during their lives if no complaints were made of them, or they did not become chargeable to the parish ...Those who could not accept such terms should, of course, be evicted at once ... It is quite essential to the welfare of this and the adjoining manors that none of these fellows should be left in the position of freeholders.

The disruptions continued until 1853 when the Bicester petty sessions finally issued warrants of ejectment against forty-two Juniper men who had no true legal claim to their land, including several members of the Moss family (some of the Moss family changed their surname in embarrassment at the connection with these rough goings-on). Some agreed to settle, so escaped ejection. Four men who could prove their ownership of their land were allocated small plots in the enclosure award. The case was reported in the *Oxford Chronicle* of 30 June 1853, which stated that the labourers who had 'resided at Juniper Hill for various periods, and then formed a colony' were charged with not giving up their land, and warrants were issued for their ejectment. They had put up such strong resistance that it was feared that the men would not leave gracefully but the fears proved unfounded:

> The Juniper Hill Ejectments – it will be remembered that a few weeks since the authorities under the Cottisford Enclosure Act obtained, at the Bicester petty sessions, warrants of ejectment against about forty working people who were holding cottages on land at Juniper Hill, in that parish, and who had there formed a colony, and who looked upon interference with their 'territorial' possessions as a measure to be resisted. From threats that had been made it was thought that on the ejectments being enforced the occupants would lawfully resist and that it would be necessary to have the assistance of those skilled in the arts of war. This, however, has not been necessary, and an arrangement has been come to. On Tuesday and Wednesday last the authorities, to the number of about twenty, proceeded to take possession of the occupancies of those who had not previously made terms with them. The constables' men had pickaxes etc., for demolishing the buildings in case such extreme measures should appear necessary. They, however, were not. All the defendants gave up possession. In return they are to have the crops from the land, and to have fourteen-year leases at 5s per year, of their residence and garden ground.

Oxford Chronicle, 20 August 1853

John Collett, a parish constable, did not at all approve of the way the squatters were being treated and was found guilty of misconduct because he dared to express his support for them, and fined £2 8s together with 12s in costs.

Flora wrote about 'Old Sally' and her husband 'Dick', who were based on Sarah and Richard Moss, who married in 1869. Both Sarah's first husband George Fox and her second Richard Moss were involved in the riots and Richard was a notorious poacher who had been specifically threatened with eviction. Surprisingly Flora does not mention the disturbances at enclosure at all in her writing, although they took place only twenty-odd years before she was born.

Watford Tunnel cottage, where Flora's aunt Harriet Sharman lived, and where Flora is said to have been born, painted by Henry Westbury.

By 1871 there were thirty-three cottages in Juniper, five of which were unoccupied. The census returns give clues about the village as Flora would have known it and to the identity of some of Flora's characters, although she has changed many of the details. In 1871 there were thirty-seven labourers, the youngest of whom was twelve, two shepherds, a shoemaker (Thomas Whiting, who became Flora's 'Uncle Tom', of whom more later), one labourer and grocer, one publican and grocer, one man with no occupation, one laundress, one dressmaker and twenty-eight scholars (schoolchildren), the oldest of whom was eleven. There was some continuity of occupation as nine of the names recorded were of the same families as in the 1801 census: Collett, Fox, Hall, Judas, Moss, Price, Sabbin (presumably the same as Savin in 1801), Tuffrey and White.

By 1881 the number of labourers had increased to thirty-nine; still two shepherds, a gardener, one publican, one tailor, and Albert Timms as stonemason, one laundress and twenty-nine scholars. In 1891 there were still thirty-nine labourers, three shepherds, one stonemason and mason (Albert Timms), one publican, two engine drivers, one carpenter, one thatcher, and female occupations included one servant (at the pub), a seamstress and a sick nurse, with only twenty-three scholars.

The Timms Family

Albert Timms, called 'Robert' in *Lark Rise to Candleford*, is said to have come to the area when he was working on the repairs to some local churches, so perhaps he rented a property in Juniper. He and his wife Emma Dibber were witnesses to the marriage of Emma's elder sister Harriet to Thomas Sharman at Cottisford church in 1873 (Thomas died young, at the age of thirty-two, in 1880, and Harriet left Juniper). Perhaps surprisingly Albert and Emma themselves married in Cottisford on 29 July 1875, rather than in Ardley where her parents lived. The witnesses at their wedding were Albert's sister Ann and Thomas Whiting, who lived in Juniper at that time and married Ann on 17 April 1876, with Albert and Emma as witnesses. Albert and Emma rented a cottage in Juniper Hill, near to Watford Tunnel Cottage where her sister Harriet was living. Albert worked as a stonemason for thirty-five years for Hawkins the builders and Coles the monumental masons in Brackley, whose premises were situated on the road to Banbury. He had to walk three miles there and three miles back, and sometimes many more miles to the site where he was working. His hours were from six in the morning until five in the afternoon.

Albert was initially proud of his ability as a stonemason, although he had not undertaken a formal apprenticeship. As a young man he built a little workshop on the side of the cottage, and Flora remembered seeing some of his carvings used as ornaments around the house – a lion, a baby's head and lilies of the valley growing at the base of a tree trunk. There was a wide variety of work in the area at that time, as country houses were being built and extended, and he may have worked on extensions to Tusmore House. As well as the elaborate work required for large houses he could turn his hand to carving a tombstone, or repairing a cottage or building a wall, or even bricklaying.

Albert married at the age of twenty-one, and Flora was born eighteen months later so it is not surprising that Flora remembers him as a handsome young man:

As Laura first remembered him he was a slim, upright young man in the late twenties, with dark, fiery eyes and raven-black hair, but fair, fresh-coloured complexion. On account of the dusty-white nature of his work, he usually wore clothes of some strong light-grey worsted material. Years after he had died, an old and embittered man, she could see him, a white apron rolled up around his middle, a basket of tools slung over his shoulder and a black billycock hat set at an angle on his head, swinging along the crown of the road on his way home from work.

Lark Rise to Candleford, p. 262.

As a craftsman he earned slightly more than the 10s a week of the agricultural labourer so when the family moved to the End House, where Flora grew up, they were able to afford 2s 6d a week to rent the double cottage. Albert was more intelligent than most of his neighbours and enjoyed himself at election time, standing on a plank supported by beer barrels to explain Gladstone's policies in an amusing way. For many years he and Emma kept talking about moving away from Juniper to find better schooling for the children, perhaps to a town, but something always seemed to happen to put it off. Albert became frustrated in his work, and his use of his skills seems to have declined as he grew older, as in 1891 he was described as a stone and brick mason. He preferred the more complex work he had done in churches to general building, but he was never able to better himself, grew depressed and turned to drink, so that the income he brought home was irregular, which must have caused the careful Emma many problems. However his sisters had married well, so parcels of cast-off clothes helped Emma to dress her family better than most.

Flora used the character of a stonemason in several pieces of her writing, though the details differ in each instance and we cannot be sure how much she drew on the character of her father in writing them. In an unpublished fragment of a book entitled *The Stithy*, she wrote about the death of a stonemason, who left a widow and two children. It was written in the first person, and contained elements of Albert's character:

My father had not been very good to us. He had been a drunkard with all the faults of his kind; weak-willed, unstable, mean and prodigal by turns; a poor broken-down creature, puffed up to the last by a fancied superiority to the labouring people amongst whom we lived. A fancy based upon a tradition of blue blood in his veins and a striking presence.

'Harry Ransom Archive', University of Texas.

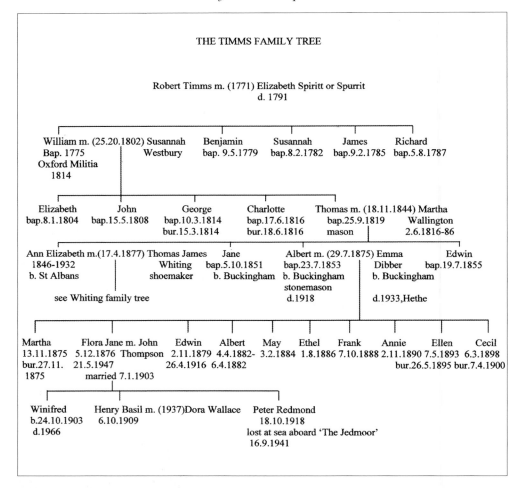

The Timms family tree.

The same stonemason character was reused, with almost the same phrases in places, in another unpublished book, *Gates of Eden*, so Flora was evidently influenced by the world of the stonemason and by the character of her father in particular.

In *Still Glides the Stream*, she featured Thomas Hearne, an elderly stonemason who took too much of a pride in his job and spent too long perfecting the work for the taste of the new owner of the firm he worked for, making his work too expensive.

Emma was a pretty girl of twenty-two when she married Albert Timms. She took care with her appearance and her clothes, and when Flora and Edwin were small delighted in taking them for walks round the local roads in their wickerwork pram, a rarity in the village. She had to develop the art of making do and mending to maintain the family's standard of living as the money she received from Albert became more erratic, but she always made sure that she kept her head high and maintained the family's reputation in the village. Having worked as a nursemaid she was good with her children; strict but fair in her discipline and kind. Flora wrote that she told wonderful fairy stories, some extending over several nights, and it was perhaps part of this imagination which flourished in her daughter. She does appear to have favoured her boys above the girls, particularly Edwin, and Flora seems to have felt that she was less loved than he was, and in consequence was not that close to her mother as she grew older.

They did share happy memories though, and confidences, particularly just before Flora went to work in Fringford, and it was to Flora that Emma would talk of her father, John Dibber, after his death.

Emma and Albert rented two cottages in Juniper before they settled on the End House, situated half way round the Rise:

> Looking at the hamlet from a distance, one house would have been seen, a little apart, and turning its back on its neighbours, as though about to run away into the fields. It was a small grey stone cottage with a thatched roof, a green-painted door and a plum tree trained up the wall to the eaves.

Lark Rise to Candleford, p. 20

The cottage had two small bedrooms, and Albert used his skills to improve it, adding a second downstairs room which they called the washhouse, and put in an oven grate so that they could roast the Sunday joint. Emma made the cottage welcoming, priding herself on keeping the furniture immaculately polished – never a lick and a promise for her – and decorating it with bright crockery and red and black rugs, (probably rag rugs), warmed the tile floor.

The Timms family were lucky in having their own well, as not all the cottages had one, and their earth closet was situated well away from the house to keep unpleasant smells to a minimum. The living room door led straight into the garden and the children often played there, relishing especially playing in the jungle-like tangle of growth of currant and gooseberry bushes and raspberry canes. Flora says that they rented the cottage from Mrs Herring, who was married to a retired stud groom and had lived in the village for a while.

Emma Timms, *née* Dibber, Flora's mother.
(Henry Westbury)

Above: The End House, home of the Timms family, as it looked in 1979. The plaque commemorating Flora can be seen on the right hand side of the wall. Queenie's cottage can be seen on the left.

Left: Flora in a typical pose with a book. (Henry Westbury)

The End House would now be almost unrecognisable to Flora, because most of it has been pulled down and rebuilt, leaving only one wall the same, and the thatch has been replaced by slates. A small plaque on the wall reveals it to be Flora's house.

Flora was born on 5 December 1876, probably in Watford Tunnel Cottage (now demolished) in Juniper, where Emma's sister Harriet lived, 'for convenience'. Later Emma often sent the elder children away when she was expecting the next baby, and there was a general pretence to the children that there was no pregnancy until the baby actually arrived. Flora was the eldest surviving daughter; her elder sister Martha, baptised on 13 November 1875, only lived for a few days. Flora grew into a quiet, dreamy child, shy and diffident compared with the bouncy village children. She never found it easy to make friends, and always felt a little different from the children around her. As she grew up she was expected to help with her younger siblings, and Emma fondly imagined that she too would become a nursemaid, but changed her mind about her suitability when she saw that Flora would much rather read a book than pay any attention to small children.

Flora's favourite brother Edwin ('Edmund' in *Lark Rise*) was baptised on 2 November 1879. They always remained close, even though separated physically in adulthood. Both were quiet children:

> Edmund was at that time a quiet, thoughtful little boy, apt to ask questions which it puzzled his mother to answer. The neighbours said he thought too much and ought to be made to play more; but they liked him because of his good looks and quaint, old-fashioned good manners ... He was a small slender child with blue eyes and regular features. When she had dressed him for their afternoon walk, his mother would kiss him and exclaim: 'I do declare he might be anybody's child. I can't see any difference between him and a young lord, and as for intelligence, he's too intelligent'.

Lark Rise to Candleford, pp. 267-8

As he grew older Edwin certainly knew his own mind. His mother wanted him to be apprenticed to a carpenter, but he had ideas of working on the land, (considered in those days a badly paid and dead-end job), being an engine driver, or becoming a soldier and travelling abroad. In the end he was able to do two of those things. He left school to become an agricultural labourer at the age of eleven, surprisingly early as he was an intelligent boy who would have benefited from the opportunity to stay on longer at school. Perhaps the growing family meant that Albert could not afford to keep him at school any longer.

His ambition to be a soldier was achieved at the outbreak of the Boer War. Edwin was staying in Yorkshire, probably with Aunt Jane, when war was declared, and the nineteen-year-old immediately went off to enlist in the Duke of Wellington's regiment, which later became the West Yorkshire Regiment. Flora, who was then working at Grayshott Post Office, saw him off one snowy Sunday at Aldershot station; she was full of apprehension for his safety, while he was glowing with enthusiasm about the great adventure he was about to undertake.

Edwin was lucky to survive the Boer War as he was taken prisoner while scouting and abandoned alone in the veldt, one enemy soldier probably saving his life by flinging him a half-empty water bottle as he rode off. It took him three days walking, parched with thirst, before he reached a Boer homestead where, despite his being her enemy, an old woman filled his water bottle.

His regiment was sent straight to India after the war, where he served for several years. He then spent a couple of years working for poor wages as a farm labourer in England before deciding to emigrate to Canada. Flora, by then married, travelled up to Juniper for a fortnight to be with the family and see him before he left. As he was working long hours on a farm, her time with him was necessarily brief. They managed to have one long walk together, talking of their childhood, and of Edwin's travels, and he claimed that the sights which had most impressed

him were York Minster and the Taj Mahal. This may have been the last time the two were to
meet. Edwin loved Canada, and seemed set to stay there for life, but the First World War took
him back into the army. He enlisted on 12 December 1914 in Winnipeg in the 32nd Overseas
Infantry Battalion, and embarked for England on 23 February 1915. Once arrived in England
he was stationed at Shorncliffe, to the renamed 32nd Reserve Battalion, which was reinforcing
Canadian units already at the front. He had some leave between March and May 1915 and was
then transferred to the Eastern Ontario Battalion on 15 May 1915. In November 1915 he spent
eight days in hospital suffering from rheumatic fever. He was allowed home leave from 20-28
March 1916 before embarking for France. Flora was unable to travel up to Oxfordshire to see
him as her children were ill and the weather was bad. Three weeks after his arrival in France,
on 26 April 1916 he was killed in action in a relative lull after the battle for the St Eloi craters.
He was buried in grave II.F.3 in the Woods Cemetery at Zillebeke near Ieper in Belgium.

    Flora heard about his death secondhand one sunny April morning. She had felt that things
were beginning to look better for her, and the children had recovered, when one of her own
letters to him was returned to her, marked in pencil 'Killed in Action'. She should have been
informed earlier, but apparently the official letter was misdirected, possibly because the Timms'
address was given as Brackley, North Hants rather than Northamptonshire. Edwin wrote to his
mother Emma in 1915, saying that if he was killed she would receive his pay, but the Canadian
army did not let her have his pension after her husband Albert had died, or give her the $20
a month separation allowance usually granted. However several years later, in 1920, Emma
received the three service medals he had earned, together with the Canadian Memorial Cross
on a purple neck ribbon which was given to widows and mothers of Canadians killed in
action. A circular bronze plaque bearing Edwin's name, known as a 'death plaque' and death
scroll number 763901 were sent to Albert Timms (although he had already died).

    Flora was devastated and grieved bitterly for the death of such a beloved brother, but later
she was philosophical:

> ... she came to feel in later life that in the matter of his death Edmund was indeed happy, for
> he was a soldier by his own choice and he died a soldier's death on the battlefield. Unlike
> some who fall in warfare he had not to relinquish life before he had well tasted it, and unlike
> others, he left behind him no brood of young children to face the world fatherless. He went
> the way of the old heroes of his childhood, in the prime of his manhood, fighting for a cause
> he wholeheartedly believed in, and went swiftly and suddenly in the heat of battle, a happy
> warrior.

Heatherley, pp. 288-9

Edwin is commemorated on the war memorial in Cottisford church. Flora never forgot her
beloved brother, and she herself commemorated him, albeit transporting him from Oxfordshire
to Hampshire, in one of her poems, entitled 'August Again', which includes the verse:

> The heather flings her purple robe
> Once more upon the hill;
> Beneath a shivering aspen-tree
> My love lies cold and still; -
> Ah, very deep my Love must sleep,
> On that far Flemish plain,
> If he does not know the heath-bells blow
> On the Hampshire hills, again!

The photograph of Flora with a book in her hands shows her wearing an early unauthorised
version of the 2nd Battalion badge which Edwin must have sent her.

Edwin Timms in uniform, taken while he was serving in India. He went back into the army, as a Private in the 3rd Company, Second Battalion, 1st Canadian Division, to fight in the First World War, and was killed in his first week in the trenches. His obituary reported that his last words to his mother were 'Don't fret, mother, when I go into battle my last thoughts are for you and my God'. (Henry Westbury)

Stone marking the grave of Edwin Timms in Zillebecke cemetery, Belgium. (Mrs Doris Lown)

Flora makes occasional references to her younger siblings in her books, but does not build up the detailed picture of them that she does of Edwin. She wrote:

> … by the time her last year at school approached, her mother had five children. One little sister shared her bed and another slept in the same room; she had to go to bed very quietly in the dark, not to awaken them. In the day-time, out of school hours, the latest baby, a boy, had to be nursed indoors or taken out for his airing. These things, in themselves, were no hardship, for she adored the baby, and the little sisters, who held on, one on each side of the baby-carriage, were dears, one with brown eyes and a mop of golden curls, and the other a fat, solemn child with brown hair cut in a straight fringe across her forehead. But Laura could no longer read much indoors or roam where she would when out, for the baby-carriage had to be kept more or less to the roads and be pushed back punctually at baby's feeding-time.

Lark Rise to Candleford, p. 374

Flora's next brother Albert was born on 4 April 1882 and buried two days later. Her sister May was baptised on 3 February 1884. She was commended by the Diocesan Inspector who visited Cottisford School in 1894, and by 1901 she was working as a domestic servant at the Coffee Tavern, a Temperance hotel in Dorking in Surrey.

Flora's sister, Ethel Elizabeth, usually known as Betty, was born on 10 June 1886. Betty, aged fifteen was living in Wraby House in Brackley in 1901, working as a general domestic servant for Wesleyan Minister John Osbourne, his daughter Lydia and his sister Frances. She went on to work in Post Offices but left in 1918 to look after her sick father Albert. She took after her in her literary leaning and had her children's book *The Little Grey Men of the Moor* published in 1926, which encouraged Flora to persevere with her own writing. Like Flora, Betty entered literary competitions and won two in 1924 and 1926. Betty married Henry Eastwood at Hungerford on 17 July 1928 and they went to live in Laurel Cottage, Henstridge, near Temple Combe in Somerset. Henry Westbury who has researched her life wrote:

> Betty continued her writing with a 55,000 word autobiographical novel entitled *A Pin to see a Pin-a-sight*, and an essay 'Golden Wedding' and a number of short stories, but it would appear that these were never published. Fortunately these works have survived in draft form and interestingly it would appear that they were typed using the same machine that Flora used. Betty also wrote a further children's book entitled *The Island of Kaboo*, but again it would appear that this book was not published. However two typewritten draft versions have survived. The first shows on the cover 'by Elizabeth Eastwood, The Outlook, Dartmouth', and the other shows 'by Elizabeth Eastwood, Lauriston, Brixham'. These were of course two of Flora's addresses, and as before the drafts appear to have been typed on Flora's machine… In spite of her humble beginnings, those who met Betty during her later years, describe her as being an elegant and refined lady. This impression was quite possibly due to the benefit of the many years which she spent as a lady's companion, following the death of her husband. Betty was still residing at Laurel Cottage in 1978 when Margaret Lane wrote to her concerning a proposed meeting, but at some time during the 1980s Betty was admitted to a nursing home in Devizes where she remained until she died.

Henry Westbury's manuscript notes.

Frank Wallington Timms was born in 1888, (he later emigrated to Australia). Annie Gertrude was born in 1890, Ellen Mary in 1893, (who died aged two), and Cecil Barrie in 1898, who died in 1900. Albert Timms died aged sixty-four in December 1918 and is buried in Cottisford churchyard, but sadly, although he was a stonemason there is no tombstone for him. Emma died aged eighty in Hethe and was buried in Cottisford on 5 December 1933.

Ethel Elizabeth Timms, usually known as Betty, Flora's younger sister, who also became a writer and had her children's book *The Little Grey Men of the Moor* published. (Henry Westbury)

Frank Timms, Flora's brother, who emigrated to Australia to become a fruit farmer. (Henry Westbury)

Neighbours

Flora later wrote that in writing *Lark Rise* she accurately described the people and places she remembered from her childhood, but she has made some significant changes in her depictions of them, perhaps deliberately to make them less readily identifiable, perhaps because she was remembering them many years later, and memory is fallible. However she draws wonderfully detailed pictures. Some can be readily identified, such as 'Sally' and 'Dick', in real life Sarah and Richard Moss, (Richard was involved in the Juniper Hill riots), although significant details about them have been altered. The pair were recorded in the 1871 census as both being fifty-eight, a good deal younger than Flora suggested in her book, though by the time she was ten in 1886 'Sally' would have been seventy-three. The couple represented for her the old pre-enclosure society, living in more comfortable circumstances than others in the village. 'Dick' was apparently a small, rather withered man who wore a smock-frock (out of fashion by this time), and spent much time tending his big garden. His wife 'Sally' seems to have been a larger than life character who left a lasting impression on the young Flora. She used her character in her writings for *The Catholic Fireside* long before she thought about writing *Lark Rise*. She vividly described 'Sally' and her cottage, giving a rare first-hand description of what life was like in a village towards the end of the Victorian era:

> Sally was tall and broad, not fat, but massive, and her large, beamingly good-natured face, with its well-defined moustache and tight, coal-black curls bobbing over each ear, was framed in a white cap frill; for Sally, though still strong and active, was over eighty, and had remained faithful to the fashions of her youth.
>
> She was the dominating partner ... the house was hers and she carried the purse; but Dick was a willing subject, and enjoyed her dominion over him. It saved him a lot of thinking, and left him free to give all his time and attention to the growing things in his garden.
>
> Old Sally's was a long, low, thatched cottage with diamond-paned windows winking under the eaves and a rustic porch smothered in honeysuckle. Excepting the inn, it was the largest house in the hamlet, and of the two downstairs rooms, one was used as a kind of kitchen storeroom, with pots and pans and a big red crockery water vessel at one end, and potatoes in sacks and peas and beans spread out to dry at the other. The apple crop was stored on racks suspended beneath the ceiling and bunches of herbs dangled below. In one corner stood the big brewing copper in which Sally still brewed with good malt and hops once a quarter. The scent of the last brewing hung over the place until the next and mingled with apple and onion and dried thyme and sage smells, with a dash of soap-suds thrown in, to compound the aroma which remained in the children's memories for life ...
>
> The garden was a large one, tailing off at the bottom into a little field where Dick grew his corn crop. Nearer the cottage were fruit trees, then the yew hedge, close and solid as a wall, which sheltered the beehives and enclosed the flower garden. Sally had such flowers, and so many of them, and nearly all of them sweet-scented! Wallflowers and tulips, lavender and sweet william, and pinks and old-world roses with enchanting names - Seven Sisters, Maiden's Blush, moss rose, monthly rose, cabbage rose, blood rose, and, most thrilling of all to the children, a big bush of the York and Lancaster rose, in the blooms of which the rival roses mingled in a pied white and red. It seemed as though all the roses in Lark Rise had gathered together in that one garden. Most of the gardens had only one poor starveling bush or none; but then nobody else had so much of anything as Sally.

Lark Rise to Candleford, pp. 76-79

Flora wrote that the house had been built by 'Sally's' grandfather before enclosure, but here she distorted the facts. Sarah herself, the daughter of John Stephens, who was not a Cottisford man, was born in Helmdon, Northamptonshire, in about 1812 and died in October 1895 aged

Aove left: Flora's sister, Annie Timms. (Henry Westbury)

Above right: Emma Timms sits front right in this photograph and it is thought that the woman next to her may be Jane Whiting (*née* Timms) possibly with two of the Whiting girls standing behind them. (The Old Gaol Museum, Buckingham)

eighty-three. She came to Cottisford after marrying George Fox, an agricultural labourer, who had built a squatter's cottage in the village in 1847, which he agreed at enclosure to lease for fourteen years. Sarah was described as a lacemaker in the 1851 census. They had one son, John, who was also an agricultural labourer. By the time of the 1861 census Sarah had given up lacemaking, and had no occupation. At that time Richard Moss, aged forty-six, an agricultural labourer, was married to Mary, and they had two sons, William and Robert, both agricultural labourers and a daughter Mary Ann. After the deaths of George Fox and Mary Moss, Sarah and Richard were married in 1869, so Flora was inaccurate in stating that they had been married for sixty years. It was Richard Moss who owned the cottage, not Sarah, and his father had been one of only four men granted the right of freeholder at enclosure, when his claim to the cottage, with a garden and an acre of land was formally recognised. It is more likely that the items which made the house so comfortable were inherited from his side of the family.

Flora suggested that 'Sally' told her about the village as it had been at the beginning of the nineteenth century, before enclosure, when the village still stood in the middle of a furzy heath dotted with juniper bushes, boasting only six houses in a ring. But Sarah Moss would not have known the village then, although 'Dick' would have done. By this time two new cottages had evidently been added to the original four cottages of the eighteenth century, and gradually more would be built. Again she used 'Sally' as a vehicle to describe how the agricultural labourers had lost much of their ability to earn money in other ways at enclosure, such as by keeping cows, geese and poultry, in addition to the pigs still cosseted in the back gardens. The grazing for these was lost at enclosure, so the wives could no longer make butter to sell. Labourers no longer had the right of cutting furze for firing, and many other advantages were lost. Again, this probably referred to 'Dick's' family rather than 'Sally's'. Richard Moss died in 1893 aged eighty and Sarah died in 1895 aged eighty-three.

Sarah and Richard Moss, (Flora's 'Sally' and 'Dick') who owned the largest and best-equipped house in the village when Flora was a child. (Oxfordshire Photographic Archive)

As some of the village houses were built as squatters' cottages, without the benefit of architects and professional builders, it is hardly surprising that many only had a short life. Flora came back to visit Juniper later in life, and must have been horrified by what she saw; the roofs of some cottages had fallen in and the only trace of Sarah and Richard's was a whitish mark in the corner of a ploughed field.

In *The Peverel Papers* she wrote about 'Old Sally' as a bee wife, possibly mingling the characters of Sarah Moss and lacemaker Eliza Massey, christened 'Queenie Macey' in *Lark Rise*. Sugar was expensive, so keeping bees for their honey was a common alternative among country people, who could also make a little ready money by selling honey and beeswax. The beehives were usually straw bee skeps at this time rather than rectangular wooden hives. The light skeps were weighted down with locally made red earthenware pans:

On a three-legged stool beside them their mistress would sit dreaming and dozing for a whole summer day together, a little old woman in a mauve sunbonnet and plaid shawl who may have dropped straight out of a fairy-tale.

Now and again, in early summer, a loud hubbub would arise in the sleepy garden – a sound of beating and drumming, tinkling and jangling; and then the villagers would smile at each other and say: 'Old Sally's bees've a'swarmed'; and anyone near enough would see the old woman rushing wildly backwards and forwards, bonnet strings flying, as she followed the flight of a column of whirling wings, banging all the time with her door key upon whatever pot or pan had come nearest.

The Peverel Papers, p. 88

Eliza Massey (Flora's Queenie Macey'),
the lacemaker and beekeeper who
lived next door to the Timms family.
(Oxfordshire Photographic Archive)

'Sally' and 'Queenie' shared several attributes, both of them in real life being lacemakers and keeping bees. Eliza and her husband Thomas Massey can be found for the first time in Juniper Hill in the 1881 census. Thomas was then aged forty-nine, working as an agricultural labourer, born in Launton, the son of William, an agricultural labourer, and Mary. His wife Eliza, aged fifty-eight was born in Lower Heyford. They lived in the tiny cottage with one room downstairs and one room upstairs set almost in front of the End House. Although Eliza cannot have had personal memories of the great period of lacemaking in the village, Flora was correct in saying that it had been important. In the 1851 census, nineteen out of the female population of 125 were lacemakers. The invention of the Nottingham lacemaking machines devastated the cottage industry of bobbin lacemaking, which was slow and labour intensive, so by 1861 no lacemakers were listed there in the census.

Eliza's maiden name was Gee, and she was probably the daughter of Thomas and Elizabeth Gee. Thomas was an agricultural labourer who was living in Fringford, next to the mill, in 1841, with his wife, Eliza and two other daughters: Sarah who was eighteen and Ann who was eight. Eliza married Thomas Massey in 1850 and by 1851 they were living in Launton with their nine-month-old son Thomas. In the 1861 census they had three sons: Mark (six), Joseph (two) and Eli (five months). They also had a daughter, Annie, born in 1855, who married James Aris, an agricultural labourer from Bicester and in 1881 Eliza's granddaughter Ellen was staying with them in Juniper Hill. Thomas died in Bicester Union Workhouse in 1899 aged seventy and was buried in Cottisford on 6 November. Eliza was living with her daughter Annie in Albert Place, Market End in Bicester in 1901 and she died aged eighty-three in 1902.

Flora wrote a vivid description of 'Queenie':

She seemed very old to the children, for she was a little, wrinkled, yellow-faced old woman in a sunbonnet; but she cannot have been nearly as old as Sally... old Master Macey, commonly called 'Twister', was still able to work part of the time, and they managed to keep their home going.

Lark Rise to Candleford, pp. 81–2

Flora wrote that 'Queenie' kept her tiny cottage clean and tidy, but once she had whitened the hearthstone and polished the brass candlesticks, if the weather was fine she would take her lace pillow and low stool out to the beehives and sit there, her face protected by her lilac sunbonnet, and make lace, or doze in the sunshine. She must have started to learn lacemaking, probably at a special lace school, when she was about four or five, as children had to start young when their fingers were still very supple, to achieve the speed required to earn money. She would have worked on a big pillow stuffed with straw, using slim bone or lace bobbins weighted with bead spangles, perhaps decorated with messages such as 'KISS ME QUICK FOR MOTHER IS COMING' or 'TAKE THIS SMALL GIFT I FREELY GIVE AND THE LORD PROTECT YOU WHILE YOU LIVE' making the highly-prized Bucks point lace:

Queenie at her lacemaking was a constant attraction to the children. They loved to see the bobbins tossed hither and thither, at random as it seemed to them, every bobbin weighted with its bunch of bright beads and every bunch with its own story, which they had heard so many times that they knew it by heart, how this bunch had been part of a blue bead necklace worn by her little sister who had died at five years old, and this other one had belonged to her mother, and that black one had been found, after she was dead, in a work-box belonging to a woman who was reputed to have been a witch.

There had been a time, it appeared, when lacemaking was a regular industry in the hamlet. Queenie, in her childhood, had been 'brought up to the pillow' sitting among the women at eight years old and learning to fling her bobbins with the best of them. They would gather in one cottage in winter for warmth, she said, each one bringing her faggot or shovel of coals for the fire, and there they would sit all day, working, gossiping, singing old songs, and telling old tales till it was time to run home and put on the pots for their husbands' suppers... In very cold winter weather the lacemakers would have a small earthen pot with a lid, called a 'pipkin', containing hot embers, at which they warmed their hands and feet and sometimes sat upon.

Lark Rise to Candleford, p. 83

Now the laceman no longer called to purchase the handmade lace and 'Queenie' was described as taking her lace to sell at Banbury Fair.

'Queenie' managed as best she could, with her husband being such a poor provider. Flora told the story of how she used to collect milk from the farmhouse in Cottisford, which was supposed to be sold at 1d a pint, but people took their own containers and the lax dairymaid just filled them, whatever the size and still charged only 1d. 'Queenie' gradually increased the size of her container until she dared to take a tin cooking boiler. 'Laura' and 'Edmund' were intrigued, suggesting that she could make a good rice pudding with it, and 'Queenie' responded that she never made rice puddings – all the milk was used to fatten her pig, who was so fat he could hardly see out of his eyes! The family pig was the mainstay of the family diet in those days, and the fatter the meat was, the better they thought it.

'Queenie' was born in 1819, the same year as Queen Victoria and Flora said that she was married the day Queen Victoria was crowned, (this was not true: she was married in 1850)

Queenie's cottage, situated next to the End House. (Banbury Museum)

Eliza Massey (Queenie) would have used a lace pillow and bobbins similar to those used here by Elizabeth Hinks of Fringford. (Oxfordshire Photographic Archive)

and because of that she was apparently taken out of Bicester Workhouse to be chaired round the town on the day of the Coronation of Edward VII in 1902. She died not long afterwards and was buried in Bicester on 21 August 1902, aged eighty-one, and the parish registers state that she was then living in Back Way, Bicester.

'Twister' was apparently not over-fond of work, unless it was beating at shoots. Thomas was only forty-nine in 1881, and probably still working, although Flora says that he had bad rheumatism which forced him to work part-time. He was described as:

> ... a small thin-legged, jackdaw-eyed old fellow, and dressed in an old velveteen coat that had once belonged to a gamekeeper, with a peacock's feather stuck in the band of his battered old bowler and a red-and-yellow neckerchief knotted under one ear ... To serve his own purposes, Twister would sometimes pose as a half-wit, but, as the children's father said, he was no fool where his own interests were concerned. He was ready at any time to clown in public for the sake of a pint of beer, but at home he was morose.

Lark Rise to Candleford, p. 85

According to Flora, 'Twister' died one winter as a result of hunting in great snowstorms for a boy who was thought to be trapped in a horse and cart in the drifts. As it happened the boy had abandoned the horse and cart and escaped home, but 'Twister' is said to have caught pneumonia and died quickly. The truth of the story is uncertain, but 'Twister' is known to have died in Bicester Workhouse and was brought back to be buried in Cottisford in November 1899.

Another identifiable character is 'Caroline Arless', a lively neighbour who liked to entertain her friends and talk about the novelettes they were reading. Flora described her as being about forty-five, but young-looking with black hair and flashing eyes, who may have had gipsy blood. She was disapproved of by the local women because she was still having children when she was a grandmother, and she did not have a high standard of honesty:

> Ways and means did not trouble her ... One night she would fry steak and onions for supper and make the hamlet's mouth water, another night there would be nothing but bread and lard on her table. When she had money she spent it, and when she had none she got things on credit or went without ... Her idea of wise spending was to call in a few neighbours of like mind, set them round a roasting fire, and dispatch one of her toddlers to the inn with the beer can ... She was so charged with sex vitality that with her all subjects of conversation led to it – not in its filthy or furtive aspects, but as the one great central fact of life.
>
> Yet no one could dislike Mrs Arless, however much she might offend their taste and sense of fitness. She was so full of life and vigour and so overflowing with good nature that she would force anything she had upon anyone she thought needed it, regardless of the fact that it was not and never would be paid for.

Lark Rise to Candleford, pp. 112–113

She was hauled up several times in the County Court for non-payment of debts, but always managed to persuade the judge that her debt was due to her large family and her generosity, and got away with it.

'Caroline Arless' was in real life Caroline Smith who married Uriah Ariss, an agricultural labourer in 1868. Both came from Tingewick in Buckinghamshire. The 1871 census of Tingewick gives astonishingly incorrect information about them, as Caroline is said to be forty and Uriah fifty-three, and their son William seventeen. However Uriah had been born in 1844 and was twenty-five and as they had married in 1868 it was more likely that William was seventeen months rather than years. They had moved to Juniper Hill by 1881 and the ages are more realistically given as thirty-one for Caroline and thirty-six for Uriah. They had five children living at home: William, aged twelve who had probably left school as he was not listed as a scholar or as a labourer, Mary, aged seven and Eliza aged five were both at school, and the youngest two, Uriah aged three and Joseph aged one, were still at home. Ten years later in 1891 Uriah was listed as a thatcher, his son William was a shepherd and young Uriah, aged twelve, as an agricultural labourer. Four more children had been born: Ernest aged eight, Amy aged six, Henry aged four and Marian aged two. This fits better with Flora's recollections, so perhaps she was remembering them from this era. In 1901 the family was living in Chesterton and had two more children: Fred (nine) and Alice (six).

The 'Waggon and Horses'

The pub, called by Flora the 'Waggon and Horses', has in fact always been The Fox Inn. Thomas Harris, the innkeeper, who was born in 1808 in Gawcott in Buckinghamshire first appears in Cottisford in the 1851 census, described as a grocer, with his wife Mary who came from Hardwick and children Agnes (eighteen), a dressmaker, Thomas (fifteen), an errand boy, Hannah (eleven), Alban (seven) and John (four). Mary must have died before 1861 as Thomas' wife then was Fanny (also called Frances in later censuses), said to have been born in 1833 either in Dundee, Scotland (according to the 1861 census) or Dinedor, Herefordshire (according to the 1871 census). In 1861 another daughter, Harriet, had become a servant, Alban was a shoemaker and John an agricultural labourer. Thomas and Frances had three children: Eliza Mary, born in 1862, Aloysius born in 1866 and Elizabeth born in 1877. A one-year-old nephew from Scotland was staying with them. Thomas Harris died in 1875 but Frances carried on running the pub. In the 1881 census she was described as a widow of seventy-two and also living at the pub were: her son-in-law Joseph Morgan, a tailor from Hethe, his wife Elizabeth, Frances' fifteen-year-old son Aloysius who had no occupation and their fourteen-year old daughter Eliza. Aloysius later became a carpenter, working at Tusmore Park and was still living in the village in 1891, when he was twenty-five with his wife Elizabeth aged twenty-seven and young daughter Winifred. In 1891 the publican was Thomas Harris, son of the original publican, Thomas, and his first wife Mary. He described himself as a pub-licensed victualler, and was living with his wife Ann, children Mary (six), Thomas (five), Roxana (three) and John (two) and their servant, Louise Buckley.

A valuation had been made of the contents when Thomas Harris the elder died in 1875 (see Appendix One for the complete text) which reveals much about the pub and the family. The taproom was furnished with a deal table, twelve Windsor chairs and three corner cupboards, and contained other items such as fifteen spittoons, twenty-three tumblers, fifteen champagne glasses, tea things and kettle and a beer warmer. It seems unlikely that there was much call for champagne in the village! The inn contained a gallon of rum, 35 gallons of 9 per cent beer and 18 gallons of mild.

In 1882 another inventory was taken, and by then the taproom was more comfortably furnished with a table and cover, six Windsor chairs, an oak table, a drop-leaf table, sofa, double-front cupboard and writing desk.

The shop was in a back room in 1875, furnished with a deal counter, scales and weights, an oak table with drawers and a mahogany table and writing desk and at the time of the inventory contained bacon, beef suet, lard, sweets and matches for sale. Sugar was probably sold too, as there were sugar nippers in the shop for cutting it up. Perhaps the stock had been run down while Mr Harris was ill. In the 1882 inventory the only stock for sale appears to have been cheese. Flora wrote that the children used to be sent to the shop to buy candles, treacle and cheese, and commented that after Queen Victoria's Jubilee in 1887 nothing seemed quite the same, and one of the changes was that the shop was selling tins of salmon and of Australian rabbit! By 1904 the shop had disappeared and the room was being used as a parlour.

The men of the village spent many convivial evenings in the Fox Inn which was one of the largest houses in the village and even boasted two four-poster beds. The Harris family who ran it were Catholics. The man in a cap sitting to the right of the door bears a strong resemblance to Edwin Timms. (David Morris)

The Fox Inn in 1979.

A shooting party outside the Fox Inn, *c.* 1900. The man fifth from the left is the Earl of Ettingham and the man in front is Anthony Wood, the publican. (David Watts)

The inn was the largest house in the village, with its own bakehouse, which contained washing trays and tub and a large rectangular lead tray for salting bacon. The field bottles mentioned as being there were probably the costrels or harvest barrels which labourers took into the fields with them filled with beer or cider, to refresh them as they worked. In the hovel were large quantities of potatoes and peas, flour and two stocks of bees with a wheelbarrow and sundry other equipment. The Dutch oven stored in there was a semi-circular metal contraption from which a joint was hung which had a dripping tray below to catch melting fat. It was placed in front of the fire and the clock jack wound up so that the joint turned backwards and forwards to cook right through. The concave metal back reflected heat from the open fire to cook the joint more quickly.

There seems to have been no private living room for the publican and his family, although they appear to have used the taproom when the pub was not open, as dishes and tea things were kept in there. The house had four well-furnished bedrooms: the main one contained a four-poster bed with feather bed and flock mattress, feather bolster, five pillows, three blankets and a counterpane and other furniture including an oak table, chest of drawers, chairs, night commode, washstand and chest. In the second bedroom was a French bedstead with flock and straw mattresses, in the third bedroom there were two stump bedsteads, and the fourth bedroom contained another four-poster and volumes of *The Tablet*, a Catholic weekly. Among the items in the loft were four skittles and a ball – perhaps the game was played by the villagers outside the pub. There was also a coal house, and Mr Harris had a sow and six pigs. The presence of four-poster beds and flock mattresses suggests that the family were a good deal better off than most of the villagers. The Harris family were Catholic, as Flora wrote, and had to go off to mass each Sunday in a nearby village – hence the presence of the volumes of *The Tablet* and the name Aloysius:

The Catholic minority at the inn was treated with respect, for a landlord could do no wrong, especially the landlord of a free house where such excellent beer was on tap. On Catholicism at large, the Lark Rise people looked with contemptuous intolerance, for they regarded it as a kind of heathenism, and what excuse could there be for that in a Christian country? When, early in life, the end house children asked what Roman Catholics were, they were told they were 'folks as prays to images', and further inquiries elicited the information that they also worshipped the Pope, a bad old man, some said in league with the Devil. Their genuflexions in church and their 'playin' wi' beads' were described as 'monkey tricks'.

Lark Rise to Candleford, pp.213-4

The men would meet socially in the pub each evening. The publican would not have got rich on what the men spent, as they could seldom afford more than half a pint each evening, which they sipped to make it last as long as possible – even that sometimes had to be sacrificed when extra feed was needed to fatten the family pig.

The men each had their own places, and women did not join them, nor did children, although they tried to listen to what was going on when they came to buy items from the shop. The men happily discussed politics, told spine-chilling tales, and above all sang folk songs. The younger men knew the popular songs of the day such as 'Tommy, Make Room for Your Uncle', while the middle-aged men specialised in long mournful ballads on topics such as thwarted lovers. All the men could join in songs such as 'The Barleymow'. Thomas Price, who was fifty-nine in 1881, may have been the 'Master Price' who excelled in singing about Lord Lovell:

> Lord Lovell stood at his castle gate,
> Calming his milk-white steed,
> When up came Lady Nancy Bell
> To wish her lover God-speed ...

Flora described Master David Tuffrey, who was indulged because of his great age of eighty-three by letting him sing about the 'Outlandish Knight' most evenings, as it was the only song he knew, which he had learnt from his grandfather:

> An outlandish knight, all from the north lands,
> A-wooing came to me,
> He said he would take me to the north lands
> And there he would marry me.
>
> Go fetch me some of your father's gold
> And some of your mother's fee,
> And two of the best nags out of the stable
> Where there stand thirty and three ...

The dastardly knight then tried to murder his innocent lady, but she managed to outwit him and he drowned instead of her. 'David' was probably David Tuffrey, actually aged seventy-one in 1881, a labourer who lived in Juniper with his wife Sarah aged seventy.

Flora's early years were spent largely in the hamlet of Juniper, but when she was old enough to go to school the mother village of Cottisford began to feature more in her life.

Cottisford – Flora's Fordlow

The tiny village of Cottisford is a mile and a half away from Juniper by road, and it was here that Flora went to school and to church. It was smaller than Juniper, and very different in character, coming under the influence of Eton College who owned much of the land. Although the road is less sunken than a century ago, the buildings are little altered (apart from the conversion of the school and some barns) from those Flora would have seen:

> The village was a little, lost lonely place, much smaller than the hamlet, without a shop, an inn, or a post office, and six miles from a railway station. The little squat church, without spire or tower, crouched back in a tiny churchyard that centuries of use had raised many feet above the road, and the whole was surrounded by tall, windy elms in which a colony of rooks kept up a perpetual cawing. Next came the Rectory, so buried in orchards and shrubberies that only the chimney stacks were visible from the road; then the old Tudor farmhouse with its stone, mullioned windows and reputed dungeon. These, with the school and about a dozen cottages occupied by the shepherd, carter, blacksmith, and a few other superior farm workers, made up the village. Even these few buildings were strung out along the roadside, so far between and so sunken in greenery that there seemed no village at all. It was a standing joke in the hamlet that a stranger had once asked the way to Fordlow after he had walked right through it. The hamlet laughed at the village as 'stuck up'; while the village looked down on 'that gipsy lot' at the hamlet.

Lark Rise to Candleford, pp. 47-48

Cottisford has a much longer history than Juniper Hill, being a Saxon village established on the western side of a ford across the Crowell Brook. The earliest forms of the name are Wolfheysford and Urlesford, based on a Saxon personal name.

At the Norman Conquest, Cottisford consisted of two manors, both eventually granted to the manor of Bec. One manor was granted to Hugh de Grantmesnil who gave control of it to Roger d'Ivry, the husband of his daughter Adeline, who in turn granted it to the abbey of Bec in Normandy, who administered the estates through the priory of Ogbourne in Wiltshire. The other manor was granted to Bec by Rohais and her husband Robert de Curcy around 1125. Some land which had been granted to St Evroult Abbey was also passed to Bec so that it ended up holding the patronage of the Church and the entire village in the thirteenth century. Bec was an important abbey, being the northern centre of the Cluniac revival; it was Bec who replaced the Saxon church by the present building.

Manorial documents give us a glimpse into the administration of the monastic estate. In 1292 oats were obviously being grown as the manor was instructed to send two bushels for the horse of the prior of Goldcliff on the vigil of the Ascension and one bushel for the horse of the sub-proper of Steventon in June. The village was at its most prosperous at the end of the thirteenth century, when there was a flock of 765 sheep. Manorial receipts for 1288-89 mention:

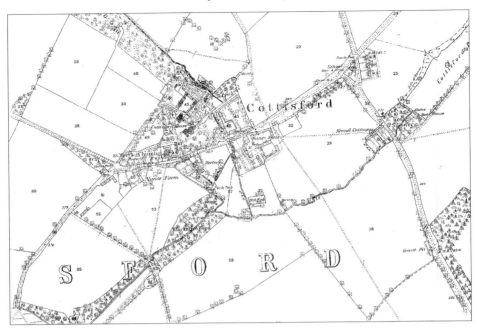

Reproduced from a late-nineteenth century Ordnance Survey map showing Cottisford. Most of the houses are built along the main village street. The village has a long history, as indicated by the medieval fishponds attached to the Manor House, known in the late nineteenth century as the Manor Farm. The village school is situated on a triangular plot at the crossroads and the houses nearby were model cottages built for agricultural labourers. (Oxfordshire Studies)

Rents (including forinsec rents)	£4	15	9
Court dues in tallage	£1	12	0
Sale of wool	£19	18	6½
Sale of corn		11	8

The estate then had 128 acres of arable, 126 acres sown and 5 acres of meadow with 195 ewes and hoggets, 220 wethers and 100 lambs, totalling 579 animals. The yields were 34 quarters and 3 bushels of wheat, 70 quarters of rye, 51 quarters of drage and 50 quarters of oats.

Many of the villagers were cottars who owed customary duties to the lord of the manor – in this case Bec. They had to work for so many weeks for their lord, including ploughing, weeding, mowing and harvest boons. Duties and any administrative problems were dealt with at manorial courts.

After the Black Death the number of available labourers was reduced so Bec land began to be leased out. In 1391 the lessee was Edward Metteley who paid £10 for a ten-year rental, subsequently renewed for the lifetime of himself and his wife Margaret. One of Bec's lessees in Cottisford was Sir Roger de Cotesford, three times High Sheriff of Oxfordshire.

The Hundred Years' War with France made the situation of manors attached to alien priories untenable so in 1404 Ogbourne and its manors, including Cottisford, were taken from Bec's ownership and granted by Henry IV to his son John, (later Duke of Bedford), William de St Vaast and Thomas Langley, who became Bishop of Durham, while England was at war with France. In 1438, three years after the death of the Duke of Bedford, Henry VI granted Cottisford to his uncle, Humphrey Duke of Gloucester, revoking his gift in 1441 to give it to his new foundation, Eton College. This gift was confirmed by Edward IV in 1462. Eton College exerted great influence over Cottisford for centuries, and retained the patronage of the church into the twentieth century when it was given to the Bishop of Oxford. Following the practice of Ogbourne, Eton leased out the manor and for sixty years from 1469 it was leased to John Samwell, whose brass of about 1500 can be seen behind the door of Cottisford church, commemorating him, dressed in armour, his wife Eleanor and their eight sons and five daughters. Various people held the lease of the manor in the sixteenth century and in the late seventeenth century it was held by Laurence Lord of Fritwell and then his son Laurence until 1731.

The medieval rabbit warren was still important in the seventeenth century, and there were deer on the heath. In 1739 the manor was leased by Richard Eyre, who had worked for the East India Company for twenty-eight years. The estate was in a neglected state, in 1759 comprising two farms which only brought in £90 and £34 a year, together with a warren worth £8, Mr Eyre's farm and a good house, plus a farm and mill in Fringford, so Eyre had to spend a good deal of money on repairs.

One activity which had died out by the time Flora was born was Cottisford Races, which ended around the 1820s. The echoes of it remained in village memory as Flora wrote to her nephew Leslie Castle that the field found on the right after turning off the main road to go down to Juniper was marked on old maps as 'The Racecourse' and that old people had a tradition about races being held there. The races must have caused much excitement locally, with lots of hustle and bustle in the village and crowds of people arriving to enjoy the races:

Replete as it was then with smug clean shaved squires, parsons, farmers, and traders from the towns and localities of Brackley, Buckingham, and Bicester, arrayed in deep white ties, kerseymere, top boots, and blue or black coats; replete also with young farmers, and farmers' sons, in bright green coats, resplendent with gilt buttons ... the spruce jocks, in jackets of various colours, the ladies in and on carriages, the grooms, all important in their own eyes, the thickly packed pedestrians, the refreshment booths, the grandstand, the extemporised stables, whose walls were fagots of gorse, and their roofs the open sky, the gambling tents, the thimble riggers, the cards with the names, weights, and colours of the riders, and other publications vended by bawlers, of a nature to tend only to the nourishment of vice and the corruption of youths ... That long looked for day at equal, the end of March or early in April, the last hunting day but one of the season, converted into a racing day, we will suppose to have arrived. Then was to come off the Farmer's Cup Race, for horses, not thoroughbred, that had regularly hunted with the packs of the Duke of Grafton or Beaufort, or that of Sir Thomas Mostyn, to be ridden by the owners or friendly non-professional riders. This was the great attraction of the day, at least, to the agricultural eye ... Nervous enough, and more than enough, looked many of the young farmer riders; albeit confident enough in their own saddles across country, as they emerged from the weighing scale, in tight-fitting leather inexpressibles, and flaunting silk jackets and caps, with their sweethearts and sisters, as well as trained jockeys engaged for other races, looking on. Half a dozen false starts were not uncommon; but at last they cry 'they are off', 'they are off' was borne upon the breeze, and the excitement became equal, among a smaller circle, to that of the Londoners on Epsom Downs on a Derby day ...

William Wing, *Brief Annals of the Bicester Poor Law Union and its Component Parishes, in the County of Oxford and Buckingham*, 1879

Although the races were long-gone by Flora's time, she did remember Cottisford Feast, an annual event until 1914, which also attracted many people from beyond the village. It was held on the weekend following 26 August, said to commemorate the joy of the villagers at the English victory at the Battle of Crecy on that date in 1346. Flora talks about it taking place on the Sunday and Monday. On the Sunday the people, friends and strangers from Brackley and nearby villages, sauntered along the road through Juniper, dressed in their best clothes, and all the families heated their ovens if they had them to provide roast beef and Yorkshire pudding

Reproduced from a nineteenth-century Ordnance Survey map, showing the site of Cottisford race course, adjacent to the turnpike road, which disappeared at enclosure, but was remembered as 'Racecourse Field'. (David Watts)

for their visitors. They tried to save a little money from harvest so they could afford to indulge in a little extra alcohol in the pub.

Although it was called Cottisford Feast, and must have originally taken place there before the hamlet developed, by Flora's time it took place largely in Juniper – perhaps because of the proximity of the pub. On the Monday and Tuesday the men had to go back to work, but the women gave tea parties at which the chief delicacy was 'baker's cake', a spicy dough cake flavoured with dried fruit.

Larger village feasts would have had a small fair and several stalls, but only one stall seems to have come to Cottisford Feast by the beginning of the 1880s, the gingerbread stall, with its canvas awning, which sold otherwise seldom obtainable delicacies such as gingerbread babies, striped peppermint humbugs, pink and white rock and various other sweets, including new-fangled items such as chocolate, hitherto unknown in the hamlet:

A visiting cousin, being fairly well-educated and a great reader, already knew it by name. 'Oh, that's chocolate,' he said off-handedly. 'But don't buy any; it's for drinking. They have it for breakfast in France.' A year or two later, chocolate was a favourite sweet even in a place as remote as the hamlet ...

Lark Rise to Candleford, p. 231

Perhaps the cousin was young Johnny Whiting from Twyford and the son of 'Uncle Tom'.

Life in the Cottisford village, Flora knew would have been dominated by the Rector, Charles Sawkins Harrison, the family of the squire Edwards Richard Kendal Rousby who lived at Cottisford House and the Waters family who leased the Manor Farm. In the 1881 census there were only twenty-six households in Cottisford (excluding Juniper). Mrs Rousby, a widow, lived at Cottisford House, and two occupiers of land were listed: Joseph Waters at the Manor Farm and Frederick Baines at the Warren. The Rector was assisted by a curate as well as twenty-one labourers, two gardeners (plus one groom and gardener and one butler and gardener), a blacksmith, mason, carpenter, tailor, schoolmistress, lacemaker and a variety of servants. The servants were: four general servants, a cook, housemaid, housekeeper, governess and coachman. There were also nine scholars (schoolchildren). This gives a much greater variety of occupations than those found in Juniper, and the description of the men as 'labourers' disguises more specialised occupations such as shepherd and carter. The men lived in tied cottages, which were cheaper than the rented Juniper ones, but gave the men less independence, as if they changed jobs they had to move immediately. Most of the labourers would have worked on the Cottisford farms.

The Farms

The principal farmhouse in Cottisford is the so-called 'Tudor farmhouse' described by Flora, which is the 'Manor Farm'. The core of it was probably built by Sir Roger de Cotesford, in the second half of the fourteenth century, and it was enlarged in the sixteenth and seventeenth centuries. The original medieval house was a rectangular block with two small projections facing west, with a first-floor hall and solar, open to the roof until the sixteenth century when it was re-roofed, a new floor inserted and a parlour built on. What Flora thought was a 'reputed dungeon' was probably the medieval garderobe tower. Some of the medieval windows have been reused in later portions of the house. The farm in Flora's time belonged to the Earl of Effingham, owner of Tusmore House.

A sale catalogue of 1944 shows the extent of the farmhouse, which was probably little changed from when Flora had known it, apart from the addition of electricity and some mod cons:

The attractive stone-built Manor Farmhouse with the original stone-mullioned windows ... fitted with electric light and modern conveniences, contains accommodation: five bedrooms, dressing room and two attics, bathroom and airing cupboard (with hot water from an independent boiler in the kitchen) and lavatory.

Ground floor: three reception rooms, kitchen (fitted with Triplex Range and an independent boiler), cloak-room with lavatory and scullery.

Sale Catalogue, Cottisford Manor Farm, Monday 8 May 1944, Auctioneers Messrs Stace and Foot, Brackley

The catalogue goes on to describe the 'well laid-out kitchen garden' and the range of farm buildings, which comprised:

Nag Stable for three horses with Harness Room adjoining and loft over.
Cow Stall with concrete floor and standing for nine cows.

18

Lot 2.

THE

COTTISFORD PART

OF THE ESTATE,

CONSISTING OF A SUPERIOR

Stone-built & Slated Farm Residence,

Containing Parlour, Sitting Room, and Kitchen ; Cellar, Pantry, Dairy, Brewhouse, 5 Bed-rooms, and 1 Attic. The Premises comprise Granary, Stabling for 20 Cart Horses, three-stall Nag Stable, 3 Barns, 2 Wagon Hovels, Cow-house, Chaff-house, Hen-house, Piggery, Yards, Garden, &c., and

616A. 1R. 19P.

OF ARABLE AND PASTURE LAND,

(CHIEFLY ARABLE,)

DIVIDED INTO THE FOLLOWING INCLOSURES :

As copied from the Tithe Commutation Plan, dated 10th of May 1856.

No. on Plan.	Description of Lands and Premises.	Cultivation.	Quantities. A. R. P.
41	Home Field Allotment...............	Arable	13 0 38
42	Two Cottages, Gardens and Allotment of Land...............	———	6 3 30
43	The Heath Allotment...............	———	35 1 24
44	Knights House Allotment	———	8 0 8
45	Ditto...............	———	6 2 37
46	Fox Cover Allotment...............	———	17 0 9
48	Woods House Allotment	———	26 2 14
49	Barn and Yard	———	0 1 20
49a	Old Driftway	———	1 3 36
51	Old Freeboard	———	1 1 0
52	Fox Cover Allotments	Arable	11 3 32
53	Cow Ground Allotments	———	16 0 18
54	Great East Allotment	———	121 2 6
54a	Reserved for Building	———	2 0 0
55	Great South Allotment	Arable	101 2 35
56	Great West Allotment	———	190 2 30
77	Mount Close	———	5 3 37
78	Rick Yard	———	0 0 39
90	Pond Piece Allotment	Arable	15 3 19
79	Dove House Piece	———	14 0 3
103	Sanfoin Ground	Grass	12 1 11
106	Rick Yard	———	0 1 34
106a	Allotment from Waste	———	0 1 30
107	Homestead, Garden, Yards, Stables, &c.	———	1 1 3
108	Garden	———	0 2 16
110	Moat Close	Meadow	2 0 16
43b	Cottage and Garden	———	0 0 29
43c	Ditto	———	0 0 35
43d	Three Cottages and Gardens	———	0 1 26
101	Five Cottages and Gardens	———	0 1 26
102	The Kennels...............	———	0 0 32
	Total. Acres		616 1 19

Of which Four of the Cottages (part of No. 101) are let to punctual tenants at £15 per annum ; one other Cottage, part of No. 101, and the Kennels, No. 102, in hand ; and the remainder of the property described in the above particulars let to Mr. RICHARD WOODS, a most respectable yearly tenant.

At £430 per annum,

Exclusive of £81 2s. 6d. tithe rent charge paid by the Tenant to the Rector.

ALSO THE UNDERMENTIONED

Cottages with Gardens, situate at Juniper Hill,

IN THE PARISH OF COTTISFORD, and not shown on the Plan,

Let on Lease for Fourteen Years from Michaelmas 1853, at the following Rents.

Extract from the sale catalogue when the Manor Farm was sold in 1853. It lists the pre-enclosure fields attached to the Manor Farm which reveal some of its history: for example 'Pond Piece' probably refers to medieval fishponds, 'Moat Close' may indicate that the medieval manor house was originally moated and 'Dove House Piece' probably indicates the site of the medieval dovecote. (Oxfordshire Studies)

Seven-bay open Cow Hovel opening into an enclosed yard and surrounded by the Cart Stable for seven horses with loft over, barn with concrete floor.

Large Barn opening on to the main road with loft over with six wood-partitioned Cornbins to accommodate 250 or so quarters of wheat and automatically fed by a blast Elevator from the Drier.

Eight-bay enclosed Cow Hovel with Loose Box adjoining and four-bay Implement Hovel.

Loose Boxes, Cow Stall and standing for cows.

Garage. Detached four-bay Implement Hovel.

Various Outbuildings.

Range of six brick-built pigsties, fitted with water troughs and feed-house adjoining, opening on to another enclosed Crew Yard with five-bay open Cow Hovel.

The Farmhouse and buildings have a continuous supply of water from the wind-pump in the Home Paddock and the pump is adaptable for engine power if required at short notice.

The land was said to be in good heart, especially suited for breeding sheep, growing barley and wheat and sugar beet. (In the late nineteenth century the principal crops were corn and turnips with much meadowland and in the 1880s there were about 800 sheep). Perhaps as important to any prospective new owner was the hunting potential:

> Good hunting is available in the immediate district, being in the heart of the Bicester country and within easy reach of the Grafton, Heythrop and Whaddon Chase hunts.
> The estate is noted for its partridge drives and the game has been preserved for many years and maintained by a keeper.

The gamekeeper would have been employed by the owner of Tusmore who owned the shooting rights. One of the cottages on the outskirts of Cottisford is called Kennel Cottage. In the 1861 census it was called Dog Kennel and its occupier was the gamekeeper, John Wilson, who came from Derbyshire, reflecting that game keeping is a specialist job. In 1871 the cottage was lived in by a labourer, James Savin. Ten years later it was being used by the curate Samuel Luffman and in 1891 it was the home of labourer Joseph Blaby.

The farm sale catalogue ties in with the description Flora gives, about the farm being several farms combined, extending beyond the parish boundaries. She wrote that there were meadows around the farm for the carthorses and a few milking cattle. The main crops were corn, especially wheat, and root crops, supplemented by hay, sainfoin and rye. Many of the farm buildings Flora knew are still there, although the barns, with enormous doors through which the blue and yellow painted farm wagons loaded with hay could be driven, have been converted to housing.

Joseph Waters, the tenant farmer Flora knew, had come to Cottisford in the 1860s, and had farmed several different holdings over the years. His father was a brewer, maltster and farmer who employed six labourers in 1851. Joseph was born in Fringford in 1833 and probably started his farming career working for his father, as he was living at home at the age of eighteen. He married Mary Painter in 1860 at Brackley, and by time of the census of 1861 they were ensconced in Cottisford, farming 590 acres, employing twenty-one men, ten boys, and one servant – Caroline Taston, aged twenty-four from Lower Heyford. Joseph must have done well as ten years later he was farming 1,200 acres, employing thirty-four men, twenty boys and five women. Their servant in 1871 was Mary Jane Golder, aged sixteen from Stoke Lyne.

Mary Waters died before 1881, when Joseph was living in Cottisford with his children Ellen (seven), George (four), William (three), housekeeper Elizabeth Lepper, aged forty-eight from Fringford and governess Marie Mobbs from Forest Hill. His older daughters Mary aged nine and Penelope aged eight were at a boarding school for young ladies run by Elizabeth Russell in Brackley High Street. In 1891 Joseph had several of his children at home: Mary, George, and William and two servants: Mary Atkins (sixteen) from North Kilbrook and Ada Gadd (twenty-four) from Buckinghamshire. The census tells us that two Waters girls, Amy (twenty) and Hannah (could this be Ellen, as the age matches and Ellen does not feature in the census anywhere else), who were presumably his daughters as theirs was the only Waters family in Cottisford, were staying with farmer Joseph Painter (possibly the relatives of their mother) at Barford St Michael. Penelope had gone further afield and was staying in Scarborough in Yorkshire with civil engineer William Millhood and his wife Sarah.

Joseph Waters farmed in Cottisford from 1861 until around the end of the century. Then he went to Home Farm, Shelswell where he was living in 1901 with his daughters Mary, Penelope and Helen and sons George and William, with one servant, Florence Wansfield from Croughton. While in Cottisford he was farming more than anyone else locally, renting some land from the Tusmore Estate and some from Eton College, to a total of about 1,400 acres.

Again Flora has made her character older than in real life, as he would only have been in his sixties in the 1890s. She described how the labourers came to the farmhouse every week to receive their wages personally from Joseph Waters:

> On Friday evening, when work was done, the men trooped up to the farmhouse for their wages. These were handed out of a window to them by the farmer himself and acknowledged

The core of the Manor House, now known as Manor Farm, was built in the fourteenth
century, probably by Sir Roger de Cotesford, and has been added to over the centuries. The
tenant in Flora's time was Joseph Waters, the principal farmer in the parish. (Oxfordshire
Photographic Archive)

by a rustic scraping of feet and pulling of forelocks. The farmer had grown too old and too
stout to ride horseback, and, although he still made the circular tour of his land in his high
dogcart every day, he had to keep to the road, and pay-day was the only time he saw many
of his men. Then, if there was cause for complaint, was the time they heard of it. 'You, there!
What were you up to in Causey Spinney last Monday, when you were supposed to be
clearing the runnels?' was a type of complaint that could always be countered by pleading,
'call o' Nature, please, sir.' ... But, just as often, it would be: 'There, Boamer, there you are
my lad, a bright and golden half-sovereign for you. Take care you don't go spending it all at
once' or an enquiry about some wife in childbed or one of the ancients' rheumatism. He
could afford to be jolly and affable: he paid poor old Monday Morning to do his dirty work
for him.

Apart from that he was not a bad-hearted man and had no idea he was sweating his
labourers.

Lark Rise to Candleford, pp. 60-61

Waters died in 1901 and his obituary in the *Banbury Guardian* on 24 October described him as:

an old and respected inhabitant has passed away – the death of Mr Joseph Waters. He was
engaged in farming here for upwards of half a century. For many years he resided at the
Cottisford Old Manor House as a tenant of the Earl of Effingham, who was then the Lord
of the Manor of Cottisford, but which is now the property of Mr John Allen of Evenley Hall.
His many acts of courtesy, and kindness, his genial disposition, his strict sense of justice, and
his straightforward manner of dealing, endeared him to the parishioners.

It is difficult to say who 'Monday Morning', the farm bailiff, could have been, as the last farm
bailiff recorded in the census returns was James Tebby in 1861, long before Flora was born.

The history of the area and the land use was encapsulated in the field names, which were shown on the 1855 Tithe Map of Cottisford, including: 'Drying Close', 'Ozier Bed', 'the Pond', 'Race Course Allotment' (recalling Cottisford Races), 'Ox pasture piece', 'the Great Warren' (where rabbits would have been bred in the middle ages), 'Great Sheep Pen Ground', 'Butcher's Meadow', 'Priests's Close', 'Dove House Piece', 'Old Driftway' and 'Moat Close' (the manor farm was probably originally defensively moated). Some of these tie up with names Flora remembered:

> The field names gave the clues to the fields' history. Near the farmhouse, 'Moat Piece', 'Fishponds', 'Duffus Piece', 'Kennels', and 'Warren Piece' spoke of a time before the Tudor house took the place of another and older establishment. Farther on, 'Lark Hill', 'Cuckoos' Clump', 'The Osiers', and 'Pond Piece' were named after natural features, while 'Gibbard's Piece' and 'Blackwell's' probably commemorated otherwise long-forgotten former occupants. The large new fields round the hamlet had been cut too late to be named and were known as 'The Hundred Acres', 'The Sixty Acres', and so on, according to their acreage. One or two of the ancients persisted in calling one of these 'The Heath' and another 'The Racecourse'.

Lark Rise to Candleford, p. 52

Long before *Lark Rise to Candleford* was begun, Flora commented on field names, remembering back to her childhood in Juniper, in *The Peverel Papers*. She regretted that field names were becoming obsolete:

> Some of these names explained themselves. 'Charlcroft's' was an echo of the reign of a once important local family. 'Lark's Lease' – poor in soil and rich in skylark's song, though at least two centuries had passed since it was named on that account. Loam Pits, Pond Piece, Sanfoin, and Forty Acres were plain straightforward names. But what could be made of Duffus Piece?

The Peverel Papers, p. 190

The family pig was an important member of the household. Most labouring families kept a pig in a sty in the back garden and this provided most of the meat they ate. This pigsty is attached to one of the model agricultural labourer's cottages near the school.

Some clues to the mystery of 'Duffus Piece' were found in large stone blocks clustered in one corner of the field, revealing that there had once been a building – the dovehouse. This was important for breeding doves for the table in the Middle Ages, when the flesh of doves counted as fish, and could be eaten on 'fish days'. Flora went on to weave a fantasy about the manor house near the ruined dovecote, describing the young squire who had been killed by tripping on his spur running downstairs to go hunting many years before, and how his now ninety-year-old widow lived in seclusion in the house. Flora wrote that she found an excuse to go to the dairy attached to the house during a milk shortage, and was amazed to see a strange circular building in the courtyard, with little 'doorways' in the walls. She found an imperious old woman who answered her enquiry by telling her that the dairy was 'round the corner by the Duffus', and it was explained to her that Duffus was a dovehouse. She was obviously fascinated by the way that the old field names revealed snippets about the history of the area.

The other Cottisford farm, entitled 'Warren Farm', was tenanted in 1881 by Frederick Baines, aged thirty-five from Souldern, son of the butler at Cottisford House, who was living with his wife Martha, aged thirty-three, and their children: Martha (ten), Frederick (nine), Ruth (six), John (three) and James (five months). Ten years earlier he and his wife and Martha were living in Eastoft, Yorkshire where he was working as a gardener. In 1891 he and his family were farming in Finmere. His eldest daughter Ruth was a mother's help, and several more children had been added to the family: Louisa (eight), Agnes (six), Bernhard (sic) (four), Harold (two) and Montague (six months). He had moved on to Lower Street, Tingewick in Buckinghamshire by 1891 and his son James was farming with him and Bernhard was an apprentice baker, aged fourteen.

Most of the labourers in Cottisford and Juniper Hill would have worked for these two men, although some may have had to travel outside the parish to find work. The 1871 and 1881 censuses list the men just as labourers, but in 1891 we can find out more about them. In Cottisford specialist workers such as an agricultural milkman, a horse waggoner and shepherd were mentioned. As superior workers they received slightly higher wages, and usually lived in tied cottages close to their work. Most of the boys, when they left school at the age of about twelve, would become farm labourers, many of them having already done odd jobs around the farm for years.

Their work was hard, and they had to be out for long hours in all weathers, protected only by crude sacking used to form a hooded cloak when it rained, working for meagre wages, but on the whole they were healthy. It was at harvest time that the men had to work the longest hours, to cut the precious grain while the weather held, and this was the last generation of men doing it by hand, before the advent of farm machinery – some of that used locally would probably have been made by the famous firm of Samuelson's of Banbury. They upheld the traditions of generations:

> ... they still kept up the old country custom of choosing as their leader the tallest and most highly skilled man amongst them, who was then called 'King of the Mowers'.
>
> For several harvests in the eighties they were led by the man known as Boamer. He had served in the Army and was still a fine well-set up young fellow, with flashing teeth and a skin darkened by fiercer than English suns.
>
> With a wreath of poppies and bindweed trails around his wide rush-plaited hat, he led the band down the swathes as they mowed, and decreed when and for how long they should halt for 'a breather' and what drinks they had from the yellow stone jar they kept under the hedge in a shady corner of the field. They did not rest often or long: for every morning they set themselves to accomplish an amount of work in the day that they knew would tax all their powers till long after sunset.

Lark Rise to Candleford, p. 235

Agricultural labourers taking a break for refreshments after building a hayrick, probably at Fringford Mill. Frederick Mansfield, who was not a labourer, is shown with his arms folded. (David Watts)

Each year the farmer provided a harvest home dinner for his men. This could be a poignant occasion, for labourers were often employed on a yearly contract, dispersing after harvest for a few days well-earned rest and then attending the nearest hiring fair to find a new job, so it might be the last time that that particular group of people got together. Many names recur through the decades at Juniper and Cottisford, but other names come and go, so there was a certain turnover of men.

The harvest supper was often the best meal the labourers had all year; a welcome change from their usual diet of meat from the family pig and vegetables grown on their allotments, supplemented by bread. Breakfast was seldom eaten that morning, to leave more room for the feast:

And what a feast it was! Such a bustling in the farmhouse kitchen for days beforehand; such a boiling of hams and roasting of sirloins; such a stacking of plum puddings, made by the Christmas recipe; such a tapping of eighteen-gallon casks and baking of plum loaves would astonish those accustomed to the appetites of today. By noon the whole parish had assembled, the workers and their wives and children to feast and the sprinkling of the better-to-do to help with the serving. The only ones absent were the aged bedridden and their attendants, and to them, the next day, portions, carefully graded in daintiness according to their social standing, were carried by the children from the remnants of the feast. A plum pudding was considered a delicate compliment to an equal of the farmer, slices of beef or ham went to the 'bettermost poor'; and a ham-bone with plenty of meat left upon it or part of a pudding or a can of soup to the commonalty.

Long tables were laid out of doors in the shade of a barn, and soon after twelve o'clock the cottagers sat down to the good cheer, with the farmer carving at the principal table, his wife with her tea urn at another, the daughters of the house and their friends circling the tables with vegetable dishes and beer jugs, and the grandchildren in their stiff, white, embroidered frocks, dashing hither and thither to see that everybody had what they required …

After the dinner there were sports and games, then dancing in the home paddock until twilight, and when, at the end of the day, the farmer, carving indoors for the family supper, paused with knife poised to listen to the last distant 'Hooray!' and exclaimed, 'A lot of good chaps! A lot of good chaps, God bless 'em!' Both he and the cheering men were sincere, however mistaken.

Lark Rise to Candleford, pp. 237-8

Flora again looked behind the surface enjoyment of the occasion to its implications, here giving it as her father's opinion, that of an outsider, as he was not employed by the farmer:

It did not do to look beneath the surface. Laura's father, who did not come into the picture, being a 'tradesman' and so not invited, used to say that the farmer paid his men starvation wages all the year and thought he made it up to them by giving that one good meal. The farmer did not think so, because he did not think at all, and the men did not think so either in that day; they were too busy enjoying the food and the fun.

Lark Rise to Candleford, p. 238

The wages paid were low, even by Oxfordshire standards, so the labourers would have had some cause for complaint. As Joseph Waters' wife died in 1879, she could only have presided over the dinners when Flora was very young, so perhaps the housekeeper took her place at later occasions.

Horseman with his team, *c.* 1900. (David Watts)

A group of labourers standing by a traction engine, probably at Shelswell Park. Flora commented that machines were gradually taking over from men in the fields. Machinery was just coming into use on the land. Every autumn appeared a pair of large traction engines, which posted on each side of a field drew a plough across by means of a cable. *Lark Rise to Candleford* p. 53 (Baroness von Maltzahn)

The Church

The little church, built in the thirteenth century and much restored by Charles Buckeridge in 1861, has a particular charm. It is tiny, consisting of a nave and chancel. The Rousbys of Cottisford House had the east and west windows ornamented with their own diaphane work in 1860 and one window was dedicated in 1870 by the Sawkins Harrison family to two of their children who had died: George Sidney who died in 1867 aged eight and Amy Catherine who died in 1868 aged fourteen. It is loved and well-tended by the villagers, and has become a place of pilgrimage for lovers of *Lark Rise to Candleford*. The interior has changed, with a different arrangement of pews, whitewashed walls instead of the roughcast stone of Flora's time, the addition of an organ, and no more unpleasant smells from the crypt!

> The Squire's and clergyman's families had pews in the chancel, with backs to the wall on either side, and between them stood two long benches for the schoolchildren, well under the eyes of authority. Below the steps down into the nave stood the harmonium, played by the clergyman's daughter, and round it was ranged the choir of small schoolgirls. Then came the rank and file of the congregation, nicely graded, with the farmer's family in the front row, then the Squire's gardener and coachman, the schoolmistress, the maidservants, and the cottagers, with the Parish Clerk at the back to keep order.
>
> *Lark Rise to Candleford*, p. 210

Flora and Edwin sat in a pew half way down the nave, probably close to where the war memorial has been placed on the wall. In 1995 a plaque was unveiled commemorating Flora herself.

A largely new Rectory had been built in Cottisford in 1821 by Peake of Fringford, for T. W. Champneys, who lived at Fulmer in Buckinghamshire. A datestone reading 1618 or 1619 can be found at the back of the house, perhaps revealing the date of the earlier one. The tithe barn behind the Rectory has a datestone recording its restoration in 1651. When Charles Sawkins Harrison (the 'Mr Ellison' of *Lark Rise*) who had studied for his MA at Durham University, came to Cottisford in 1853 he lived there, and spent £400 enlarging the house. Revd Sawkins Harrison was born in 1816 in Chester and attended Eton College. In 1851 he was staying in Lambeth with Charles Bice, an annuitant, and described his profession as 'Conduct of Eton College'.

In 1861 he was aged forty-five and lived at the Rectory with his thirty-eight-year-old wife Margaret and their children Grace, aged nine, Richard aged eight, Amy aged seven, Edmund aged four, Clement aged three, George aged two and infant Basil. To help in the house they had twenty-one-year-old governess Joanna Goodall, forty-year old Martha Mortley as cook, twenty-three-year-old nurse Jane Clayton, housemaid Emily Austin aged eighteen and nurse Eliza Mansfield, aged fourteen. In December 1867 their son George died aged eight and in March 1868 Amy died aged fourteen. In 1867 he became Rector of Hardwick as well as Cottisford.

In 1871 the only children at home with their parents were Grace and Richard, the latter still a scholar at the age of eighteen. The family employed two servants: Jane Berry aged twenty-six from Farborough, Buckinghamshire and Sarah Newitt from Broughton, Oxfordshire. Their son Edmund, aged fourteen, was at school at the District Russell College North Church of England School in Thornton, Lancashire, while his brother Clement was staying at the Rectory in Erbistock, Flintshire, with Revd Peter Price and his family.

Margaret Sawkins Harrison died in 1878 and was buried on 5 November, but Revd Charles Sawkins Harrison had his elder daughter Grace, then aged twenty-nine, living at home to help with his parish work in 1881, and they kept two servants: twenty-three-year old Maria Price from Cottisford and Annie Cripps, aged seventeen, from Birmingham. At the time of the census Richard, at the age of twenty-nine, said to be 'living on the interest of moneys', was staying at Willoughby in Lincolnshire with farmer William Brooks, while Clement, now twenty-eight, was following in his father's footsteps, serving as Curate at Temple Balsall, Warwickshire and being looked after by his sixty-six-year-old servant Susannah Lawrence from Balsall. Revd Sawkins Harrison died in 1896 aged eighty-one and was buried in his beloved Cottisford. It is noted in the Parish Register that he was the first Rector of Cottisford buried in his own parish since 1720. Unfortunately the *Bicester Advertiser* of 10 August 1896 which records his death is almost illegible, but it comments that he was 'the late venerable and revered rector'.

Grace never married. She had moved to Kingston Road in Oxford by 1901, living on her own means. She was living at 71 Woodstock Road when she died in 1923 aged seventy and her body was brought back to Cottisford for burial on 4 May. Her brother Clement became vicar of St Peter and St Paul parish in Dagenham, Essex.

Revd Sawkins Harrison was a well-known figure to Flora and Edwin, as he came into the school at ten o'clock each morning to teach the children scripture:

> He was a clergyman of the old school; a commanding figure, tall and stout, with white hair, ruddy cheeks and an aristocratically beaked nose, and he was as far as possible removed by birth, education, and worldly circumstances from the lambs of his flock. He spoke to them from a great height, physical, mental and spiritual. 'To order myself lowly and reverently before my betters' was the clause he underlined in the Church Catechism, for had he not been divinely appointed pastor and master to those little rustics and was it not one of his chief duties to teach them to realise this? As a man, he was kindly disposed – a giver of blankets and coals at Christmas, and of soup and milk puddings to the sick.

Lark Rise to Candleford, p. 179

Above: Cottisford church, although small, is full of character. Edmund Timms is commemorated on the brass war memorial inside. (Oxfordshire Photographic Archive)

Right: Charles Sawkins Harrison, Rector of Cottisford from 1853–96, who was rechristened 'Mr. Ellison' in *Lark Rise to Candleford*. (Cottisford and Hardwick Parochial Church Council)

Flora Thompson's connection with Cottisford has been commemorated with a plaque in the church.

He regularly preached on the duty of regular church-going, forgetting that his congregation did that already, and those to whom he wanted his message to go were not there to hear it! He also imprinted on their minds the importance of the social order and that each one should be happy to stay in his own niche. He worked his way regularly round the parish, visiting each family at least once each year, but was not always a welcome visitor, as the house had to be rapidly tidied as news came of his approach. The local diocese commented that he taught scripture very satisfactorily:

> The Condition of Religious Knowledge is satisfactory and the answering generally was very creditable. The written work (in the Lower Standards especially) was decidedly above the average.

Diocesan Inspectors' Report, 1882, Oxfordshire Record Office OxCRO T/SM 6 ii

His daughter Grace actively helped him in the parish. She had the responsibility for taking care of the box of baby clothes lent out to mothers who needed it, with its half dozen of everything, 'tiny shirts, swathes, long flannel barrows, nighties, and napkins', which she made and repaired between each use. She prepared little packets as welcome gifts for the new mothers, with tea, sugar and patent oats to make gruel. She helped the mothers find places as servants for their daughters, by asking round to see where there were local vacancies, and if necessary placing advertisements in the *Church Times* or the *Morning Post*. She also visited the hamlet families often, carefully visiting each in turn lest any should become jealous, not realising that, to many, her visits were unwanted:

> Considering her many kindnesses to the women, she might have been expected to be more popular than she was. None of them welcomed her visits. Some would lock their doors and

pretend to be out; others would rattle their teacups when they saw her coming, hoping she would say, as she sometimes did, 'I hear you are at tea, so I won't come in'.

The only spoken complaint about her was that she talked too much. 'That Miss Ellison, she'd fair talk a donkey's hind leg off', they would say; but that was a failing they tolerated in others, and one to which they were not averse in her, once she was installed in their best chair and some item of local gossip was being discussed.

Perhaps at the root of their unease in her presence was the subconscious feeling of contrast between her lot and theirs. Her neat little figure, well corseted in; her clear high-pitched voice, good clothes, and faint scent of lily-of-the-valley perfume put them, in their workaday garb and all blowsed from their cooking or water-fetching, at a disadvantage.

Lark Rise to Candleford, pp. 221-2

Grace was friendly with Emma, Flora's mother, whom it was said she had known from birth, and at the time when Emma worked at Fewcott Rectory. Flora was incorrect in saying that she was the only daughter, but she was the eldest, and her sister Amy Catherine died in 1868 aged thirteen, so the task of caring for her father may naturally have devolved on her.

An interesting insight into life in the Rectory is given by the catalogue of the sale of its contents after the death of Revd Sawkins Harrison on 25 August 1856 (see Appendix Three for the full list), although presumably some of the contents, particularly his books and personal objects, were kept by his children. The catalogue shows the rooms in the house, listing an entrance hall, outer hall, a study, a library, a drawing room, a dining room, servants' hall, kitchen, pantry, scullery cellar, laundry, landing and staircase store room, six bedrooms, a dressing room and a dairy and hovel. The hip baths and sponge bath probably indicate that there was no bathroom. Much of the bedroom furniture was described as being painted, perhaps because the wood used was not good enough to have bare. The bed furnishings included straw palliasses and flock mattresses, as well as feather beds, bolsters and pillows, a white knotted quilt and coverlids, but no eiderdowns. One bedstead was described as Arabian. In one bedroom there was a hanging press. There were fire irons in the bedrooms, so fires were probably lit there in cold weather. The house was lit by various different types of oil, benzoline and colza lamps, with chamber candlesticks to light the way upstairs. Carpets were used on most floors, but in some rooms, including one bedroom, linoleum was laid, and the kitchen floor was covered with cocoa matting.

The study had a tapestry carpet and furniture which included two bookcases and a walnut inlaid chess table and a smoking chair. It also had a five-foot bed, so perhaps Revd Sawkins Harrison slept there in old age. There were quite a lot of large and small swing mirrors throughout the house. The library contained a timepiece and chimney ornaments, a Brussels carpet, an Indian rug and a sheepskin rug, tables and chairs including a prie-dieu chair, a couch, a walnut stationery case and brass letter scales.

The drawing room had a Brussels carpet and a Kidderminster square and one of the cushions on the easy chair was embroidered. The chesterfield was upholstered in figured damask with a satin cretonne cover. One chair, described as being Elizabethan, but more likely a Victorian copy, had a stuffed seat and back upholstered in plush, a fabric manufactured in Banbury and Shutford. The Broadwood Cottage piano was in here, with a mahogany music canterbury. Pictures included engravings of 'Marriage of St Catherine', 'The Annunciation' and 'Dying Douglas'.

The dining room had a set of extending mahogany dining tables, over eleven feet long, and a library table with inkstand and stationery case and blotting pad. For some reason there was a patent mangle in the servants' hall, together with warming pans, water cans, a housemaid's box and cutlery. Although there was a deal table, no chairs were mentioned, so perhaps the servants ate in the kitchen. No dinner service was mentioned in the kitchen; presumably it was retained by one of the family. Plated goods included a swan salt cellar, pickle-jar stands and dessert knives and forks. Some of the cups and saucers were willow pattern. Among the

Cottisford Rectory, the home of Charles Sawkins Harrison and his family. Previous rectors had been non-resident, so when he moved in a brick extension was built on the back of the building.

cutlery in the kitchen was an oyster knife. The kitchen table was deal, and there was also a deal dresser. Utensils included a tea kettle and iron boiler, fish kettle and brass kettle, copper preserving pans, smoothing irons and a box iron, dish covers and a painted flour bin. Iron saucepans and frying pans were kept in the scullery with buckets and a small churn (perhaps indicating that the servants made butter, possibly using cream from their own cow, or from one of the neighbouring farms – this is reinforced by the cream pan, butter prints and butter kiver stored in the dairy). Beer barrels and wine casks were stored in the cellar.

The laundry would probably have been a dry laundry where the ironing was done. It had a stove for heating flat irons, an ironing board, clothes horses and washing trays. The washing dolly was stored in the dairy or the hovel.

The brown nag was described as being very fast, with a good action. It was probably used for riding, as there was an ordinary saddle and a side-saddle for ladies' use, but it probably also pulled the spring trap and pony trap, unless a pony had been kept who was not included in the sale. Other items for sale included harness, carriage lamps, a lawn mower, garden engine, agricultural tools including a one-horse plough by Ransome, horse hoe, winnowing machine, turnip drill, root pulper, chaff machine and dung dray. Hens were kept (the cockerels were termed 'Toms') and they, together with their troughs and coops were for sale. On a more domestic note, there were three wooden pig troughs, a yoke and two buckets. Even the firewood, the manure heap and nine water butts were on sale. Perhaps the most unexpected items in the sale were a double-barrelled breech-loading gun and a spear in bedroom seven (actually bedroom six as the dressing room was counted as a bedroom) and the single-barrelled gun and double-barrelled guns in the scullery.

The villagers must have been fascinated to see the contents laid out for the sale, and some may have bought souvenirs.

Flora mentions the curates – 'Mr Alport' the 'big, fat-faced young man, who had been a medical student', keeping a dispensary at his lodging, may perhaps have been Samuel Luffman, aged twenty-six, who lived with his wife Maria in 'Dog Kennel Cottage' in 1881. Ten years later he was clergyman at St Swithuns, Lewisham in London. 'Mr Marley', the old man with a grey beard, who was an Anglo-Catholic, may have been William R. Almond, aged fifty, who is found in the 1891 census, lodging with labourer William Cross. William Russell Almond, born in 1855 was the son of another clergyman of the same name who was vicar of Stapleford, Nottinghamshire when William was born. He came from a large family, with six brothers and three sisters in 1861. In 1871 at the age of twenty-one he was a student at St Augustine's College, Canterbury and ten years later he was a Church of England clergyman living with his widowed mother in Bedford.

Cottisford House

Next to the church stands Cottisford House – there have been several big houses on the site over the centuries, the current one being built about 1700 by Laurence Lord, as a square building of coursed rubble decorated with ashlar quoin stones, with a hipped roof and attic dormers. At one time there was a lane with several cottages between the church and the house, but Squire William Turner, a member of the Irish Bar who held Cottisford House from 1825 decided to use the £20,000-dowry brought by his Welsh wife Maria Meares on their marriage in 1825 to enlarge the house and extend the grounds. As part of this refurbishment he demolished the cottages, closed the lane and laid out fine pleasure gardens, rebuilding the cottages well away from the house, as was fashionable at the time: Earl Harcourt had moved and rebuilt the entire village of Nuneham Courtenay in the eighteenth century as it spoiled his view. Turner drastically overspent on his improvements, and was unable to enjoy the fruits of his labour; he had to flee to Belgium to escape his creditors, dying in Bruges in 1836. He sold his lease of the house and in 1838 Eton leased it to Susanna Ingram of Warminster.

From 1842 the lease was in the hands of the Rousby family, first James Edwards Rousby, who died in 1848, then his son James Edwards Rousby, who died in 1875, followed by his son Edwards Richard Kendall Rousby, who purchased the manor house and Warren Farm from Eton College in 1885. He would have been the squire that Flora knew, although she rechristened him Bracewell. In 1851 Edwards Rousby, born in 1819 in Souldern, and described as a landed proprietor, was living at Cottisford House with his sisters Helen (born in 1825) and Lucy (born in 1827). The servants were: James Baines, their footman, aged thirty-six, who had been born in Souldern (and had been living in the house in 1841 as well), the groom, Robert Clarke, aged sixty-seven from Fringford, their cook, Mary Bowerman from Chesterton, aged forty-six and the housemaid Sophia Herring aged forty-nine from Shabbington in Buckinghamshire. Ten years earlier Sophia had been an agricultural labourer.

In 1861 Edwards Rousby had become head of the family and a landed proprietor. His thirty-one-year-old wife Louisa came from Portsmouth and their children were Edith L.C., aged six, Edward Richard Kendall Rousby aged four and Josephine aged three. Their visitors – cousins Maria Seaton, a widow aged forty-one and A.R. Wilmot aged eight were accompanied by a lady's maid (a luxury Louisa was unable to afford) while the live-in staff of the house were Sophia Herring, who had risen to the rank of cook, Helen Shakespeare (thirty-three) from Ladbroke, Warwickshire who was a nurse and Emma Hegson (nineteen) from Hethe was a housemaid.

In 1871 Edwards Rousby, then fifty-two, was living at the house with his wife Louisa (aged forty-one), and their daughters Edith (sixteen), and Josephine (thirteen). Their live-in servants were Elizabeth Hexamer (thirty-eight), the German governess, Mary Ann Greenwood (thirty-seven) from Bicester who was the cook, Isabella Cripps (thirty-five) from Cottisford was the housemaid and fifteen-year-old Catherine Thame from Fringford was the children's maid.

In 1881 their son Edwards Rousby, aged twenty-four and a student of Magdalen College, Oxford, was staying at the Rectory at Great Hampden in Buckinghamshire. His father had

Cottisford House seen after the improvements made by William Turner in the early-nineteenth century. When Flora knew it as a child it was the home of the Rousby family whom she called the Bracewells. (Oxfordshire Photographic Archive)

died in 1875 and his widowed mother was living at Cottisford House with her daughter Josephine and seven-year-old niece Evelyn Johns. Mary Greenwood was still cook and the other live-in servants were Ruth Freeman, the twenty-four-year old housemaid from Fringford, Ellen Jones (aged fourteen) a servant from Deddington and James Baines (aged sixty) who was working as butler and gardener and presumably 'living in' so that there was a permanent male presence in the house.

Edwards Richard Kendal Rousby purchased the house from Eton College in 1885 and in the 1891 census was living there aged thirty-four, with his mother, their cook Mary Langley, aged forty-nine from Clewer, Berkshire and two domestic servants, Jane Clist, aged twenty-two, from Bantripp, Somerset and Elizabeth Higgs, aged nineteen, from West Hanney, Berks.

The Rousbys performed the role of squire and family in the village. Flora wrote that 'Mrs Bracewell' (really Louisa Rousby) visited the village school to examine the girls' needlework. She describes the lady as:

> ... a haughty, and still handsome old dame in a long flowing, pale-grey silk dust cloak and small close-fitting black bonnet, with two tiny King Charles spaniels on a leash.
>
> It would be almost impossible for anyone born in this century to imagine the pride and importance of such small country gentlepeople in the eighties. As far as was known, the Bracewells were connected with no noble family; they had but little land, kept up but a small establishment, and were said in the village and hamlet to be 'poor as crows'. Yet, by virtue of having been born into a particular caste and of living in the 'big house' of the parish, they expected to reign over their poorer neighbours and to be treated by them with the deference due to royalty.

Lark Rise to Candleford, pp. 194–5

Flora wrote that 'Mrs Bracewell' had been brought up during the Regency, but in fact she was born in 1831. She commented that she was generous in her way, despite her shortage of money, providing for two old women, organising soup for the 'deserving poor' in the winter and providing a special tea and magic-lantern show for the schoolchildren at Christmas.

In the 1860s there were two gamekeepers employed in Cottisford, and one in 1871 (probably working on the Tusmore Estate), but the male members of the Rousby family would have enjoyed shooting, and presumably hunting. The fact that the Rousbys did not maintain a large household, and that some of their retainers were elderly, echoes Flora's comment that they were not well-off. Living in the house at the time of the 1861 census were a cook, a nurse and a housemaid, and in 1871, when they had two daughters – Edith, aged sixteen, and Josephine, aged thirteen – living at home, they had a governess, a cook, a housemaid and a children's maid. The Rousbys probably also employed Henry Price, aged thirty-seven, who described himself as a groom and gardener. When she was widowed, Mrs Rousby obviously decided that she needed a male servant, so she employed sixty-five-year-old James Baines as butler and gardener, plus a cook, housemaid and general servant. Baines was married, but seems to have lived at Cottisford House. His wife Charlotte, aged sixty-two from Aston Clinton, Buckinghamshire, who lived in a nearby cottage in the Warren, described herself as head of the household and butler's wife in the census. Thomas Mansfield, aged seventy-eight, who was described as a groom and coachman, probably also worked for the Rousby family. The family may also have had girls from the village coming in daily to clean the house.

In 1901 Edwards Rousby, unmarried, was still living at Cottisford House with his widowed mother, both living on their own means. Their servants were: Elizabeth Hall (seventy), a cook from Hethe; Ruth James, a housemaid aged twenty-five from Stoke Lyne and Amy Ashton (fifteen), a housemaid from Cottisford. Coachman Thomas Mansfield, now aged eighty-eight was also described as their groom.

James Baines was employed at Cottisford House in 1841 (and at that time had his wife Charlotte living with him at the house with their baby Charles). In 1841 his job in service was not specified but by 1851 he had become footman, (and Charlotte was living elsewhere in Cottisford, as she seems to have been for quite a lot of their married life, since servants were seldom allowed to have their children living in their employers' houses) and in 1861 he was working as gardener (presumably still for the Rousbys). He rose to become their butler in 1881 again 'living in' at the 'big house'. James and Charlotte had lived in Aston Clinton before James became footman to the Rousbys, and their eldest son Charles was born there in 1841, and their next children James and Frederick were born in Souldern, (where the Rousbys lived before coming to Cottisford) in 1843 and 1846 respectively. Henry was born in Cottisford in 1850. James died on 14 December 1882 and his tombstone attests the esteem he was held in by the Rousby family, 'He was a faithful servant and friend in the family of James Edward Rousby Esq., for fifty-eight years'.

The School

The triangle of land at the crossroads in the village was allocated for a school at the time of enclosure in 1854, and the little school, paid for by Charles Sawkins Harrison, with grants from Eton College and the National Society for the Education of the Poor in the Principles of the Established Church, opened in 1856. Flora described it minutely:

> Fordlow National School was a small grey one-storied building standing at the crossroads at the entrance to the village. The one large classroom which served all purposes was well-lighted with several windows, including the large one which filled the end of the building which faced the road. Beside, and joined on to the school, was a tiny two-roomed cottage for the schoolmistress, and beyond that a playground with birch trees and turf, bald in places,

the whole being enclosed within white-painted palings ... The school ... had a lobby with pegs for clothes, boys' and girls' earth-closets, and a backyard with fixed wash-basins, although there was no water laid on. The water supply was contained in a small bucket, filled every morning by the old woman who cleaned the schoolroom, and every morning she grumbled because the children had been so extravagant that she had to 'fill 'un again'.

Lark Rise to Candleford, p. 177

As the logbooks of Cottisford School have disappeared without trace, there is little direct information about the school in Flora's time apart from her vivid chapters. There were about forty-five pupils, varying in age from about four to fourteen, although most children left school at the age of twelve. All had to be taught by the one teacher in the single classroom, helped only by untrained pupil-teachers chosen from amongst the elder children. The first teacher Flora knew was Susannah Holmyard, who she said had been at the school since the mid-1860s, and had been engaged to the squire's head gardener for most of that time:

She was at that time, about forty, and was a small neat little body with a pale, slightly pock-marked face, snaky black curls hanging down to her shoulders, and eyebrows arched into a perpetual enquiry. She wore in school stiffly starched, holland aprons with bibs, one embroidered in red one week, and one with blue the next, and was seldom seen without a posy of flowers pinned on her breast and another tucked into her hair.

Lark Rise to Candleford, p. 178

Susannah Holmyard was not the first teacher, as Ann Walter, aged twenty from Bicester, held that post in 1861. Susannah, who was the daughter of a London saddler, was born in May 1844. She worked for two years as a monitor and was a pupil-teacher in Malvern before coming to Cottisford in November 1867 as an uncertified teacher, earning only £27 10s a year in the early 1870s, mitigated slightly by the fact that she could live rent-free in the tiny cottage attached to the school. She worked for her teacher's certificate by external examination, gaining it in 1872, which raised her salary to £32 4s a year. She was much younger than Flora suggested, being thirty-four in 1881. Henry Tebby, her fiancé, (called 'Tenby' in *Lark Rise to Candleford*) was twenty-eight in 1881, and described as a servant in 1871 rather than a gardener. Ten years later he had advanced to being a gardener, and lived on his own. They married in April 1885, when Mrs Rousby graciously acted as a witness. While Susannah, as a married woman, had to give up work, Henry carried on working as gardener at Cottisford House. They did not have children.

   None of the teachers after that stayed so long. Flora called the next teacher 'Matilda Annie Higgs'. She was a progressive teacher who tried to treat the children as friends, but by doing this disastrously lost all authority over them:

They hid her cane, filled her inkpot with water, put young frogs in her desk, and asked her silly, unnecessary questions about their work. When she answered them, they all coughed in chorus.

Lark Rise to Candleford, p. 185

This behaviour often reduced the poor woman to tears and it was obvious that the situation could not continue indefinitely. It was when the Rector arrived at the school in time to witness a pitched battle between some of the older boys in the classroom that the end came. He easily restored order, but 'Miss Higgs' had to go. For a while Mrs Tebby was recalled, until 'Miss Shepherd' was appointed. She was much older, but again not strong on keeping

Cottisford School, which opened in 1856, was built at the crossroads to cater for about forty-five pupils and one teacher. (Oxfordshire Photographic Archive)

discipline, but she kept things going. She obviously liked Flora, and must have got to know her well, as Flora stayed on a year longer than most of the other pupils, and helped her teach the younger ones. Once, after the Bishop had come to consecrate an extension to the churchyard, 'Miss Shepherd', disappointed at not having been invited back to the Rectory for tea, instead invited Flora to tea in her little cottage attached to the school. She had transformed the tiny one-up, one-down cottage to suit 'artistic taste', with a green-serge tablecloth hiding the old deal table, cushions and antimacassars, and masses of fashionable decorations and examples of her craft work such as wool-work, hanging pincushions and letter racks, plus Japanese fans, pictures and photographs, covering the walls. In 1891 the schoolmistress was Alice Davis, aged thirty from 'Loughor' in Gloucestershire, who may have been Flora's teacher, but it is not known when she began work at the school.

Apart from the daily scripture lessons, taught by Mr Sawkins Harrison, the main subjects for the children were reading, writing and arithmetic. Additionally, each afternoon the boys did drawing while the girls were taught needlework; as most of them would end up in service it was important to be able to darn and mend, and be able to embroider cross-stitch names on clothes, if they wanted to rise above menial duties. Flora loathed the sewing and commented wryly that while the other girls were busy making their pinafores she was still struggling with her grubby, blood-stained hemming strip. Writing lessons were used to inculcate morality as well as teach a copperplate hand, with maxims such as, 'a fool and his money are soon parted'. Essays were set to teach composition and spelling. Other subjects were taught on a more informal basis:

> History was not taught formally; but history readers were in use containing such picturesque stories as those of King Alfred and the cakes, King Canute commanding the waves, the loss of the White Ship, and Raleigh spreading his cloak for Queen Elizabeth.

The interior of Cottisford School with the teacher's desk on the left and the rows of benches for the children. The room was heated by one turtle stove, (just visible in front of the fireplace) so must have become very cold at the back in winter. *c.* 1905. (Oxfordshire Photographic Archive)

There were no geography readers, and, excepting what could be gleaned from the descriptions of different parts of the world in the ordinary readers, no geography was taught. But, for some reason or other, on the walls of the schoolroom were hung splendid maps: The World, Europe, North America, South America, England, Ireland, and Scotland. During long waits in class for her turn to read, or to have her copy or sewing examined, Laura would gaze on these maps until the shapes of the countries, with their islands and inlets became photographed on her brain. Baffin Bay and the land around the poles were especially fascinating to her.

Lark Rise to Candleford, p. 180

Flora had been taught the rudiments of reading by her father before she went to school, but was too shy to tell the teacher, who on finding she could not recite the alphabet decided she could not read either. She did not enjoy arithmetic, but must have been reasonably good with figures to be able to work in the Post Office in later life. It is astonishing, and a tribute to her tenacity, that with the handicap of such a basic education she was able to pursue such a successful writing career.

The day the children dreaded most was the annual visit of Her Majesty's Inspector, who came to examine each child. Their results materially affected the future funding of the school, as if they performed badly, the funds would be reduced for the next year. The Inspector was an elderly clergyman, of 'autocratic demeanour and scathing judgement', and little understanding of children, confusing them utterly by enunciating the punctuation as well as the words in giving dictation. A School Inspector appears again in Flora's novel *Still Glides the Stream*, where the heroine is 'Charity', who is a pupil-teacher who very much wants to become a teacher:

The time of the annual visit of Her Majesty's Inspector of Schools was drawing near and she had extra lessons of her own to prepare, as well as to help Miss Fowkes coach some of the backward

Needlework was taught to the girls each afternoon, and was the bane of Flora's life; while the other girls were busy stitching pinafores she was still struggling with her first blood-bespattered hemming strip. The needlework illustrated here, which is similar to that done in Cottisford School, was submitted by Cherwell British Schools, Banbury, for the Oxford Prize Scheme for Needlework. Each sample is labelled with the name, age and standard of the pupil. (Oxfordshire Museums Service)

pupils... That year, too, she had fears and apprehensions on her own behalf, for the time of her probation as monitress had expired and upon the decision of the great man her whole future depended. For it was he, and only he, who could accept or reject her application for the advanced post of pupil-teacher. But for her personally all went well on the day of judgement.

Mr Findlater was a learned man, an historian, with a leaning to the already becoming-less-popular Right. It happened that Charity's history paper dealt with the events leading up to the Civil War, and, unwittingly, she gained her examiner's favour by supporting the royal cause. At the end of her *viva voce*, he grunted, 'Very creditable', and, instead of going away and leaving her in suspense, as he often did with such candidates, he told her at once that the appointment was hers. After he had gone, Miss Fowkes kissed and congratulated her upon 'passing with honours', and she bounded home to tell her parents the good news with her head in the air. It was years later, when she came to read Mr Findlater's *England in the Seventeenth Century* that she recognised the working of Chance.

Still Glides the Stream, pp. 123–4

It is possible that the Inspector Flora is referring to here was the Revd James Blomfield, a learned man who was Rector of Launton, and Rural Dean of Bicester, who wrote extensively about the local history of the area in the 1870s and '80s although not so far as is known about England in the seventeenth century.

As the logbooks have disappeared it is not possible to see what the Inspector thought of the school. However some of the reports of the Diocesan Inspector, who was a much more welcome visitor, who actually encouraged the children instead of terrifying them, have been preserved. On the day assigned for the visit the teacher would dress in her best and watch while he asked the class scripture questions and gave them a written essay on some biblical topic. Revd Sawkins Harrison had done his work well, and the children were easily able to answer.

Flora won the Diocesan prize in 1888, inspired by the subject of the life of Moses. The Report of Charles E. Adams, Diocesan Inspector for that year read:

> The Religious Instruction has been painstaking and the children are evidently interested in their work. The 1st Class especially passed a very creditable examination, both in Holy Scripture and Catechism – Catechism, passages of Holy Scripture etc. were very well repeated and the written work was, on the whole, good.
> Diocesan Prize: Flora Timms
> Commended Isabel Blaby, Sarah A. Cripps, Charles E. Adams

Oxfordshire County Record Office reference OxCRO T/SM 6 ii

Flora had been commended for her work in 1886 and 1887, while Edwin was commended in 1889 (not actually receiving the prize as Flora wrote) and her younger sister May was commended in 1894, in the last report to have been preserved.

May Day

The highlight of the children's year were the May Day celebrations which were organised by the school. Several weeks beforehand, the May queen, usually aged about ten or eleven, was chosen. Making the garland took longer. Instead of the usual crossed hoops of most Oxfordshire garlands, the Cottisford one was pyramid-shaped, based round a light wooden bell shaped about 4ft high which required many flowers, bunched together and attached closely together and a lot of work to decorate. The weekend before the boys would have walked to a wood about six miles away to gather primroses in readiness, and on 30 April the children arrived at school heavily laden with all the flowers they had been able to lay their hands on, cowslips and violets gathered from the fields and wallflowers, oxlips and red flowering currant from their gardens. Greenery was culled from the sweetbriar hedge in the school mistress's garden.

The flowers they had brought invariably proved insufficient and parties of children were despatched to Cottisford House, the Rectory, farms and cottages – anywhere that might produce more flowers for them. Everyone gave generously. Eventually the garland was finished, the top decorated with the coveted crown imperial lilies, and the garland was sprinkled with water and left overnight. The next morning a large china doll in a blue dress was installed sitting on a ledge in the centre of the front of the garland, covered with a white muslin veil, which could be lifted on receipt of payment:

> The attitude of the children to the lady is interesting. It was understood that the garland was her garland, carried in her honour. The lady must never be roughly handled. If the garland turned turtle, as it was apt to do later in the day, when the road was rough and the bearers growing weary, the first question was always, 'is the lady all right?' (Is it possible that the lady was once 'Our Lady', she having in her turn, perhaps, replaced an earlier effigy of some pagan spirit of the newly decked earth?).

Lark Rise to Candleford, p. 203

The queen was dressed up in a white frock with a crown of red and white garden daisies, holding her veil in position, while the other girls dressed in white or pale frocks – with veils if possible – both boys and girls being arrayed in bright knots, sashes and bows of ribbon. They were allotted roles, and paraded in order:

May Day was the highlight of the school year for the children. Here the May king and queen are shown with the pyramid-shaped garland containing a doll, referred to as 'The Lady' outside Cotmore House, near Fringford. (Baroness von Maltzahn)

Boy with flag   Girl with money box.

The garland with two bearers.
King and queen.
Two maids of honour.
Lord and lady.
Two maids of honour.
Footman and footman's lady.
Rank and file, walking in twos.

Girl known as 'Mother'.   Boy called 'Ragman'.

Lark Rise to Candleford, p. 204

The 'Mother' was a responsible girl who was made the children behave well, and carried the lunches in a big basket. The 'Ragman' carried the children's coats, in case of rain. The children first paraded round the village, starting at the Rectory, at about 7 o'clock in the morning, while the Rector was still shaving, where the children would sing the traditional:

A bunch of May I have brought you
And at your door it stands.
It is but a sprout, but it's well put about
By the Lord Almighty's hands ...

Lark Rise to Candleford, p. 203

After the Rector's daughter had given them a silver coin, and admired the lady, the children went on to Cottisford House, where more silver would be forthcoming, and a different song sung. They visited all the rest of the houses in the village, carrying on beyond the parish boundary on a seven-mile circuit which would have included Shelswell House. It made a long and tiring day for the children, but one they would not have missed for the world, and even when the day was over they could look forward to the money they had collected being shared out the next day at school, and the girls could give the precious doll one last stroke before she was lovingly stored away until the next year.

The description Flora gives of the May celebrations, although it may be slightly embroidered, is one of the most complete, and is invaluable to students of folklore, as are other insights into customs in the book.

Twyford: Uncle Tom

Until recently it was believed that the character Flora described in her books as 'Uncle Tom' was the prosperous owner of a shoemaking firm in Market Square in Buckingham by the name of Rechab Holland. Rechab's father Henry Holland, from Stowe or Westbury in Buckinghamshire, had arrived in Buckingham by 1851 and opened a boot and shoe manufactory in the Market Square, employing seventy-six people. By 1871 he had flourished and was employing eighty-eight men, women and children. His eldest son Rechab was brought into the family business at an early age, working as a 'clicker' on the shop floor at the age of sixteen in 1861. Gradually some of his other children were brought into the family firm, and in 1871 Martha (nineteen) was a shop-girl and Hannah (seventeen) was a machinist. In 1881 Rechab was a commercial traveller, selling his father's wares and by 1891 he had taken over the firm and settled down with his wife Elizabeth and his children Harold (eight), Gurth (seven), Elail (five), Rupert (four), Reginald (one) and Violet (six months).

However it transpires that 'Uncle Tom' was in fact Flora's uncle Thomas Whiting, so when Flora wrote about him and his family being in 'Candleford' she was drawing one of her red herrings over his real home of Twyford, a small village south-west of Buckingham, about halfway between there and Bicester. Interestingly she is thought to have come to work here herself for a short time at Twyford Post Office when she left Fringford. Twyford is thus part of the 'town' of Candleford, which is a mixture of several different places.

Like Cottisford it was settled before the Norman Conquest but the oldest remaining building is the late twelfth-century church of the Assumption of the Blessed Virgin, which has been much altered over the centuries. The Wenman family were lords of the manor in Twyford from 1550 until 1800 when Philip, the last viscount died, after which it passed to a nephew. The Wenmans enclosed Twyford soon after acquiring it. The family moved from Twyford to Oxfordshire in the eighteenth century and their manor house was turned into a farm, which was demolished in 1857, to be replaced by Twyford Lodge.

With the loss of the Wenman family the village declined in status and by the late nineteenth century when Flora would have known it, was quite small. In 1899 most of the land was owned by Lincoln College, Oxford, Edward James Athawes of Nevill House, Chatham, Owen Clark, a grazier, who lived at Twyford House and Walter Woods of Portway Farm. The population was 349. The land was heavy clay, about two thirds of it farmed as arable, with 200 acres of woodland. The Post Office only opened in the mid-1890s, and was listed in *Kelly's 1899 Directory of Buckinghamshire*:

Post Office. Miss Elizabeth Cross, sub-postmistress. Letters received from Buckingham at 8.40 a.m.; dispatched at 4.40 p.m. week days only. Postal orders are issued here, but not paid. The nearest money order and telegraph office is at Steeple Claydon.

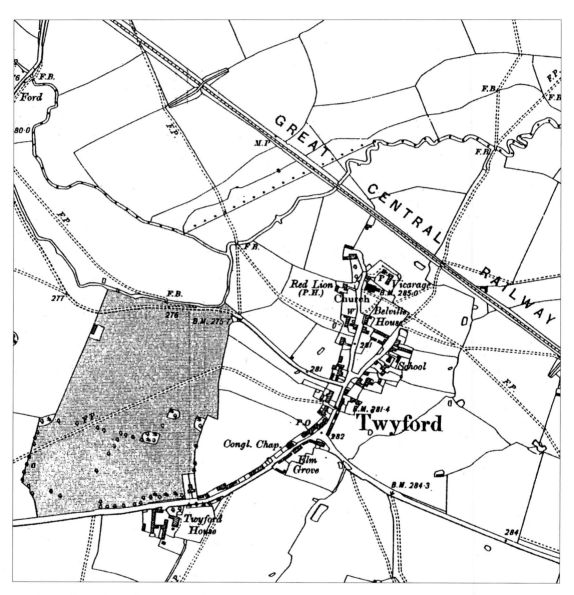

Reproduced from a late nineteenth-century Ordnance Survey map of Twyford, home of 'Uncle Tom' Whiting, the shoemaker, who lived near the school. (David Watts)

Apart from farming, there were few occupations in the village – two carpenters, three public houses (the Crown, the Red Lion and the Seven Stars), a blacksmith, carrier, haulier, coal merchant, miller, baker, grocer, butcher and shopkeeper, plus Thomas Whiting, shoemaker.

Thomas Whiting was the son of Austin Masters Whiting, a linen and woollen draper from Roade in Northamptonshire who was born in 1820 in Ashton, Northamptonshire. Austin Masters was the eldest son of another Thomas Whiting, born in about 1801 in Northamptonshire and living in Ashton in 1841, working as an agricultural labourer. His wife was called Mary and his other children were John (born in 1826), James (born 1828), George (born 1830), Thomas (born 1832), Elizabeth (born 1839) and Harriet (born in 1841). Also living with them was Elizabeth Whiting, aged thirty and a lacemaker, perhaps Thomas' sister. Austin's job is not listed in 1841, when he was living with his parents, aged twenty, but he may have been an agricultural labourer like his father. The family dispersed round the country as so many did at this time with more industrial jobs becoming available and the decline in agriculture; his brother James was working in an iron foundry in Kimberworth, Yorkshire in 1861 and 1881. By 1871, he was working as a labourer in Leeds. William was working for a tailor in Roade in 1851, while Elizabeth and Harriet were still living in Ashton in 1851, described as being the daughters-in-law of John Warst, a fifty-eight-year-old agricultural labourer who was married to Mary, a lacemaker aged fifty. Perhaps Thomas Whiting had died and Mary had remarried.

In 1851 Austin Masters Whiting was living in Roade, working as a draper. By this time he had married Mary Batchelor from Hethe, Oxfordshire, had three children: John (six), Sarah (four) and Thomas (one) and earned enough to employ Ann Spencer from Callington in Northamptonshire as a house servant. However Austin's career declined, and he was later described as a hawker. Perhaps seeing no future for himself in England he decided to emigrate to America, and as his wife did not like the idea, he left her behind. It is not known what happened to him.

In the 1861 census Thomas (Flora's 'Uncle Tom'), aged ten, is found in Cottisford living with his grandparents Thomas Batchelor, an agricultural labourer aged sixty-eight and born in Buckingham, and his wife Harriet, aged sixty-three from Blackthorn. His elder brother John was serving in the Royal Navy aboard the *District Eagle*. Ten years later Thomas was in Juniper Hill, then aged twenty-one and working as a shoemaker, living with his mother, Mary Whiting, a widow aged fifty-two whose occupation is listed as a dressmaker. He was still there in 1876, described in *Harrod's Royal County Directory of Oxfordshire* as a boot and shoemaker of Cottisford (Juniper Hill was not mentioned separately, so he was probably still living there rather than in Cottisford). In 1871 his sister Sarah was a laundry maid in Ruabon, Denbighshire in Wales.

Thomas' mother Mary still described herself as married in 1861, when she was a housemaid in Hethe, in the home of James Mitchell, a gentleman and his wife Jane, but by 1871 she had either given up completely on her husband Austin, or heard news of his death, as she described herself as a widow. In 1881 she was living alone in Hethe, which is described in some of the census returns as her birthplace (in others it is Cottisford). No occupation is given so as she was sixty-three she may have retired before this time. However the money must have run out as in 1891, still living alone in Hethe, she was once again a domestic servant. She appears to have gone to live with Thomas in Twyford at the end of her life as she died there in 1902 aged eighty-three.

Thomas was friendly with the Timms family by 1875, when he and his future wife Ann Timms, Albert's elder sister, were the two witnesses at Emma and Albert Timms' wedding in Cottisford. He married Ann Timms in Buckingham on 17 April 1876, and Albert and Emma Timms acted as their witnesses. Their eldest daughter, Mary Martha, was born in Cottisford in 1877, but shortly after that they moved to Twyford, where he spent the rest of his life, and Ellen Jane was baptised in Twyford on 1 September 1878, Anne Elizabeth on 23 May 1880, Amy on 29 February 1882 and John Austin Whiting on 5 July 1885.

Flora grew to know her uncle and aunt and cousins well, and in *Over to Candleford* she recalls her first visit with her parents to see them. The family got up early in the morning,

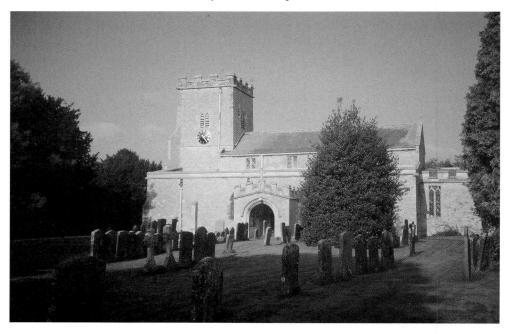

Twyford church.

dressed in their best, and set off in the innkeeper's spring cart. She mentioned going past some earthworks:

> Their father pointed out some earthworks, which, he said, were thrown up by the Romans and described those old warriors in their brass helmets so well that the children seemed to see them; but neither he nor they, dreamed that another field within sight would one day be surrounded by buildings called 'hangars', or that one day, within their own lifetimes, other warriors would soar from it into the sky, armed with more deadly weapons than the Romans ever knew.

> *Lark Rise to Candleford*, pp. 302-3

The earthworks mentioned were probably those known as Fringford Lodge, where Blomfield wrote that an important villa was built on rising ground, to the left of the road:

> When the ground was disturbed here about 1860, two human skeletons were found at a depth of two feet below the surface, the skulls being quite perfect; and several remains of tessellated pavements were laid bare, some tesserae being large and coarse, and others smaller and of different colours, red, blue, and white, the latter probably forming the floor of the hall or other chief room of the house. An underground chamber close by the pavement, with two or three steps leading down to it, was also discovered, which looked as if it might have been the site of the hypocaust (warming apparatus) or a bath; and broken pottery abounds. There are also evident signs of an embankment at a short distance in front of this house, over which the present road now runs, and in the adjacent field small coins, mostly copper have been constantly turned up in such numbers as if the ground had been sown broadcast with them.

> J.C. Blomfield, *History of the Present Deanery of Bicester*, 1882

Bicester was once a Roman town called Alchester, so it is not surprising that villas are found in the area. The airfield referred to is RAF Bicester, situated on the Buckingham road, north of the town, which was laid out as a Royal Flying Corps training station in 1916. Several large hangars were built in the 1920s and '30s and bombers were stationed there from 1935.

Flora wrote that 'Uncle Tom' lived in the town of 'Candleford', and it is possible that she knew of Rechab Holland through visiting her grandparents in Buckingham and blended a little of his character with that of Thomas Whiting as the latter was probably not as prosperous as Flora suggests. Flora described her uncle's shop as being the last in the street leaving the town, with one beautiful lady's top boot on a velvet cushion in the shop window and a sign reading: 'Ladies' boots and shoes made to order. Best Materials. Perfect Workmanship. Fit Guaranteed. Ladies' Hunting Boots a Speciality'. In a survey of Twyford made in 1910 he is listed as living at 9 Chilton Place, where he had a cottage and garden, 14 perches in size, gross annual value £18, rateable value £2 8s 9d, original value £85, with £79 deducted for buildings.

Most people had their shoes made to measure in those days, so Uncle Tom would have been able to build up a good business in the locality, being the only shoemaker in the village. What is not so certain, however, is that he would have had the workshop Flora describes with workmen and apprentices, although he may have had a small number of employees. He cannot have been very prosperous as his daughters went into service. Flora grew very fond of her uncle, and sketched his character:

> If Laura's Uncle Tom was a snob by trade, there was nothing else snobbish about him, for he was one of the most liberal-minded men she was ever to know and one of the wisest. He was a Liberal in politics, too ...

Lark Rise to Candleford, p. 313

Uncle Tom was to have a great influence on Flora. He loved books, and had amassed quite a collection. He was disappointed that his own children did not show much interest in reading, and delighted to help Flora. However, Flora exaggerated when she wrote that he considered them dunces, as they were in fact well educated and well read. Both girls attended a nearby school, and were sent for a year to 'Miss Bussell's' school to be 'finished'. This could have been Misses Harriet and Louisa Baylis' ladies' school in West Street, Buckingham or that of Miss Lydia Mary Roper in Bourton Road, or Miss Anne Warne, St Peter's College.

When Flora and Edwin went to stay in Twyford on their own for the first time, aged eleven and nine, Flora discovered a cache of books in the attic. From it she extracted the eighteenth-century novel *Pamela, or Virtue Rewarded*, by Richardson, which she brought down and devoured eagerly, being dubbed a bookworm by her cousins. Uncle Tom got her to read Mrs Gaskell's *Cranford* to him, and it became a regular thing. Each time she went to stay with her cousins she would sneak into his workshops when she could in the afternoons and read to him while he worked. As she did not have access to such a wealth of books at home, Flora's innate love of books would have been nurtured by her reading with Uncle Tom and by being able to borrow some of his books. He was perhaps the first to recognise that she had a special gift, and in consequence encouraged her to develop it.

Flora's Aunt Ann was a very slim woman, well educated as she had stayed at school until she was fifteen. She was an affectionate woman, and enormously kind:

> No one who heard her gentle voice or looked into her fine dark eyes could doubt her loving nature. Her husband laughed at what he called her 'softness' and said that customers calling in a great rage to complain that their shoes had not been delivered to time had stayed to tell the full story of their lives. For her own children she had sweet, pet names, and Edmund was soon her 'little lover' and Laura her 'Pussikins'. Except for her eyes and the dark satiny hair which

rippled in waves flat to her head, she was a plain-looking woman, pale and thin of face and of figure so flat that, with her hair parted in the middle and in the long straight frocks she wore, she reminded Laura of Mrs Noah in the toy ark she had given Edmund at Christmas.

Lark Rise to Candleford, p. 313

Ann and Albert's mother, Martha Timms seems to have come to live with the Whitings in her old age, as she was buried at Twyford on 10 August 1886. Flora does not mention having seen her when she came to stay with the family.

Flora's cousins were a little younger than her. Mary Martha, called Molly in the book, was in fact known as Polly, described by Flora as 'a motherly little person with a plump, soft figure, red-gold hair, and freckles on the bridge of her nose'. Red hair was not liked in those days, but apparently Revd H.C. Collier, the vicar of Twyford (this was his real name), admired it. Polly's eldest son, Ernest Arthur, born in 1899, lived with Thomas Whiting as a child and followed in his grandfather's footsteps as bootmaker in Twyford. In 1891 Mary was working as a domestic servant for farmer Henry Tanner in Chesterton, Oxfordshire. Ten years later she had become a cook in the home of Isabel Lake and her clergyman son, Kinsopp Lake in St Cross Cottage, St Cross Road, Holywell in Oxford. In 1903 she married Edwin Cherry a groom, who was working at Waddesdon in 1901.

Ellen Jane, known as Nellie, was two years younger than Flora who said that, 'she was dark, quick in her movements, and said things that made people laugh. "Sharp as a needle", said Laura's father afterwards'. (*Lark Rise to Candleford*, p. 314). She played the piano well. Ellen went on to marry William John Bryan, a railway porter, in 1905. William was the son of Felix Bryan, an agricultural labourer from Stratton Audley in Oxfordshire who was living in Twyford in 1891 which is probably where the couple met. In 1901 William was living in Hackney in London working as a capstan attendant on the railways.

Anne Elizabeth (Annie), baptised in 1880, was not as fond of school as her elder sisters, but although she was not so good academically, she excelled at needlework. In 1901 she was employed as a cook in the household of Dr Quainton in Steeple Claydon in Buckinghamshire. She later married John Beckett, an agricultural labourer from Steeple Claydon in Buckinghamshire, on 25 September 1907 and their son John Austin was baptised in Twyford in 1915.

Amy was the youngest daughter, baptised in 1882, and Flora mentions little about her except that she was good at schoolwork. She never married. She too went into service and in 1901 was a house parlour maid working for Ann Wood and her two sisters in St Giles Street in Oxford.

John Austin (Johnny), the last born, in 1885, but the only son, was far more important in the eyes of his parents, and in Flora's eyes, thoroughly spoilt:

Johnny must have anything he wanted, no matter to whom it belonged. If Johnny fell down, he must be picked up and comforted ... He was young for his age and slow in developing; but there was fine stuff in Johnny. As a young man he was deeply religious, a non-smoker, a non-drinker and a non-card player, and served the altar set up on many a battlefield during the 1914-18 war, and all this needed character in the atmosphere of Army life.

That Sunday afternoon Laura saw only a little boy with a pale, freckled face and thin fair hair. A spoilt child, of whom even his parents looked a little ashamed. But, in after years, she also saw Johnny as a sick soldier shut up in Kut, emaciated by illness and hunger and tormented by heat and flies; and that same soldier, once the adored little boy with his bodyguard of sisters, thrown out bodily after an exchange of sick prisoners with a last kick from his native jailer and a 'you can have this one for a makeweight. He's no good.' Or the same Johnny, lying for a whole summer on a long chair in the orchard, fed, every few minutes, as it seemed, with broth, or eggs beaten up in milk, out of teacups, until home and

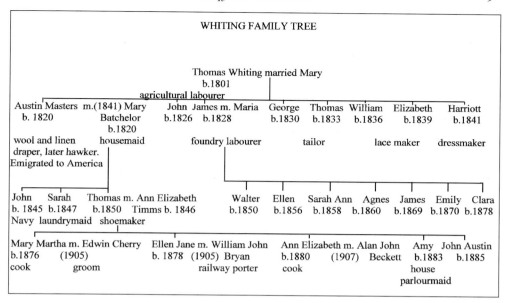

Whiting family tree.

rest and his mother's nursing had strengthened him sufficient to pass his Board and be sent to the trenches in France. For, as we grow older, we see in memory not only our friends as they appeared to us as children, but also as they were to become in later years.

Lark Rise to Candleford pp. 314-18

Johnny was in fact considerably younger than Edwin, who was born in 1879. Flora's visits here became some of the highlights of her childhood, with the pleasure of seeing her Uncle Tom who gave her so much encouragement and her affectionate Aunt Ann and her cousins – even spoilt Johnny. She seems to have visited them regularly too while she was working at Fringford, as she wrote that on the Sundays when 'Miss Lane' could spare her she would walk into 'Candleford' for tea with her relatives, enjoying seeing her uncle and aunt, although her cousins were no longer at home. It is also possible that she worked for a while at the Post Office in Twyford before spreading her wings and leaving Oxfordshire.

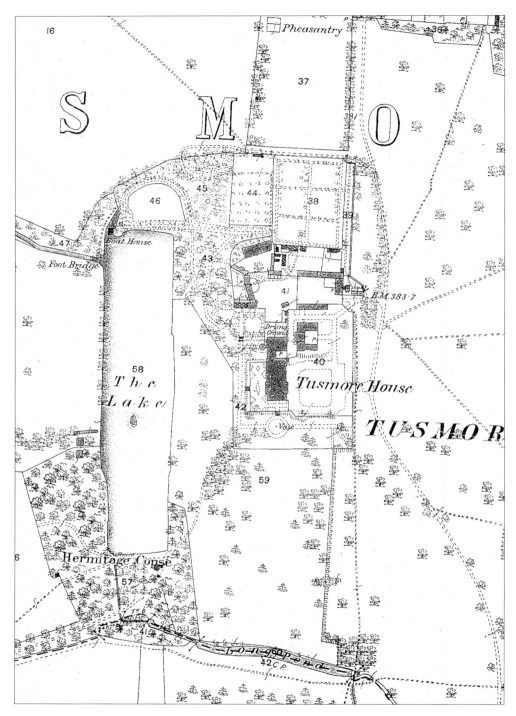

Reproduction of a late nineteenth-century Ordnance Survey map showing Tusmore House (Park) and grounds. (Oxfordshire Studies)

Tusmore Park

Tusmore Park situated just down the road from Juniper Hill, must have seemed a remote place to Flora, being the nearest 'great house'. It is unlikely that the Timms family would have had much to do with the aristocracy, but indirectly they had a great influence over the villagers. The aristocracy spent 'the season' in London, but when living at their country houses acted as local magistrates and oversaw the farming of their estates, employing some local people. On their shoulders rested the prosperity of the lower classes, so many of whom they employed. On the whole they were respected, but that respect had to be earned, and there was plenty of local gossip about the excesses of the wealthy – gambling away estates, heavy drinking, and the odd orgy! The remoteness was increased by the fact that very few of the servants, except for those working on the farm, were born locally, so the house was a self-contained community, with even the servants considering themselves a cut above the locals.

Tusmore House was a peaceable place, although the village had a fascinating history. The name means 'Thurl's Pool' or perhaps, more romantically 'a lake haunted by a giant or demon'. It was one of the villages which had been devastated by the Black Death, being so deserted in 1358 that Sir Roger de Cotesford was able to enclose it and build a house in the park. Nothing of the medieval house is left today, but in the grounds there are earthworks indicating house platforms and possibly a church, and two hollow ways and two rectangular enclosures which may have been field systems of part of a later park. The house that Flora would have known, which replaced the one built for Sir Richard Fermor in 1625, was built 1766-70 for William Fermor at a cost of £11,305 12s 5½d. The next nine years were spent completing the interior and the gardens. It was designed by Robert Mylne, a Scottish architect, in Italianate style with the principal rooms on the first floor to command better views. Stone for the house came from Fritwell Quarry and Headington, with freestone from Glympton and Tottenhoe near Dunstable for features such as columns.

The Fermors were a noted Catholic family, several members of whom entered religious orders, and were connected with the prominent Jacobites John and Francis Towneley whose mother was Ursula Fermor. They usually kept a resident priest, often a Jesuit. Mrs Fitzherbert was a frequent guest and according to tradition clandestinely married George IV at Tusmore. However after the death of William Fermor in 1806 the house was let to tenants.

In 1857 the Tusmore Estate was sold so that the proceeds could be divided between the children of the late owner, Captain Ramsay, who had married into the Fermor family. It was described as follows by Messrs Jonas and Thomas Paxton as being:

> ... situated about five miles from Bicester, and four from Brackley, near to five railway stations, and within easy distance of the metropolis; comprising the entire parishes of Tusmore and Hardwick, and portions of the parishes of Stoke Lyne, Fritwell, Cottisford, Souldern, North Aston and Goddington in the county of Oxford, and of Croughton in the county of Northampton, with the capital Mansion of Tusmore, substantially built of stone,

TUSMORE.

The Particulars & Conditions of Sale

OF MOST IMPORTANT AND DESIRABLE

FREEHOLD ESTATES,

COMPRISING THE WHOLE OF THE PARISHES OF

TUSMORE AND HARDWICK,

AND PORTIONS OF THE PARISHES OF

Stoke-Lyne, Fritwell, Cottisford, Souldern, North Aston, and Goddington, in the County of Oxford,

And CROUGHTON in the County of Northampton,

About 5 miles from Bicester, and 4 from Brackley, and within easy reach of 5 Railway stations,

COMPRISING THE

CAPITAL MANSION OF TUSMORE,

With its corresponding Offices and Premises, built of fine Stone, and suitable for the accommodation of a Nobleman or Gentleman's Family,

BEING PLACED IN ITS OWN GROUNDS, WHICH ARE SURROUNDED BY A

RICHLY TIMBERED PARK,

AND WITH

LARGE WALLED GARDEN, VINERY,

Beautiful Lake, Pleasure Grounds, Woods & Plantations.

ALSO SEVERAL

HIGHLY CULTIVATED FARMS,

WITH

EXCELLENT FARM RESIDENCES, AND NUMEROUS COTTAGES,

CONTAINING IN THE WHOLE UPWARDS OF

4700 ACRES,

TOGETHER WITH

The Perpetual Advowsons of the Rectories of Tusmore and Hardwick,

Which will be Sold by Auction,

BY MESSRS.

JONAS & THOS. PAXTON

AT THE AUCTION MART, LONDON,

On Wednesday, the 15th of July, 1857, at 12 o'clock,

By direction of the Trustee under the Will of WILLIAM FERMOR Esquire, deceased.

The Mansion and Estates can be viewed by Ticket only, which with Plans and Particulars can be obtained of Messrs. Tooke, Hallowes and Price, Solicitors, 39 Bedford Row, London; of John M. Davenport, Esq., Clerk of the Peace, Oxford; or of the Auctioneers, Bicester, Oxon. Particulars also at the Queen's Hotel, Manchester; at the Midland Counties Herald Office, Birmingham; or at the Mart.

R. SMITH AND SON, PRINTERS AND STATIONERS, BICESTER.

An extract from the sales catalogue of 1857, when Henry Howard, Earl of Effingham, purchased Tusmore Park, indicating the extent of the state. (Oxfordshire Studios)

Drawing of Tusmore Park as it was in 1857 from the sale catalogue. (Oxfordshire Studies)

erected in 1770 in the Grecian style of architecture, and containing an excellent entrance hall, good breakfast room, spacious dining room 36 feet by 24 and 13 high, a magnificent drawing room 48 feet by 24 and 18 high, a splendid library 36 feet by 24 and 18 high, study, eleven principal bedrooms, eleven secondary apartments, two staircases and numerous and suitable offices of the most convenient description, five coach houses, capital stabling for twenty-four horses, gamekeeper's and gardener's cottages, large walled kitchen garden, pleasure grounds, lake, vinery etc. The whole surrounded by a richly timbered park. Adjoining which are several extensive and well-stocked game preserves ...

Quoted in J.C. Blomfield, *History of the Present Deanery of Bicester*, 1877

Henry Howard, 2nd Earl of Effingham, purchased the estate for £152,000, moving there from 'The Grange', near Rotherham, where he felt the area was becoming too industrialised, so the rural situation of Tusmore seemed more congenial. He may have known the area previously, as he was educated at Christ Church, Oxford. He came from an eminent family; the first Baron, William Howard, was the first English ambassador to Russia in 1553 and Lord High Admiral of England, while the second baron commanded the English fleet which destroyed the Spanish Armada. The first Earl of Effingham of the second creation of the earldom was Henry Howard's father Kenneth Alexander Howard (1767-1845) who married Lady Charlotte Primrose, the eldest daughter of Neil, 3rd Earl of Rosebury. They had five sons and four daughters. He died in 1845 and Charlotte remarried Thomas Holmes in 1859. She died on 17 September 1864.

Kenneth Alexander Howard's son Henry was born at Southampton in 1806. He studied at Orial College, Oxford, and in 1832 he married Eliza, the only daughter of Sir Gordon Drummond, who was born in Montreal, Canada. In *Kelly's Handbook to the Titles* of 1883 he was described as Second titular baron Howard of Effingham, DI, Justice of the Peace for the West Riding of Yorkshire, Liberal MP for Shaftsbury (1841-45). His addresses were given as:

57 Eaton Place, London SW
Travellers' Club
Tusmore House, Bicester
The Grange, Rotherham, Yorkshire

The Grange was a large establishment, where the Howard family would have lived in some style, as befitted their rank. At the 1851 census the Earl was in residence there with his wife Eliza and their children, all born in London: Lady Maria (aged fifteen), Lord Howard (aged fourteen), the honourable Frederick (ten), Lady Alice (aged eight) and the honourable Kenneth (aged five). All except Lady Maria were described as 'scholars at home'. Henry's brother Charles was also living with them. They had an army of household servants living in The Grange to care for them: a butler, a governess, a housekeeper, a cook, two lady's maids, three housemaids, two laundry maids, a laundress, two nursery maids, a still room maid, a dairymaid, a kitchen maid, a scullery maid, under butler, footman, coachman, groom and page. There would also have been outdoor servants and gardeners. This was a world away from the few servants kept by the Rousbys at Cottisford House.

The Earl sold some of the outlying estates at Tusmore, but retained 3,376 acres. He added an office wing to the main house which spoiled the original symmetry of the design and changed the main entrance to basement level instead of first-floor level, removing the floor of the original entrance hall to construct a large internal staircase. The library became the new dining room. Flora wrote that her father was employed on these renovations.

The Earl's wealth and status is revealed by the number of servants he employed at Tusmore. In 1861 both the Earl and his wife were in residence there, with their unmarried daughters Maria and Alice and son Kenneth. They drew their servants from a wide geographical area. Samuel Gardol, their butler (aged thirty-five) and the senior male servant, came from Old Swinford, Worcestershire, George Clarke, the footman (aged twenty-six) came from Cuxham, Oxfordshire, Thomas Manners, another footman (eighteen) was from Westminster, Elizabeth Macuerson, the housekeeper (aged fifty-nine), Anne and Caroline Sharp the lady's maids (aged twenty-nine and twenty-seven) were from London, Elizabeth Whiteker, the cook (thirty-two) was from Church Stretton, Shropshire, Mary Mecar, the still room maid (thirty) was from Harrietsham, Kent, Harriet Allen, kitchen maid (twenty-six) and Mary Tidler the scullery maid (twenty) came from London, Emma Price the dairymaid (twenty-six) came from Ewhurst in Surrey, Jane Garnett, a housemaid (forty-three) was from Lincolnshire, Mary Guest, also a housemaid (thirty-one) came from Kimberworth, Yorkshire, Emile Smith, a housemaid (twenty-nine) came from Middlesex, laundry maids Mary Ann Hellms (twenty-three), Susan Budd (twenty-three) and Elizabeth Harrison (seventeen) came from Elvetham, Hampshire, Kensington and Clapham, Surrey respectively and Annie Brysson, a housemaid (seventy) was from Ersol, Scotland.

Living in the Tusmore stables were: the coachman George Packett (forty-one) from Wortley, Yorkshire, Frederick Shaw, the groom (thirty-three) from Norfolk and Emmand Wilson the stable man (thirty) from Stoke Dayle, Northamptonshire. Nearby were the farm bailiff Joseph Fifield (thirty-three) from Kiddington, Oxfordshire and his wife Frances who had living with them Thomas Barton, the twenty-one-year-old carter from Ardley, John Coles (twenty-nine) the shepherd from Wroxton, Joseph Brock (twenty-three) the under carter from Fewcott and Charles Keen, a groom aged fifteen from Fewcott. The shepherd William Whate (thirty-eight) and his wife Barbara (thirty-nine) lived next door, and next to them were the estate bailiff, James Wilson (twenty-five) from Derbyshire, his wife Ann from Kings Sutton and their infant son Arthur. Thomas Hart (thirty-three) from Scotland, the clerk of works, lived alone, and next to him was the farmer Thomas Borridge (twenty-three) from Somerton who farmed 610 acres with twenty men and boys and six women. He and his wife had three servants. This, with a newly built uninhabited cottage completed Tusmore. There were few opportunities here for local girls who went into domestic service – perhaps the Howards did not want local gossip about their lives.

In 1871 the Earl of Effingham was again in residence with his wife Eliza, their unmarried daughters Lady Maria (thirty-five), and Lady Alice (twenty-eight), and their four-year-old grandson Henry Alexander Gordon Howard.

Tusmore Park. (David Watts)

The bridge over the ornamental lake at Tusmore in winter. (David Watts)

The household staff had all changed since 1861. The butler Henry Dobson (forty-one) from London was married to the housekeeper, Eleanor (thirty-nine) from Exeter. At the time of the census their children William, a fifteen-year-old solicitor's clerk and Fanny, a pupil, were visiting them. The Welsh cook Catherine Roberts (thirty-eight) came from Carmarthenshire; the lady's maids were two sisters, Hannah (twenty-eight) and Mary Dixon, from Wantage. Lower down the scale there were three housemaids: Elizabeth Pudner (twenty-five) from Newton Farrer, Devon, Eliza Wadham (twenty) from London, and Sarah Williams (twenty-two) from Bryngwn, Radnorshire plus one kitchen maid, Mary Roberts (twenty-eight) from Willcom Merrifield, Cornwall and a scullery maid, Maria Mattwood (twenty-one) from Griston, Norfolk. They also kept four laundry maids – Elizabeth Randall (twenty-four), Martha Kirby (twenty-five), Elizabeth Roffe (seventeen), and Anne Cowley (sixteen) – a nursery maid, Betsy Fathers (nineteen), a still room maid Ann Giles (twenty-six) and a dairymaid Rachel Waters (twenty-seven). Other male servants were coachman James Rapple (thirty-five), two footmen – William Poolley (twenty-three) and Edmund Moore (twenty-two) – and a page, George Wickham (fourteen).

It is interesting to note that the butler and the housekeeper were married to each other, as female servants usually had to leave their employment when they married, so the Dobsons were fortunate in that they were able to live together as a married couple. As in most households, there were more female than male servants – sixteen female to five male. In the greatest households male cooks were preferred, but the Earl had a female cook. The lady's maids would have had higher status than other maids, often coming from the middle rather than lower classes, and had the privilege of travelling with their mistresses. There must have been a lot of washing to justify four laundry maids when there were only three housemaids and one kitchen and one scullery maid. Still room maids were not common by this time – Ann Giles would probably have been involved in making preserves and perhaps herbal remedies. Most of Flora's female contemporaries would have gone into service and many mothers liked their daughters to go into service in a big house like Tusmore; there was more chance of promotion up the servant ladder than there was working in a farmhouse – 'once a farmhouse servant, always a farmhouse servant,' as they used to say.

The young men working as footmen had probably been chosen for their good physique, as they would open the door to visitors, accompany the family on visits, and thereby reflect credit on their employers. They were seldom selected from among the local boys.

In 1881 the Earl and his wife were ensconced in their house at 57 Eaton Place in London in a much smaller household which included their unmarried daughter Maria, their son Kenneth who was working as a clerk in the Foreign Office and their grandson Henry Alexander Gordon Howard who was a scholar at fourteen. Eleanor Dobson (now widowed) was still their housekeeper. The servants were Henry Wanstall (fifty-one) the butler, Sarah Gibbs (twenty-eight) the cook, Alice Fielden (seventeen) the lady's maid, Sarah Hatton (nineteen) working as needlewoman and Anna King (thirty-six) and Annie Macdonald (twenty-two) the two housemaids. Emily Haywood (twenty-two) was kitchen maid, Alice Bilney (twenty) was scullery maid and Anne Thomson (thirty-six) was still room maid. It seems that the groom and coachman were living in the mews nearby.

They had left a skeleton staff awaiting their return at Tusmore: laundry maids, Ellen Wood (thirty) and Emma Lovett (eighteen) from London and Jane Anstiffe aged eighteen from Aston Rowant, Oxfordshire, housemaids Mary Edwards (forty) from Herefordshire and Caroline Speed (twenty-seven) from Somerset, dairymaid Mary Buckingham (twenty-four) from Devon, house porter Thomas Hitchman (forty-six) from Souldern and gardener Walter Wiliams (twenty-five) from Williamscote.

Although the villagers had little to do with the aristocracy, they noticed when the flag was flying from the tower, indicating that the family were in residence. Flora recalled seeing Henry Howard, Earl of Effingham:

The lavishly decorated saloon of Tusmore Park. (David Watts)

A group of great house outdoor servants in the courtyard at Tusmore Park, showing, from left to right: Joseph Walby, the gamekeeper, Mr Rouse, a footman, Jack Allan (brother of Richard Allan, who later served as land agent to the Earl of Effingham), with a jug of beer, and another footman and a groom. Characters were identified by Gordon Allan. (David Watts)

They sometimes saw him pass through the hamlet in his carriage, an old, old man, sunk deep in cushions and half-buried in rugs, often too comatose to be aware of, or acknowledge, their curtsies. He had never spoken to them or given them anything, for they did not live in his cottages, and in the way of Christmas coals and blankets he had his own parish to attend to; but the men worked on his land, though not directly employed by him, and by some inherited instinct they felt they belonged to him.

Lark Rise to Candleford, pp. 289-90

Lord Effingham was not nearly as old as Flora remembered – he would only have been sixty-nine when she was born. His death on 5 February 1889 was reported in the *Bicester Advertiser* of Friday 8 February:

With much regret we have to announce the death of the Earl of Effingham which took place at his town house 57 Eaton Place, Pimlico, London at about 5 o'clock on Tuesday morning. Deceased, Henry Howard, was in his eighty-third year, was the second earl, succeeding his father in 1845, having been educated at Harrow… The deceased nobleman represented Shaftesbury in Parliament from 1841 till 1845 and was deputy lieutenant of the West Riding of Yorkshire and patron of the livings of Whiston and Paul in Yorkshire, Albury, Foracett St Peter and Foracett St Mary in Norfolk. He had not taken any prominent part in public life of late years but had recently had the church at Hardwick restored. The living of Hardwick was also in the gift of the Earl of Effingham…

By the time the Earl moved to Oxfordshire he had ceased much of his public life, so was not prominent in Oxfordshire affairs. However his elaborate funeral was described in detail in the *Bicester Advertiser* of 15 February 1889:

Amidst many demonstrations of respect and esteem, the funeral of the late Earl of Effingham took place at Hardwick churchyard on Saturday afternoon last. The remains of the deceased were conveyed from his London residence on Friday by rail and arrived at Brackley station in the evening. The coffin was then placed in a mourning hearse and taken to Tusmore House and from thence to Hardwick church. Here it was met by the Revd C.S. Harrison, Rector, who read the opening sentences of the burial service. The coffin was placed in the central aisle and on Saturday morning several members of the bereaved family visited the church and placed beautiful wreaths upon it. The floral tributes were beautiful and costly, and included a large cross from the Countess of Effingham … [here followed a list of the donors of the floral tributes] … At half past two o'clock, the time fixed for the funeral, the church was crowded with those anxious to show their respect for the deceased nobleman. Soon afterwards the mourners arrived and took their places in the centre of the church. They included: the Countess of Effingham, Lord and Lady Howard, the Hon. Henry Howard, Lady Maria and Lady Alice Howard, the Hon. Frederick Howard, and Mr Gordon Howard. The service was commenced by the Revd C.S. Harrison and after the choir had sung the appropriate hymn 'A Few More Years Shall Roll' the lesson was read in an impressive manner by the Revd W. Russell Almond, Curate. The choir then sang 'Lord Now Lettest Thou Thy Servant Depart in Peace', Mr Rouse presiding at the harmonium. At the grave the burial service was resumed by the Revd W. Russel Almond and after the choir had sung 'The King of Love My Shepherd Is', the Rector pronounced the Benediction. At the close of the service the Countess of Effingham, who was deeply affected, retired to the chancel for a few minutes after prayer. Amongst those present at the church and at the grave were – Lord Valentia, Colonel Griffith (Croughton), Mr Beville Ramsay (Croughton), Mr H. Tubb, Mr E. Slater Harrison, the Revd E. Withington, Mr E.R.K. Rousby … Miss Harrison, Miss Waters … Mr T. Ayriss (steward). There were also present several of the servants from Tusmore House and a large number of residents in the

A shoot at Tusmore Park. The Earl of Effingham is second from the left at the back. (David Watts)

neighbourhood including the deceased's tenantry – Mr J.W. Tubb, Mr Waters (Cottisford), Mr Radford and Mr Taylorn (Croughton), Mr W. Goodwin (Stoke Lyne) and Mr Hiorns (Hardwick). The coffin, which was borne to the grave by workmen on the estate, was of polished oak with brass furniture and an inner leaded shell and the inscription was:

Henry
Second Earl of Effingham
Born 2nd August 1806
Died 5th February 1889

It was deposited in a new brick vault, lined with moss, on which was placed a cross of narcissus and snowdrops, and the ground was selected by the late Earl to the north of the church. The London undertakers were Messrs Hailes of Buckingham Palace-road, but the vault was constructed and the arrangements satisfactorily carried out by Messrs T. Grimsley and Sons, Causeway, Bicester …

The obituary went on to describe the renovations to Hardwick church financed by the Earl. He was succeeded by his son Henry Howard, 3rd Earl of Effingham (1837-98, who was educated at Christ Church, Oxford). He was buried in London, at Kensal Green cemetery and the funeral was conducted by Revd Herbert Holmes, Rector of Whiston.

The way of life in great houses was more ritualised than that of the village. The ladies of the house would go out in the carriage to pay calls each afternoon at three o'clock, leaving visiting cards if they found no one in, or else invited friends round to drink tea and play croquet. The family would have had little to do with the local villagers.

The girls who went to work in such houses as servants must have been dumbfounded to see the elaborate decoration and furnishings of these houses compared to the stark furnishings of their own homes. Flora's family were once given a beaded footstool which came from 'Tusmore House' after a fire there, acquired by their landlady 'Mrs Herring', who had no room on the cart for it when she removed the last of her belongings from the End House which Flora's family rented from her:

> But Mrs Herring was back in the closet and, since she could not take all her things away with her, was determined to be generous. 'Now, here's a nice little beaded footstool. Come out of Tusmore House that time the fire was, so you may be sure it's good. You have it, my dear. I'd like you to have it'. Their mother eyed the little round stool with the claw legs and beaded cover. She would really have liked that, but had made up her mind to accept nothing. Perhaps, she reflected, too, that it would be hers in any case, as what Mrs Herring could not take she would have to leave, for she said again, 'it's very kind of you, I'm sure, but I don't know that I've any use for it'.

Lark Rise to Candleford, p. 296

There are few direct references to Tusmore in *Lark Rise to Candleford*, and Flora is unlikely ever to have set foot inside it, but she was delighted to discover after her book was published that Lady Bicester, wife of the then owner of Tusmore Park, liked it, and commented to her sister '... such praise makes me feel very humble. It is rather amusing to think of my books being read at Tusmore. Father helped to finish rebuilding that house'. (Quoted from a letter in a private collection by Gillian Lindsay).

The house Flora knew was demolished in 1960 and a new house built, designed by Claud Phillimore in Georgian style, but looking woefully small in the vast landscape of the park, itself now destroyed, although some of the old farm buildings, including a half-timbered barn on staddle stones, still remain. The current owner, Wafic Saïd, a Syrian billionaire, who donated money to build the Saïd Business School in Oxford, has rebuilt the house in grand style as a Palladian villa, designed by eighty-four-year-old Sir William Whitfield. The house, built of white stone imported from Burgundy, is set on rising ground, with the front banked up so that there are only three steps to the front door, but as the ground falls away on the other three sides, French windows open out into the garden. The front elevation features a portico with 20-ft high classical columns and the interior is arranged around a grand staircase set in a rotunda. The Whitfield Partners brochure describes it as:

> A Palladian Villa constructed to the most exacting standards of dimensional tolerance and fine detail, standing 20m above the existing ground level. There are four main floor levels giving a total floor area of 500m square. The house has exceptional storey heights, the reception floor being the highest at nearly six metres. It boasts the tallest scalable columns made in this country. It incorporates other magnificent features including sweeping cantilever stone staircases, beautifully ornate and grand fibrous ceilings, niches, columns and pilasters, polished plaster walls, curved stone and marble flooring, fine natural oak flooring, fine carved fitted joinery and furniture, fine marble bathrooms, fair faced brick cellars, and a highly complex service installation including under-floor heating, a/c units and ducting, audio visual, lighting, security and control systems.

The building has been described as 'perhaps the finest country house built since the Second World War'. The house cost £300 million and was awarded the Georgian Architectural Award.

Shelswell Park

Shelswell Park was the second great house which featured in Flora's life. It is situated between Cottisford and Fringford, and her first experience of the house must have been as one of the group of Cottisford schoolchildren carrying their May garland both here and to Tusmore each year:

It was at the back door of large houses that the fun began. In country houses at that date troops of servants were kept, and the May Day procession would find the courtyard crowded with housemaids and kitchen maids, dairy maids and laundry maids, footmen, grooms, coachmen, and gardeners. The songs were sung, the garland was admired; then to a chorus of laughter, teasing and urging, one Maid of Honour snatched the cap from the King's head, the other raised the Queen's veil, and a shy, sheepish boy pecked at his companion's rosy cheek, to the huge delight of the beholders.

'Again! Again!' a dozen voices would cry and the kissing was repeated until the royal couple turned sulky and refused to kiss any more, even when offered a penny a kiss. Then the lord saluted his lady and the footman the footman's lady (this couple had probably been introduced in compliment to such patrons), and the money-box was handed round and began to grow heavy with pence.

The menservants, with their respectable side-whiskers, the maids in their little flat caps like crocheted mats on their smoothly parted hair, and their long, billowing lilac or pink print gowns, and the children in their ribbon-decked poverty, alike belonged to a bygone order of things. The boys pulled forelocks and the girls dropped curtseys to the upper servants, for they came next in importance to 'the gentry'...

After the mansion, there were the steward's, the head gardener's and the stud-groom's houses to visit with the garland; then on through the gardens and park and woods and fields to the next stopping-place.

Lark Rise to Candleford, p. 208

There was no real village of Shelswell in the nineteenth century, only a few houses near the house, lived in by important employees such as the gardener, gamekeeper, blacksmith and the two farmers, William Ladler and Thomas Badam, who leased their farms from the Harrison family who owned Shelswell. The area was probably settled in Saxon times, as the place name means the spring or stream of *Scield*, an Anglo-Saxon personal name. Only traces of moats and humps and bumps indicate the site of the medieval manor house near Home Farm, the site of St Ebbe's church (it was not used after the seventeenth century and was demolished by 1796) and the deserted medieval village nearby. Like Tusmore, the land was enclosed early, here in 1601. In the early eighteenth century the Trotman family built a new manor house.

Gilbert Harrison, a London merchant, purchased the estate in the eighteenth century, and was succeeded in 1790 by his son John who died in 1834. The house then descended to John's

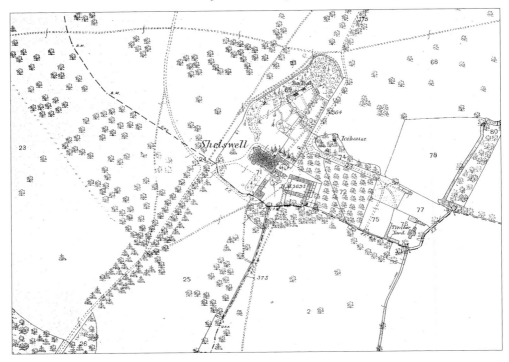

Above: Reproduction of a late
nineteenth-century Ordnance
Survey map of Shelswell Park,
showing the wooded gardens and
the ice house. (Oxfordshire Studies)

Left: A detail of Shelswell House,
built in 1875 and demolished in the
1980s, illustrating the crest of the
Slater-Harrison family. (Bodleian
Library)

nephew, another John and the son of his sister Ann Harrison and John Slater of Margate, on condition that he use the surname Harrison so he complied by changing his name to John Slater-Harrison. He married Louisa, daughter of the second Earl of Clonmell, grand-daughter of the second Earl of Warwick, who died in 1873 aged sixty-six. John Slater-Harrison died the following year in 1874, aged seventy-one. Shelswell was not as large as Tusmore, but in 1841 there were four male servants and nine female servants, but their jobs were not described. In 1851 Slater-Harrison was described as a landowner, and his wife Louisa as a Peer's daughter, and their children —Louisa (nineteen), Edward (eighteen) and Augusta (fourteen) – were living at home. The only servant given a title was Charlotte Hendre, the governess who was thirty. In total, there were five male servants and eight female servants.

Years later in 1861 he was described as a landed proprietor and for the first time the servants were detailed: Sarah Edwards (forty-nine) from Worcestershire was the housekeeper; there were two lady's maids, Eliza Mary Taylor (thirty-one) from Brighton, Sussex and Mary Paddington (thirty-three) from Bloomsbury, London. The two housemaids, Mary Waddington (aged sixty-two and unmarried) and Mary Ann Barnett (twenty-seven) came from Leeds and Shalstone in Buckinghamshire. Both the young kitchen maids, Esther Freeman (eighteen) and Mary Morgan (seventeen) were hired locally from Hethe. Thomas Best, the butler, aged forty-seven, was described as married, but his wife was not living with him. He came from Walling, Kent. The other male employees were Joseph Franklin (twenty), the footman from Mixbury, John Clark (sixteen), the house boy, from Hethe and John Gee (twenty-six) the stable man from Fringford. John Tarsman (forty-five) from Gawcott, Buckinghamshire was gardener and appropriately lived in the Gardener's Cottage next door, while John Simmons (thirty-six) the keeper from Ivinghoe Aston, Buckinghamshire lived next door to him in the Keeper's Cottage with his family.

John was succeeded by his son Edward Slater-Harrison, the 'Sir Timothy' of *Lark Rise to Candleford* who was born at Shelswell. Edward had two sisters. One of them, Louisa Mary Ann, born in 1832, married Edward Roland Forman, son of Edward Forman of Hensol Castle, Glamorgan. She was widowed by 1861. Her sister Augusta, born in 1837, married while still a minor in 1857. Her husband was William Wemyss Methven Dewar, son of the Chief Justice of Bombay, who was born in India. In 1861 they were living at 1 Ardley Road, Middleton Stoney, where William Dewar was described as Lieutenant in the OVR, a fund holder and farmer of 243 acres, employing nine men and four boys. They employed a butler, lady's maid, housemaid and nursery maid. By 1871 they had five children, Florence (twelve), Arthur (ten), James (nine), Edward (eight) and Charles (five) and had moved closer to Shelswell, to Cotmore House near Fringford. William Dewar was by this time a magistrate, still farming and employing nine men and five boys. They must have become more affluent, as although they had no butler, they kept two male servants and seven female servants plus a governess, Ann Wilson, aged twenty from Harrogate. In 1901 he and Augusta were in Torquay, with Louisa's lady's maid, so they were probably on holiday. William died in 1903 aged seventy-three and Augusta died in 1911 aged seventy-four.

Edward Slater-Harrison was born at Shelswell in 1833. His first wife was Cecilia Selina Carhampton Saunderson, the daughter of Hardress Saunderson, a Lieutenant Colonel in the army in the 1851 census, who was born in County Cavan, Ireland. He and Cecilia married in 1865 in Fareham, Hampshire. She died in July 1899.

In 1900 Edward married Emma Cecilia Cartwright, daughter of Richard Aubrey Cartwright who lived at Edcott House, Northamptonshire in 1861, when he was a landed proprietor, a Justice of the Peace and Deputy Lieutenant for Northamptonshire and Oxfordshire. He was affluent enough to support a large establishment with a governess, housekeeper, upper nurse, three nurses, a nursery maid, schoolroom maid, two housemaids, kitchen maid, scullery maid, footman, groom and houseman. In 1881 when his daughters no longer required nursery maids his household had altered to consist of Richard and his wife the Hon. Mary (*née* Fremantle, and born in Little Marlow, Buckinghamshire), and his unmarried daughters Harriet Louise (thirty), Emma Cecilia (twenty-six), Frances Emily (twenty-four) and Beatrice Anna (twenty-two), his butler, footman, under footman, coachman, groom and eight female servants.

Above: All that remains of Shelswell House is the stable block.

Left: Edward Slater-Harrison, owner of Shelswell Park, the magistrate to whom Flora had to swear official oaths of loyalty to the Post Office when she first went to work at Fringford Post Office. (Baroness von Maltzahn)

Edward Slater-Harrison played an important role in county affairs, acting as High Sheriff in 1882, as a Justice of the Peace on the Bicester Bench, and an elected member of the first Oxfordshire County Council in 1888. He was also Colonel of the Bicester Corps of the Oxfordshire Yeomanry Cavalry.

The 1881 census indicates the composition of his household, which was much smaller than that of the Earl of Effingham: Edward Slater Harrison, head, aged forty-eight, magistrate and Captain of Yeomanry, was in residence with his wife Cecilia, aged forty-eight. Their staff consisted of butler Oliver Damp, (fifty-four), housekeeper Maria Holfman (thirty-five), German lady's maid Maren Wiegand (twenty-seven), housemaids Ellen Kay (forty-one) and Sophie Savin (twenty-two), kitchen maid Emily Cook (twenty-four), scullery maid Mary Fensmore (aged twenty), footman Charles Hadland (twenty-four) and under footman, Charles Ansford (seventeen).

The house that Flora would have known was very modern, having been built for Edward Slater-Harrison in 1875. He demolished most of the eighteenth-century house and commissioned architect William Wilkinson, famous for his many North Oxford houses, to design his new one, Italianate in style, in Bath stone, which was embellished with the Slater and Harrison family crests and a datestone that read '1875'. Part of the eighteenth-century house was incorporated into the new building, housing the billiard room. (This house in its turn has been demolished, and all that is left is the stable block). Slater-Harrison enlarged Shelswell Park and made several plantations, increasing the size of the gardens and laying out new ornamental gardens north of the house. Blomfield, who knew him, evidently considered him to be a good influence on the area, as he wrote in his *History of the Present Deanery of Bicester*, pp. 17-18:

> These houses of the squirearchy, who are in residence on their estates the greater part of the year, are elements of considerable blessing to the country. Their families are always in the midst of the people, knowing and attentive to the history, wants and infirmities of everyone. The ladies look after the sick, the schools, the young girls at home and those gone to service; the squire takes an interest in the general good of the parish and district; holds important offices connected with their management. Money is freely spent on the estate, and a considerable amount of culture and moral restraint is acquired in the classes below, in the farmhouses and the cottages. Those persons only who have known parishes that have been for generations squireless, and also those where a good squire and his family have been settled for a similar time, can appreciate the difference in general tones among the people.

It was to Shelswell Park that Flora and her family went for the celebrations in honour of Queen Victoria's Jubilee in 1887. Having been almost forgotten for years, Queen Victoria suddenly became a popular figure, her name on everybody's lips; people were proud to contribute a penny each, collected by Miss Sawkins Harrison, the vicar's daughter, to buy their Queen a present, and, most exciting of all, a big celebration for the villagers from nearby parishes took place at Shelswell Park.

At midday on the day of the Jubilee the family at the End House began their preparations for the great day: the children and their mother were washed and brushed and put in their best clothes, and only given a snack lunch so that they would not spoil their appetite for the treat. Flora's father refused to come on principle and went to work instead, so Emma, accompanied by Flora, aged ten, Edwin, aged eight, and three-year-old May with new-born baby Elizabeth in the baby carriage, walked to Shelswell.

It must have been quite daunting to see the milling crowds on their arrival in the Park – in the ordinary course of events they would not see many people, so they must have had feelings of both excitement and fear. As well as the expected feast, they were greeted by the sight of a small fair in progress, with roundabouts, swings and coconut shies, and music from hurdy-gurdies and a brass band.

A group of people dressed in their best, thought to be on their way to celebrate Queen Victoria's Golden Jubilee in 1887 in Shelswell Park. (David Watts)

A marquee erected in Banbury with food laid out to celebrate Queen Victoria's Jubilee. A similar one was set up in Shelswell Park in 1887 so that members of each parish could eat in turn. (Oxfordshire Photographic Archive)

To control the numbers, each parish in turn was invited into the marquee for their tea – after the meagre fare at home the quantity of food must have been almost unbelievable – clothes baskets filled with slices of bread spread with butter and jam and dough cakes washed down with tea from watering cans. There was so much there that few could resist slipping some food into their pockets to take home after they had eaten their fill.

After tea there were the usual sports and entertainments: races and high jump competitions, sideshows such as dipping heads into water tubs to bring up sixpences with the teeth, and traditional country games such as grinning through a horse collar – in other words the winner was the one who could make the most hideous face – and the one the housewives hated, because climbing the greasy pole to take the leg of mutton (almost roasted in the sunshine) from the top was an activity that ruined trousers.

The celebrations ended with fireworks as it grew dark, but what fascinated Flora most was the tightrope dancing, and for ages afterwards she delighted in pirouetting along five-barred gates.

When she visited Shelswell Park for the jubilee celebrations she could have had no idea that only four years later she would be going into the house and meeting the owner! When she went to work for Mrs Whitton at Fringford Forge at the age of fourteen, before she was permitted to so much as handle a letter in the Post Office she had to be sworn in before a Justice of the Peace – in this case Edward Slater-Harrison at Shelswell:

The interview next morning did not turn out so terrifying as Laura had expected. Sir Timothy smiled very kindly upon her when the footman ushered her into his Justice Room, saying: 'The young person from the post office, please, Sir Timothy.'

'What have you been up to? Poaching, rick-burning, or petty larceny?' he asked when the footman had gone. 'If you're as innocent as you look, I shan't give you a long sentence, so come along,' and he drew her by the elbow to the side of his chair. Laura smiled dutifully, for she knew by the twinkle of his keen blue eyes beneath their shaggy white eyebrows that Sir Timothy was joking.

As she leaned forwards to take up a pen with which to sign the thick blue official document he was unfolding, she sensed the atmosphere of jollity, good sense, and good nature, together with the smell of tobacco, stables, and country tweeds he carried around, like an aura.

'But read it! Read!' he cried in a shocked voice, 'never put your name to anything before you have read it or you'll be signing your own death warrant one of these days.' And Laura read out, as clearly as her shyness permitted, the Declaration which even the most humble candidate for Her Majesty's Service had in those serious days to sign before a magistrate.

'I do solemnly promise and declare that I will not open or delay or cause or suffer to be opened or delayed any letter or anything sent by the post', it began, and went on to promise secrecy in all things.

When she had read it through, she signed her name; Sir Timothy signed his, then folded the document neatly for her to carry back to Miss Lane, who would send it on to the higher authorities.

Lark Rise to Candleford, pp. 402–3

For a few months in her career at the Post Office she acted as letter carrier and so frequently visited Shelswell Park with 'Sir Timothy's' post in a locked private postbag. The footmen, who resented the fact that their private mail was also locked in the bag, gave Flora a hard time, teasing her unmercifully, but she did not dare complain to Mrs Whitton.

It was while she was walking in the grounds in the course of her duties that she had an interesting encounter, which could have changed the future course of her life, with a young gamekeeper, armed with a shotgun, who accused her of trespassing. Flora christened him 'Philip White' in Candleford Green:

He was a tall, well-built young man, apparently in the middle twenties, with a small fair moustache and very pale blue eyes which, against his dark tanned complexion, looked paler. His features might have been called handsome but for their set rigidity.

Lark Rise to Candleford, p. 518

They got chatting once he realised that she was no threat to his precious pheasants and he told her all about his family, including his gamekeeper father and his sister who worked in a draper's shop in Oxford. After that he contrived to meet her in the course of her journeys through the park most days, and even kissed her shyly when they went through the kissing gate. He was her first boyfriend, and she supposed they counted as sweethearts, daydreaming that as his wife she could help him feed the pheasant chicks and live in a little cottage. However the thought of Philip being there too brought her down to earth; she was not truly in love with him, and was old enough to realise that he was a selfish and self-centred man. Much to her surprise and embarrassment he turned up to see her at the Post Office one evening, and talked to her within Mrs Whitton's hearing, demanding that she take a few days off to come and visit his mother. This was tantamount to a proposal of marriage and Flora was dumbfounded, terrified of what Mrs Whitton would think. Philip continued, 'you are my girl, aren't you, Laura?' to which Flora responded rather desperately, 'you've never asked me'. At this Philip took her hand and said: 'Well, I thought you understood. But don't be frightened. You will be my girl, won't you, Laura?' Flora commented rather sadly:

> That was inadequate enough as a declaration of love, but Laura's answer was even more inadequate. 'No – no thank you, Philip,' she said, and the most unromantic love scene on record was over, for, without another word, he turned, went out of the door and out of her life. She never saw him again to speak to.

Lark Rise to Candleford, p. 522

To her great relief, Mrs Whitton was not censorious or reproachful of her behaviour and little was made of the incident.

While she was working in Fringford she encountered Cecilia Slater-Harrison, Sir Edward's second wife, the greatest lady in her immediate area, to whom she gave the name of 'Lady Adelaide':

> For Lady Adelaide, Sir Timothy's wife, the footman usually did business while she sat in her carriage outside, but occasionally she herself would come rustling in, bringing with her a whiff of perfume, and sink languidly down in the chair provided for customers on their side of the counter. She was a graceful woman, and it was a delight to watch her movements ... She was tall and thin and, Laura thought, aristocratic-looking.

Lark Rise to Candleford, p. 465

Flora was embarrassed when Lady Cecilia spoke to her and invited her to join the Conservative Primrose League, of which she was local patron, because her parents were Liberals and would greatly disapprove of her doing so, but she plucked up all her courage to decline politely. She only realised afterwards that her ladyship had done her a kindness. Her father had imbued her with his independence of spirit, which shone through her shyness and gave her the strength and perseverance to work hard to achieve her aims in life, particularly in her writing.

Fringford: Candleford Green

When Flora left 'Lark Rise' behind, and began to write about 'Candleford' and 'Candleford Green', she openly admitted that she took a lot more liberties with her material, and deliberately combined several places into one. She wrote:

> In *Over to Candleford* and *Candleford Green* I wrote more freely than on *Lark Rise* and do not think I described any house or place exactly as it actually existed excepting Miss Lane's post office and forge, and Shelswell Park, where I used to carry the letters.

Margaret Lane 'Flora Thompson', from *The Cornhill Magazine*, No. 1101, Spring 1957

It was to 'Candleford Green' that Flora went to work in the Post Office for 'Miss Lane' at the age of fourteen in 1891, living away from home for the first time, and enjoying her first taste of independence.

'Candleford Green' is partly based on Flora's knowledge of Fringford, with elements drawn from her work in other Post Offices in different parts of the country, probably including Twyford, where her Uncle Tom lived, but many of the physical characteristics of Fringford are nothing like those of 'Candleford Green'. She depicted her Candleford Green as a suburb of the town of Candleford, whereas in reality it is a medium-sized village, well away from the nearest town of Bicester, so her descriptions have to be treated with circumspection. However Fringford, like 'Candleford Green', is a much larger and more varied village than either Juniper Hill or Cottisford, so Flora was able to widen her experience of life. It was described in the 1880s by Blomfield:

> This village, as it now appears, is prettily situated on the slope of a gentle eminence northwards. It is a quiet spot, remote from public traffic, there being no highway through it. The only approach to it is from the west. Three roads (a branch from Buckingham and Bicester road, a road from Stoke and Caversfield, and a third descending from Hethe) meet close to one point, where is the only access to this village. This opens on the Green, and then divides into two roads, which cross it in different directions. On two sides of the Green are some old, picturesque houses, and in a hollow at its north end is a large pond, near which may generally be seen a few representatives of the geese tribe, who through many long years have fed and quacked upon the greensward. Here, too, stands the schoolroom, unenclosed. The road, passing these, leads on to some of the cottages, and beyond them to the rectory house. The church is not visible from the Green, but the second road, running eastward, leads to it, and to the present manor house, and some other houses of the villagers. There is no street here, as in most other villages, the various buildings being scattered apart from each other.

History of the Present Deanery of Bicester, vol. 5–6, p. 26

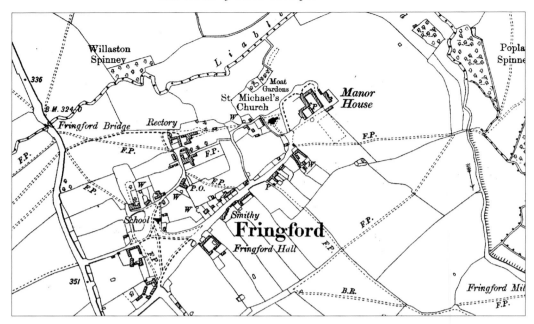

Reproduced from the 1879 Ordnance Survey map of Fringford. Flora lived with Mrs Whitton in the building marked 'Smithy'. The Mansfield's grocery store was on the corner near the church. (David Watts)

A notable family were the Addingtons who moved to the village in the sixteenth century; in 1597 William and Henry Addington, a yeoman and husbandman, bought 2,000-year leases to two-and-a-half yardlands (measured in the archaic units) from the manor. Henry Addington held the important posts of constable and churchwarden in 1662 and 1664, and his son William was the first of the family to call himself a gentleman and to aspire to a family pew in the church. His son Dr Anthony Addington (1713-90), was William Pitt's doctor. He and he and his wife Mary who died in 1778 are commemorated on a monument in the church designed by Richard Westmacott which shows the arms of the Addington family. Addington and the Rector started a school in the village in 1768, and his family continued to support it. The house he lived in on the Green, which is now incorporated into Hall Farm, near the forge, is basically sixteenth century although it has been much altered over the years. Flora described it as a 'tall old red-brick Georgian farmhouse, where judging by its size and appearance, people of importance must once have lived, but where then only an old cowman and his wife occupied one corner'. (*Lark Rise to Candleford*, p. 418). Addington's son Henry was Prime Minister from 1801-4 and was created Lord Sidmouth.

Many different families held the manor over the next few centuries, until 1815 when it was purchased by John Harrison of Shelswell Park. The land had already been enclosed in 1762, which increased its value and the population increased from 252 in 1801 to 479 in 1871. In 1901 there were ninety-four dwellings. The village grew up round a large green, with the church and manor house to the north, where the village pond was situated.

As at Juniper Hill and Cottisford the principal occupation in Fringford was farming, although Fringford boasted a much wider range of employment. The main farms were Manor, Glebe and Waterloo Farm, (the house there was built by John Harrison and named after Wellington's victory over Napoleon), and the outlying Cotmore Farm which has the remains of a medieval moat. In 1891 there were fifty-four agricultural labourers, one cowman, five shepherds (one retired), five carters, one plough boy and one field woman, plus one farm bailiff and three farmers, (Henry King of Waterloo Farm, John Simons at the manor house and George Gibbard who was also a maltster and brewer and employed one assistant). Connected with farming were two agricultural machinists, a woodman and a hurdle maker.

Several people worked as servants, including four housekeepers, twelve domestic servants, three farm servants, one housemaid, one laundry maid, two footmen, two coachmen, two grooms and six gardeners. Other occupations included a carrier and two assistants, a coal haulier, shoemaker, army reserve, timber carrier, two brick makers and one assistant, bricklayer, stonemason, painter, plumber and decorator, decorator, four blacksmiths (one also postmaster), three carpenters, two wheelwrights, five general labourers, butcher, baker, grocer, one licensed victualler (Richard Hood at the Butcher's Arms), timber carter and interestingly, two lawyers. Three lived on their own means. There are also records of a midwife, a charwoman, two laundresses and a letter carrier. The range is far bigger than that of Cottisford. Flora appreciated this and commented of Fringford:

> In the hamlet there lived only one class of people; all did similar work, all were poor and all were equal ... The village was a little world in itself; the hamlet was but a segment.

Lark Rise to Candleford, p. 416

Flora must have been fascinated by the variety of shops in the village, having been used to only a tiny store in the back room of the pub. The 1891 census lists a butcher, a baker and a grocer in Fringford, but not some of the stores described by Flora. For example, the shop owned by 'Ruby' and 'Pearl', selling smart clothes, is one which she must have seen in another town and transposed.

Flora's description of Tarman's the grocers is based on the Fringford grocers' shop run by John and Mary Mansfield. John Mansfield was born in Fringford in 1830, the son of George Mansfield, a carrier, and he took over his father's business before 1861. According to family records he fitted Flora's description of being 'a burly giant in a white apron'. Around 1855 he married Mary, who came from Lacock in Wiltshire. Their children were Matilda (born in 1856), Alfred (born in 1858) who became a carpenter, Edwin (born in 1860) who ran a baker's shop in Warmington, Warwickshire in 1891, Mary Ann (born in 1863) and Frederick (born in 1866) who began as a carpenter and went on to make railway carriages in Wolverton, Buckinghamshire. The family must have been relatively well-off as Frederick and probably the other boys attended boarding school in Northampton. Flora wrote:

> This family was not liked by all; some said they had ideas above their station in life, chiefly because the children were sent to boarding school; but practically everyone dealt at their shop, for not only was it the only grocery establishment of any size in the place, but the goods there could be relied upon.

Lark Rise to Candleford, p. 463

John Mansfield opened the shop, probably in the 1860s, and described himself as a butcher and grocer in the 1871 census. He died in 1886 but Flora described the Mansfield's shop, which was situated near the church and John Clarke's butcher shop:

> ... the grocer catered for all. At that time the more important village people, such as the doctor and clergyman, bought their provisions at the village shop as a matter of principle ... and even the rich who spent only part of the year at their country houses or their hunting boxes believed it their duty to give the local tradesman a turn. If there happened

Mary Mansfield ran the grocery store after the death of her husband John. Their shop was referred to as 'Tarman's' in *Lark Rise to Candleford*. Here Mary Mansfield is seen with her son Frederick outside the shop. The signboard reads 'Mansfield, Grocer and Licensed Dealers in Tobacco'. (Peter Morrall)

to be more businesses than one of a kind in a village, orders were placed with each alternately …

A grocer had to be a grocer then, for his goods did not come to him in packets, ready to be handed over the counter, but had to be selected and blended and weighed out by himself, and for quality he was directly responsible to his customers. The butcher, too, received no stiff, shrouded carcasses by rail, but had to be able to recognize the points in the living animal at the local market sufficiently quickly and well to be able to guarantee the succulent joints and the old-fashioned chops and steaks would melt in the mouth. Even his scrag ends of mutton and sixpen'orth of pieces of beef which he sold to the poor were tasty and rich with juices which the refrigerator seems to have destroyed in present-day meat.

Lark Rise to Candleford, pp. 462–3

John's widow Mary continued to run the store as a grocery well into her old age; she was still there in 1901 at the age of seventy-two. Flora described her:

His wife was what was called there 'a little pennicking bit of a woman', small and fair … She was a generous open-handed creature who gave liberally to every good cause. The poor had cause to bless her, for their credit there in bad times was unlimited, and many families had a standing debt on her books that both debtor and creditor knew could never be paid. Many a cooked ham-bone with good picking still left on it and many a hock-end of bacon were slipped by her into the shopping baskets of poor mothers of families, and the clothes of her children when new were viewed by appraising eyes by those who hope to inherit them when outgrown.

Lark Rise to Candleford, p. 463

Frederick Mansfield married Emily Price, whose grandfather was a gardener at Cottisford House. Her Uncle John worked for the East India Company and became a soldier during the Indian Mutiny, returning to Oxfordshire as a Quarter Master Sergeant. He was referred to when Flora wrote about the visit of the cheap jack to Cottisford:

'How much did you say, mister? Twelve bob? I'll give you ten.' It was John Price, who, only the night before, had returned from his soldiering in India. A very ordinary sort of chap at most times, for he was a teetaller and stood no drinks at the inn, as a returned soldier should have done; but now, suddenly, he became important. All eyes were upon him. The credit of the hamlet was at stake.

Lark Rise to Candleford, p. 132

Eventually, Flora wrote, a deal was struck and he bought the pink rose painted tea set for 11s 6d. Curiously Matilda also married a John Price, but this one was a plumber in Fringford and his father was from Burford, so it was probably not the same person.

John Clarke the butcher, who was born in Ardley, was thirty-seven in 1891. He had taken over the shop from his father James and was living with his mother Eleanor, his sister Elizabeth and his brother James. Flora also referred to a baker:

The baker and his wife were chiefly remarkable for their regularity in adding to their family every eighteen months. They already had eight children and the entire energies of the mother and any margin the father had left after earning their living were devoted to nursing the younger and keeping in order the elder member of their brood. But theirs was a happy-go-lucky household.

Lark Rise to Candleford, p. 464

She may have been writing about Harry Lapper who came from Wendlebury, although he and his wife Thurza only had four children: Alice, Walter, Elsie and Maud, in 1891.

The national school, built in 1866 by Henry de Salis, then rector, on land granted by John Slater-Harrison in 1863, was on the far side of the Village Green from the Post Office. It was a typical village school, big enough to justify two teachers, the average attendance in 1871 being seventy-three. The building is no longer used for the school, which now occupies a modern building on the other side of the Green.

South west of the village on the road to Bicester are Cotmore House, built in 1857 by William Dewar and his wife Augusta (*née* Slater-Harrison), and Fringford Lodge, built in 1814 by Revd Herbert John Beaver, and enlarged by Revd E. Withington in the 1870s, in the grounds of which are the remains of a Roman villa, mentioned by Flora's father Albert as they drove past it on the journey to 'Candleford'. Revd Withington was born in Culcheth Hall, Lancashire in 1837. He attended Eton College and was ordained. He married Mary Ann Green from King's County, Ireland and had moved to Fringford Lodge by 1871. Although he was a clergyman he was living on private means and did not have a benefice. His children were: Edith (born in 1866), Frederick (born in 1869) and Archibald (born in 1870).

In *Kelly's Directory of Berkshire, Buckinghamshire and Oxfordshire*, 1895, Edward Withington was noted as one of the principal residents. In 1871 he employed Mary Wright (thirty-seven)

The site of the Mansfield's shop, taken in the 1970s. (Peter Morrall)

A photograph taken from Fringford church tower showing the position of the Mansfield's shop on the right. The house on the left was built in 1898 by the firm of Thomas Grimsley of Bicester. Their foreman Arthur Edward Waine built the arcading. (Peter Morall)

Fringford village green, looking east, *c.* 1910. (William Plumb)

from Ridgmont, Bedfordshire and Jane Rogers (twenty-three) from Aldingbourne, Sussex as housemaids, Selina Steeder (twenty-six) from Tingewick, Buckinghamshire as cook and Margaret Mac Orson (sixteen) from Scotland as nursemaid. He carried on employing four servants, but their jobs were not differentiated in later censuses. In 1891 Frederick Withington was described as Lieutenant in the 4th Battalion of the Oxfordshire Regiment. Edward Withington died in 1901.

The Church

The church, dedicated to St Michael and All Angels, is tucked away at the bottom of the village. There was a church here at least as early as 1103, and the earliest remaining portion – the restored south door and two arches in the nave – date from the twelfth century, and some delightful carved heads feature on the thirteenth-century south piers. Much of what one can see today only dates from the nineteenth century when substantial repairs were made as the church had been allowed to decay by many non-resident lords of the manor.

The Rectory, approached by a footpath from the church, is a large, mainly nineteenth-century house, incorporating a much earlier kitchen wing. The Rector when Flora arrived was Cadwallader Coker, a wealthy man, aged sixty-six in 1891, who came from Bicester House, Bicester, and had been there since 1874, living with his wife Emily Harriet (*née* Gould, aged sixty-nine from Ilfracombe), their spinster daughters Marianne and Emily (aged thirty-nine and thirty-five) and three domestic servants. They had two sons, James Gould, born in 1858 who became a solicitor, and Lewis Cadwallader, born in 1860 and two other daughters – Mary Aubrey, born in 1862 and Jessie Aubrey born in 1864. Flora would have attended church regularly with Mrs Whitton and gave her usual cogent description of Revd Coker and his wife:

He was an elderly man with what was then known as a fine presence, being tall and large rather than stout, with rosy cheeks, a lion-like mane of white hair, and an air of conscious

Fringford church, which was largely rebuilt in the nineteenth century, but retains a doorway and two arches from the Norman period.

authority. His wife was a dumpy little roly-poly of a woman who wore old, comfortable clothes about the village because, as she was once heard to say, 'everybody here knows who I am, so why bother about dress?' For church and for afternoon calls upon her equals, she dressed in the silks and satins and ostrich feathers befitting her rank as the granddaughter of an earl and the wife of a vicar with large private means. She was said by the villagers to be 'a bit managing', but, on the whole, she was popular with them.

Lark Rise to Candleford, p. 424

Flora wrote that Mrs Coker contracted a fatal illness at a summer bazaar, which rapidly killed both her and her husband. They did indeed die within a few days of each other, but in the spring – Emily Coker on 14 April aged seventy-one and her husband on the 23 April 1894, aged sixty-nine.

His successor was Revd C.G. Thompson – rechristened 'Revd Delafield' by Flora – and a very different character; a young man in his early thirties, who apparently always looked untidy, he was 'somewhat inclined to premature bulkiness, whose large, pink, clean-shaven face had a babyish look, which his fair hair, worn rather long and inclined to curl, did nothing to dispel. Dignity did not enter into his composition'. (*Lark Rise to Candleford*, p. 523). The Delafields did not have the private means of their predecessors, but Mrs Delafield was notable for wearing Bohemian clothes – long loose dresses very different in style from the corseted clothes worn by most of her contemporaries.

Post Office and Forge

The Post Office where Flora was to live occupied a prominent position near the green:

> Miss Lane's house was a long, low white one, with the post office at one end and a blacksmith's forge at the other. On the turf in front of the door was a circular iron platform with a hole in the middle which was used for putting on tyres to wagon and cart wheels, for she was a wheelwright as well as blacksmith and postmistress. She did not work in the forge herself; she dressed in silks of which the colours were brighter than those usually worn by women of her age and had tiny white hands which she seldom soiled. Hers was the brains of the business ... She was then about fifty, a little birdlike woman in her kingfisher silk dress, with snapping black eyes, a longish nose, and black hair plaited into a crown on top of her head.

Lark Rise to Candleford, pp. 362-3

Flora added that there was a scarlet-painted letter-box let into the wall and a signboard reading 'Candleford Green Post and Telegraph Office', with another one above the forge reading 'Dorcas Lane, Shoeing and General Smith'. This cannot have been entirely accurate, as at that time, contrary to what Flora wrote, there was no telegraph machine in Fringford, and John Whitton would probably still have been in charge when she first arrived, although he was very ill and died on 28 August 1891 at the age of sixty-one.

John's wife Kezia was baptised in Stoke Lyne on 11 January 1835, the youngest of three daughters of Elizabeth and Alexander Kirby, the village blacksmith, who was buried in Stoke Lyne in 1864. Elizabeth died aged seventy-five in 1873. Alexander does not appear ever to have been the blacksmith in Fringford, but in 1851 another Kirby was in charge there, who may have been a relative. The 1851 census tells us that in Fringford John Kirby, aged seventy-eight from Fritwell, lived at the forge with his son John, aged forty-nine, born in Croughton, and his grandsons Thomas aged nineteen, John aged seventeen and William aged eleven, who were all blacksmiths born in Fringford, and his nine-year-old granddaughter Elizabeth. Thomas appears in all the censuses except 1891 as a blacksmith in Fringford, probably on a smaller scale than the Whittons as he appears to be working on his own.

In the 1851 census Kezia was living in Stoke Lyne with her father Alexander (aged fifty-six from Fritwell), her mother Elizabeth (aged fifty-three from Somerton), her sisters Mary Ann (twenty-eight) and Louisa (eighteen) and her cousin Jeremiah Kirby, an apprentice blacksmith from Stoke Lyne. Louisa married farmer Matthew Killby and in 1891 they were living in Fritwell. Jeremiah was a journeyman blacksmith in Stoke Lyne in 1861 but ten years later was described as 'formerly blacksmith' and was living with his wife Fanny, from Yorkshire.

Kezia Kirby married John Whitton in 1857 and they moved to Fringford to run the forge. John, who was born in 1830, was the son of Edward Whitton, a saddler from Weston by Welland, Northamptonshire and his wife Elizabeth. In 1851 John, one of two apprentice blacksmiths, was working for and living with William Gascoigne, the master blacksmith at Weedon Lois, Northamptonshire and his family. In 1859 John Whitton took on nineteen-year-old John Gibbs for a five-year apprenticeship at Fringford. The indenture of apprenticeship declared John Gibbs must not waste his master's goods, or lend them out. He must not commit fornication or marry during his apprenticeship, or play at cards or dice on any other unlawful games without permission, or haunt taverns or playhouses. John Whitton was paid £40 to train John, and had to provide him with full blacksmith's training, plus 'meat, drink, clothing, washing, lodging, medical attendance and medicine and other necessaries (except pocket money)'.

Kezia Whitton was, like her husband, (but unlike 'Miss Lane' who was a 'tiny birdlike woman'), very large, weighing over eighteen stone, although Flora later wrote that the mental

The post office and forge, Fringford, before 1891. John Whitton, the postmaster and blacksmith, stands in front of the spring cart while his wife Kezia, (Flora's 'Miss Lane') holds the horse's head. Zilpha Hinks, at that time their servant, stands in the doorway. The little girl cannot be identified. The man with the sledgehammer on the left is William Elderfield, the man next to them is unidentified, and the third is Frederick William Plumb, (Flora's 'Matthew' the foreman). The rectangular area of metal on the grass in front of the forge is the tyreing platform. (William Plumb)

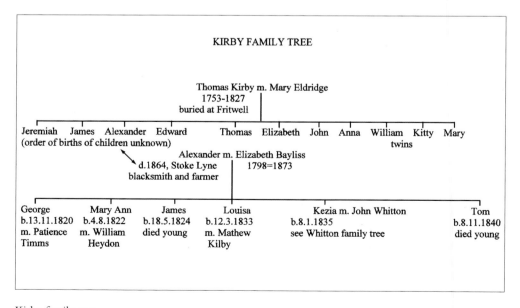

Kirby family tree.

attributes she gave to Miss Lane were all those of Kezia Whitton. The Whittons had several children, all but two of whom died in infancy: Alexander, born on 2 January 1858 lived only three days; Elizabeth, who was born on 16 February 1859 and died on 3 March 1859; Annie Louisa baptised on 29 January 1860 and buried on 11 February that year; John, who was born on 14 December 1860 and died on 29 August 1861; George, born in 1863 and Alexander born in 1866. Alexander died at the age of twenty-four in Africa, when working as accountant on the Gold Coast. George elected not to become a blacksmith, becoming a Customs and Excise Officer in Liverpool instead.

It was most unusual at that time for a woman to choose to carry on her husband's business, let alone something like a smithy, but Kezia had no hesitation, and being a blacksmith's daughter and wife, she must have known a great deal about the business. She had a strong personality which fitted her for an important role in village life, and Flora had immense respect for her:

I knew Mrs. Whitton well. About the time you were born she was teaching me the rudiments of the post-office business and there is a good deal of her in my Miss Lane. The character as it stands in my books is a mixture of her and of another postmistress I served under in Surrey, but the mental attributes are entirely those of Mrs. Whitton, and the blacksmith's business of course was hers. She was a wonderful woman. She had the most observant eye and the keenest brain of anyone I have known, and had she been born later must have left her mark on the world. What a psychologist she would have made! She was very good to me … and had more influence than anyone in shaping the outward course of my life.

Letter by Flora Thompson, quoted in Margaret Lane, 'Flora Thompson', 1976

Kezia enjoyed running the Post Office because it gave her the opportunity to find out legitimately all about the village affairs as both the smithy and the Post Office were central to village life. Her work gave her a position of authority locally. She was an organised person, and her Post Office reflected this, with all the forms neatly arranged in pigeon-holes. The Post Office counter was fixed across the through-passage of the house, and could be folded down against the wall with wooden shutters constructed so as to close it off.

Flora came to the job with no experience, only an aptitude for figures. She would have found it difficult, if not impossible, to have obtained a job in a bigger town Post Office as women of higher birth were preferred, and the Post Office expected female employees to pass Civil Service exams, which Flora did not have the basic education to be able to take. However, the experience she acquired in Fringford enabled her to take temporary work in other Post Offices including her husband's during the war.

When she first arrived in the Post Office she was petrified – at her first tea there she was offered a Banbury cake, a great luxury at home, but was too nervous to eat it, letting it crumble in her fingers! She realised that she had many things to learn:

Even in that small country post office there was in use what seemed to her a bewildering number and variety of official forms, to all of which Miss Lane who loved to make a mystery of her work referred by a number, not name. But soon, in actual practice, 'AB/35', 'K.21', 'X.Y.13', or what not became 'The Blue Savings Bank Form', 'The Postal Order Abstract', 'The Cash Account Sheet' and so on, and Laura found herself flicking them out of their pigeon-holes and carrying them without a moment's hesitation to where Miss Lane sat doing her accounts at the kitchen table.

Then the stamps! The 1d and ½d ones she already knew by sight were in tens and fives, sheets which hot, nervous hands were inclined to tear, and those of higher value, neatly hinged in a cardboard-leaved book, ready to be sold for parcels and telegrams, had to be detached just so, working up from the left-hand bottom corner. And the cash drawer, with its

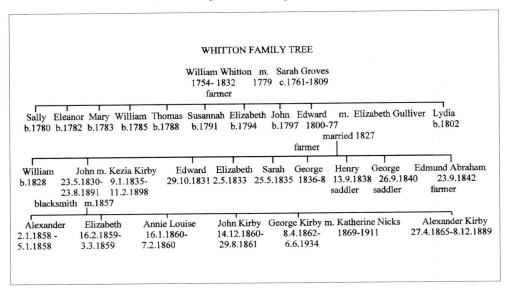

WHITTON FAMILY TREE

William Whitton m. Sarah Groves
1754- 1832   1779 c.1761-1809
farmer

Sally   Eleanor Mary   William Thomas   Susannah Elizabeth John Edward   m. Elizabeth Gulliver Lydia
b.1780   b.1782   b.1783   b.1785   b.1788   b.1791   b.1794   b.1797 1800-77   b.1802
                                                                       married 1827
                                                                          farmer

William   John m. Kezia Kirby   Edward   Elizabeth Sarah   George   Henry   George   Edmund Abraham
b.1828   23.5.1830- 9.1.1835-   29.10.1831 2.5.1833   25.5.1835 1836-8   13.9.1838 26.9.1840 23.9.1842
          23.8.1891   11.2.1898   saddler   saddler   farmer
          blacksmith m.1857

Alexander   Elizabeth   Annie Louise   John Kirby   George Kirby m. Katherine Nicks   Alexander Kirby
2.1.1858 - 16.2.1859-   16.1.1860-   14.12.1860- 8.4.1862-   1869-1911   27.4.1865-8.12.1889
5.1.1858   3.3.1859   7.2.1860   29.8.1861   6.6.1934

Whitton family tree.

John Whitton (1830-1891) the blacksmith and his wife Kezia (1835-98) who ran the post office with their sons Alexander Kirby Whitton (1866-89), local auditor of the Gold Coast Co. and George Whitton (born 1863), a customs and excise officer in Liverpool. Behind them stands their blacksmith foreman Frederick William Plumb (1859-1930) who took over the forge after Kezia Whitton's death. (William Plumb)

Mr Hornsby, the postman to Hethe, Fringford, Stratton Audley and Stoke Lyne, *c.* 1900. (David Watts)

three wooden bowls for gold, silver, and copper, and all three bowls at least half-full, even the one for sovereigns and half-sovereigns! What a lot of money there must be in the world! Laura would run her fingers through the shining gold coins when the cash was counted at night and placed in the black japanned box ready to be taken upstairs, wrapped in an old woolly shawl as disguise, and stood on the top shelf of Miss Lane's clothes cupboard. Occasionally there was a banknote in the japanned box, but no Treasury notes, for there were none issued.

Lark Rise to Candleford, pp. 404-5

In those days notes were issued by small local banks not by the Bank of England. The morning mail was brought on foot from Bicester at 7 o'clock. The postman in 1891, according to *Pankhurst's Almanack and Directory*, was Postman Plater, whose round included Hethe, Fringford, Newton Morrell, Willaston and Shelswell. Flora opened up his sack in what had once been a wash house, which had sorting benches arranged around it. The postman waited while the village mail was sorted out for him to take and female letter carriers were employed for outlying places. Flora called the morning postman Thomas Brown, 'a stockily built man with greying hair, who had, as far as was known always led a quiet, respectable life. Until recently he had taken great interest in local affairs and had such good judgement that he had occasionally been asked to arbitrate in local disputes'. (*Lark Rise to Candleford*, p. 407). He had been converted to Methodism, which altered his outlook on life. According to the almanack another postman, Hudson, delivered midday to Stratton Audley, Fringford, Hethe and Stoke Lyne.

Flora caught the eye of Walter Joseph French, the postmaster in the main Post Office in Bicester Market Place, whom she christened 'Mr Rushton'. He was born in 1846 in Buckingham, the son of Joseph French, a toy dealer and rag merchant. In 1861 he lived in Bridge Street, next door to his uncle William Walford, who was the postmaster and a watchmaker, which may have inspired him to work in the Post Office himself. Ten years later he had moved in with his uncle and was the telegraph clerk. By 1881 he had risen to the rank of postmaster in Bicester Post Office and was living next door in the market place in 1881. He and his wife Sarah had three sons: Walter, born in 1874, Frederick, born in 1878 and Harold, born in 1989. In 1891 his nieces Kate and Rhoda French were living with him and Kate was a postmaster's clerk, aged twenty-three.

He came to visit the Fringford Post Office twice a year to ensure that the business was being conducted properly. All the account books, cash and papers were neatly laid out for him on the kitchen table ready to be checked:

> It was an old-fashioned way of conducting business and Mr Rushton was an old-fashioned postmaster. He was a neat, middle-aged little man, very precise in his speech and manner, and with what many considered an exaggerated sense of his own importance. Pleasant, if somewhat patronising to well-doers on his staff, but a terror to the careless and slipshod worker. He was under the impression that his own office staff adored him. 'The crew of my little ship know who is captain.' It is sad to have to record that the crew in private spoke of their captain as 'Holy Joe'.

Lark Rise to Candleford, p. 410

This last reference is to the fact that he was a Methodist, and wore black or dark grey clothes. He spotted Flora's potential and had hoped to be able to offer her promotion to Bicester Post Office, but neither of his female clerks, who were in fact Miss Wrapson and Miss Tooley, married, so no vacancy arose for Flora. Beatrice Wrapson was born in 1876 in Yately in Hampshire, and came to Bicester with her father, who was a clothier, and his family. In 1891 they were living in The Causeway, and fourteen-year-old Beatrice was still at school. In 1901 she was still living at home in Field Street, Market End, and was a sorting clerk and telegraphist. One of her fellow Post Office workers, Albert Rowe, aged twenty-one from Pinner, Middlesex, who was also a sorting clerk and telegraphist, was boarding with the family. Perhaps it was frustration at not being able to find a better job locally that made Flora decide that it was time to see a little of the world when she left Fringford.

Flora did not, as she wrote, see a telegraph machine on her visit to the forge as a child, and Kezia Whitton wrote to her son George in 1897:

> I don't know what alteration they are going to make in postal work again … they do say every office is to be made a telegraph office (if so I shall have to give up). I can't learn that.

Quoted from a letter belonging to Norman Whitton

Perhaps it was in another Post Office that Flora saw the telegraph machine carefully housed in the front room, given an air of domesticity by being hidden under a cover similar to a tea cosy:

> The telegraph machine had been installed in the parlour, where its scientific-looking white dials and brass trimmings looked strikingly modern against Miss Lane's old rosewood and mahogany furniture. It was what was known as the ABC type of instrument … it served very well in its day, being easy to learn and reliable in working … The ABC was read by sight. A handle, like that of a coffee mill, guided a pointer from letter to letter on a dial which had the alphabet printed round it, clockwise, and this came out and was read on a smaller dial at the other end of the circuit. Surrounding the operating dial were brass studs or keys, one for each letter, and the operator, turning the handle with one hand, depressed the keys with the finger of the other, and by doing so spelt out the words of a telegram. A smaller dial above, known as the 'receiver', recorded incoming messages.

Lark Rise to Candleford, p. 412

Flora described two letter carriers, but only one was listed in the 1891 census, and surprisingly that one was Zilpha Hinks, who must be the person Flora described as Zillah, Kezia Whitton's crusty rheumatic servant. Zilpha appeared, aged sixteen, as a pupil-teacher in the 1871 census, the daughter of an agricultural labourer. In 1881 she was indeed living with the Whittons, aged twenty-six, as a general servant, but by 1891 she was back at home with her widowed mother, four grown-up sisters who worked as servants and two brothers who were agricultural labourers. Flora described her as old and flat-footed, with a bit of a temper and a shrill laugh and said that her darning was so crude that it could be seen across the room. She tolerated Flora's presence and was glad of her help running errands around the house, but she always treated her with a measure of suspicion. There is obviously a good deal of artistic license in this depiction of Zillah as Zilpha would only have been thirty-six when Flora came to the forge. As she had been intelligent enough to be a pupil-teacher, perhaps she would have liked to have had Flora's job rather than that of letter carrier. It is ironic that she became a letter carrier in real life because Flora wrote about an incident when 'Mrs Macey', the letter carrier, had to go off and see her husband who was dangerously ill in Dartmoor Prison, leaving 'Miss Lane' with a dilemma:

> The thing now is what we are going to do about the letters and Sir Timothy's private postbag. Zillah shan't go. I wouldn't demean myself to ask her, after the disgraceful way she's been banging away upstairs, not to mention her bad feet and her rheumatism.

Lark Rise to Candleford, p. 505

The upshot of that exchange was that Flora, to her delight, became a letter carrier. This gave her a chance to wander the countryside and extend her knowledge of natural history, which proved a deep interest throughout her life. Zilpha Hinks was certainly not the old woman of 'Candleford Green', as she died in January 1900 aged only forty-five. Mrs Whitton's servant in the 1891 census was Winifred Waring, a Fringford girl of only fourteen, who was termed 'general servant' – again nothing like the old woman described in the book. In 1901 Winifred was working as general servant for Beverley McKeen, a whisky and wine merchant in Finchley, London.

Flora enjoyed the new freedom and independence she found working at the Post Office. She must have delighted in the access she had to Mrs Whitton's books, which she eagerly read at every spare moment. She even found time to do a little writing of her own, which she later destroyed in Grayshott when she met 'real' writers, and felt how inadequate her own attempts had been.

She noted how Kezia Whitton ran her household on the same strict old-fashioned lines as she ran the Post Office. This presented Flora with a problem; Kezia followed the traditional method of having a washerwoman in to do her washing every six weeks, and poor Flora did not have enough clothes to last that long, so she had to parcel up her dirty washing and send it home to her mother each week via two different carriers' carts. However it was a treat to get the parcel of clean clothes back with a little present of cakes, homemade food or flowers from her mother, and it gave her a link with home.

Kezia's traditional attitude was wonderfully exemplified by her style at table:

> At the head of the long, solid oak table sat 'the mistress', with an immense dish of meat before her, carving knife in hand. Then came a reserved space, sometimes occupied by visitors, but more often blank table-cloth; then Matthew's chair, and, after that, another, smaller blank space, just sufficient to mark the difference in degree between a foreman and ordinary workmen. Beyond that, the three young men sat in a row at the end of the table, facing the mistress. Zillah, the maid, had a little round table to herself by the wall. Unless important visitors were present, she joined freely in the conversation; but the three young

The Forge, Fringford, *c.* 1898. Frederick William Plumb is sitting in the cart and the boys may be Mrs Whitton's grandsons. (William Plumb)

men seldom opened their mouths except to shovel in food. If, by chance, they had something they thought of sufficient interest to impart, they always addressed their remarks to Miss Lane, and prefixed them by 'Ma'am'. 'Ma'am, have you heard that Squire Bushford's sold his Black Beauty?'... But usually, the only sound at their end of the table was that of the scraping of plates, or of a grunt of protest if one of them nudged another too suddenly. They had special cups and saucers, very large and thick, and they drank their beer out of horns, instead of glasses or mugs. There were certain small delicacies on the table which were never offered them and which they took obvious pains not to appear to notice. When they had finished their always excellent meal, one of them said 'Pardon, Ma'am,' and they all tiptoed out. Then Zillah brought in the tea-tray and Matthew stayed for a cup of tea before he, too, withdrew.

Lark Rise to Candleford, p. 367

The horns the men drank from were beakers made from cow's horn. In 1891, in addition to John Whitton himself, there were two blacksmiths living at the forge, Frederick Plumb, aged thirty-one, from Fritwell and Tom North aged thirty, from Leicester, not as many as Flora suggests, but perhaps more arrived to help out after John Whitton's death. Flora's Matthew, the foreman, who was also an experienced farrier, a 'bow-legged, weak-eyed little man with sandy whiskers,' was based on Frederick William Plumb, who was born on 2 December 1859 at Fritwell, the son of blacksmith William Plumb and his wife Agnes (*née* Wiggins). In 1871 he was living with his widowed mother Agnes, aged thirty-eight and sisters Emily and Agnes, aged six and five, and his grandfather William Plumb, aged seventy-four, who was a master blacksmith employing two men and a boy. He must have begun to learn his trade from his grandfather before he came to live and work the forge at Fringford as an apprentice at the age of sixteen in 1875.

Details about the contents of Kezia's four-bedroomed house and the business can be found in an inventory drawn up after Kezia's death in 1898 (detailed in Appendix 3). The first bedroom contained a 4ft 6in stump bedstead with flock mattress and pillows and a feather bed, four blankets, a coloured quilt, Windsor chair, rush-seated chair, round oak table, towel rail etc. The second bedroom had a slightly narrower wooden 4ft 3in bedstead, this time with a straw palliasse and coloured quilt, with better furniture including a mahogany chest of drawers, painted dressing table, mahogany night commode and two rush-seated chairs etc. Both third and fourth bedrooms had wooden bedsteads with flock beds and the usual furniture.

The parlour was lit by benzoline lamps and comfortably fitted out with a tapestry carpet, several tables made of oak and mahogany, a work table, easy chair and an elbow chair. Ornaments included a weather glass by Ortelli and two coloured fruits. Glass and china was stored in here.

The kitchen, lit by paraffin lamps, was the room used everyday, and to which the smiths would have access, so instead of carpet there was cocoa matting on the floor. Mrs Whitton and her staff probably ate off the oak stand table, and her servant off the two-leaf oak table. There were three Windsor elbow chairs and five ordinary ones, together with a thirty-hour clock in an oak case, a bureau made from mahogany and oak and a painted corner cupboard. The china for tea was blue and white and the teapots of block-tin. The pantry was well stocked with thirty-nine packets of cashmere soap, wine, jars of ketchup, lard, beer cans, plus perforated, meat-safe baking tins, red earthenware pans, pewter plates, oil tins, stills and a wire egg basket.

Frederick William Plumb (1859–1930), Flora's 'Matthew the Foreman'. (William Plumb)

The wash-house was also used for storage, housing the salting lead and odds and ends like a fish kettle, saucepans, Bradford's mangle, wet hams and wet bacon. The entire contents of house and forge were valued at £163 2s 9d. As the valuation was made to show what was being taken over by Frederick Plumb, who was going to rent the forge and house, some furniture and personal effects may have been removed by Kezia's son George before the inventory was made; however it bears out Flora's description of Miss Lane's house, with her taste for inherited items rather than new-fangled plush-covered suites and Japanese fans. Here she is talking about the front kitchen, which served as a living room, cooking being done in the back kitchen:

> So the grandfather's clock in the front kitchen still struck the hours as it had done on the day of the Battle of Waterloo. The huge, heavy oak table at the head of which she carved for the workmen and maid, sitting in higher or lower seats according to degree, was older still. There was a legend it had been made in the kitchen by the then village carpenter and was too large to remove without taking it to pieces ...

Lark Rise to Candleford, p. 364

This clock, made by John Fardon of Woodstock and Deddington, is still in the Plumb family. Flora exaggerated a little by mentioning four-poster bedsteads – perhaps she had seen the ones in the pub at Juniper Hill and was thinking back to those. One of the items acquired from the forge by the Plumbs was a book entitled *The Complete Farrier*, which Flora mentions seeing:

> A few books, such as *Cooking and Household Management*, *The Complete Farrier*, and Dr Johnson's *Dictionary*, were kept on one of the kitchen window-seats, but all the best books were kept behind glass doors above the bureau in the parlour. When one of these was lent to Laura, it had first to be fitted with a brown-paper jacket, for Miss Lane was most particular about her books, most of which had belonged to her father.

Lark Rise to Candleford, pp. 413-4

Running the forge was as important to Kezia as running the Post Office. The low part of the building to the left of the house was used for shoeing the horses. The separate blacksmith's shop had two forges served by one central anvil. There was also a wheelwright's shop with a tin roof behind the house. The forge served most of the local gentry including the Chinnerys of the manor house, the Goslings of Stratton Audley and the Harrisons of Shelswell Park.

As well as shoeing horses and doing general repairs at the forge, Frederick William Plumb ('Matthew') and two assistants drove off three times a week in the spring cart to visit local hunting stables to shoe horses there. The men were skilled at shoeing all sorts of animals, from the carthorses to gipsy nags and even donkeys:

> Many of the horses were very patient; but a few would plunge and kick and rear when approached. These Matthew himself shod and, under his skilful handling, they would quiet down immediately. He had only to put his hand on the mane and whisper a few words in the ear. It was probably the hand and voice which soothed them; but it was generally believed that he whispered some charm which had power over them, and he rather encouraged this idea by saying when questioned: 'I only speaks to 'em in their own language.'

Lark Rise to Candleford, pp. 371-2

The 1898 valuation also shows the range of equipment used in the forge. There was a blacksmith's shop which contained one pair of bellows, various tools, horseshoes and shoeing

The frontispiece of Mrs Whitton's copy of The *Complete Farrier*, which was kept on the kitchen window seat. (David Watts)

equipment, veterinary items such as docking irons and bull-ringing irons and a quantity of iron, staples etc. The second forge had another pair of bellows, described specifically as circular bellows (so perhaps the one in the blacksmith's shop was pear-shaped) as well as more tools, horseshoes, tin man's tools, presumably used for repairing tin items, more veterinary items such as bull's-feet parers and tooth file.

In the storeroom were quantities of wood for stales, or handles, suggesting that an important part of the work was repairing tools for local farmers (Flora wrote that the men were adept at mending not only tools but household objects). It also contained a vast quantity of various types of screws, bolts, nails, sheets of tin, hoop iron for making tyres for wagon wheels and tools and coal to fire the forges. There was another room described as a shoeing house which only contained an iron manger.

Mrs Whitton owned a bay cob, housed in her stable, to pull her spring cart, and kept four stocks of bees and a patent hive – presumably a rectangular wooden one rather than the straw bee skeps used by Sally, and stored 'outside' were items such as a pig trough, hog tub, portable forge, other blacksmith's tools and garden tools. On the grass outside the forge was a rectangular tyreing platform, on which a wagon wheel would be placed so that the red-hot iron tyre could be placed over it, then quickly doused with water to cool it down and shrink it to fit the wheel exactly. There were stores of potatoes, garden produce, wood and coal, and the remains of a rick of hay from Mrs Whitton's meadow.

Kezia Whitton died in February 1898 aged sixty-three. Frederick Plumb had to take out the left-hand upstairs bedroom windows so that her heavy coffin could be laboriously lowered down a ladder, as it was too big to carry down the stairs. He had been working as a blacksmith there for more than twenty years and was able to lease the forge from the Whittons' son George. He carried on the work as blacksmith, wheelwright and farrier largely on his own, employing additional labour as and when he required it, also doing odd jobs such as repairing pots and pans. Frederick Plumb was good at tending sick animals, probably cattle as well as horses judging by the veterinary equipment listed in the inventory, and he carried on with this work after he took over the forge. Frederick William married Elizabeth Ashby in 1900 and

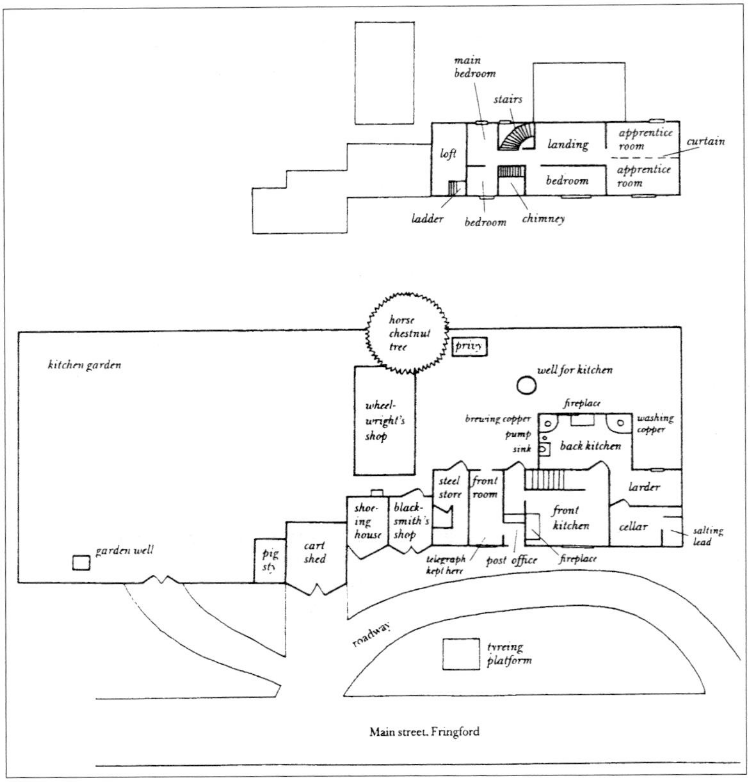
main bedroom
stairs
loft
landing
apprentice room
curtain
bedroom
apprentice room
ladder
bedroom
chimney
horse chestnut tree
privy
kitchen garden
well for kitchen
wheel-wright's shop
fireplace
brewing copper
pump
sink
back kitchen
washing copper
steel store
front room
larder
shoe-ing house
black-smith's shop
front kitchen
cellar
salting lead
garden well
pig sty
cart shed
telegraph kept here
post office
fireplace
roadway
tyreing platform
Main street, Fringford

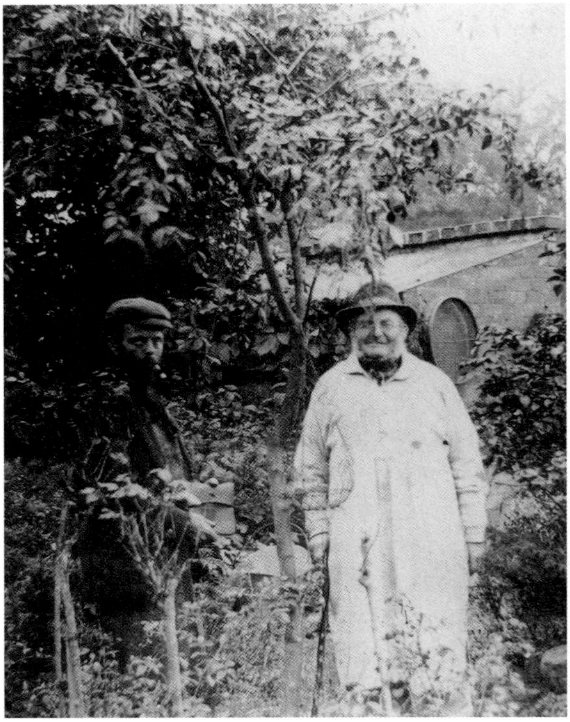

Above: Plan of the layout of the forge and post office, based on a sketch by William Plumb.

Left: Frederick William Plumb, left, and Thomas Deeley in the back garden of the forge, with its narrow flower-lined paths, one of which leads to the privy, the building behind Tommy, *c.* 1900. (William Plumb)

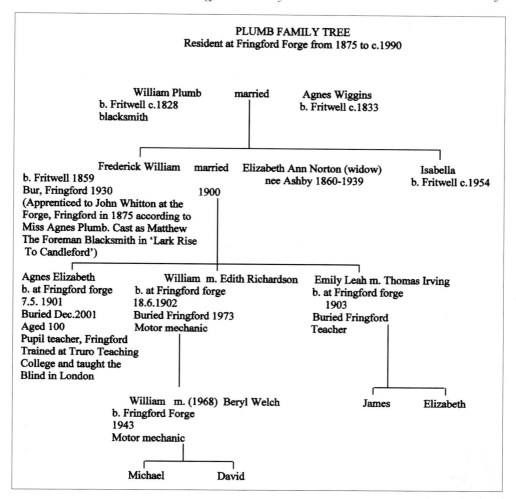

PLUMB FAMILY TREE
Resident at Fringford Forge from 1875 to c.1990

William Plumb — married — Agnes Wiggins
b. Fritwell c.1828 / b. Fritwell c.1833
blacksmith

Frederick William — married — Elizabeth Ann Norton (widow) / Isabella
b. Fritwell 1859 / nee Ashby 1860-1939 / b. Fritwell c.1954
Bur, Fringford 1930 / 1900
(Apprenticed to John Whitton at the
Forge, Fringford in 1875 according to
Miss Agnes Plumb. Cast as Matthew
The Foreman Blacksmith in 'Lark Rise
To Candleford')

Agnes Elizabeth / William m. Edith Richardson / Emily Leah m. Thomas Irving
b. at Fringford forge / b. at Fringford forge / b. at Fringford forge
7.5.1901 / 18.6.1902 / 1903
Buried Dec.2001 / Buried Fringford 1973 / Buried Fringford
Aged 100 / Motor mechanic / Teacher
Pupil teacher, Fringford
Trained at Truro Teaching
College and taught the
Blind in London

William m. (1968) Beryl Welch / James / Elizabeth
b. Fringford Forge
1943
Motor mechanic

Michael / David

The Plumb family tree.

they had three children: Agnes Elizabeth, born in 1901, William born in 1902 who became a motor mechanic and chauffeur, and Emily, born in 1903. Both the girls became teachers.

Frederick William purchased the forge and house from George Whitton in 1923 for £500, stimulated into doing so by the fact that his rent was about to be increased from £16 a year to £20. He obtained a mortgage of £222 15s at 51.2 per cent interest payable quarterly from the Grenville Lodge of the Oddfellows Friendly Society in Buckingham, which he paid off over three years. He ran his blacksmiths' business largely single-handedly, employing occasional part-time workers when he had large jobs. Most of his work involved his wheelwright and farriery skills and he also repaired pots and pans. There was a shoeing house at the north-east end of the building adjacent to the blacksmith's shop. He died in 1930 aged seventy and was buried in Fringford churchyard. The house remained in the possession of the Plumb family until 1994, although the forge was leased to Ernest Perrin from 1928-53 when he bought the other blacksmith's shop in Fringford, situated near the pub.

After Kezia Whitton's death the Post Office was moved to Rectory Lane where it was run first by James Henry Wyatt and later by Mr and Mrs Edward Price.

People gathering to watch a hunt meet in North Oxfordshire. (David Watts)

The Friendly Society procession leaving Fringford church on feast day, after the service, on their way to enjoy the entertainment on the village green, *c.* 1900–10. (William Plumb)

Entertainments

There were few organised entertainments, apart from the penny readings and church socials, but most people turned out to watch the annual meet of the Bicester Hunt on the first Saturday in January, which met outside the Butcher's Arms on the outskirts of the village. It must have looked very colourful with the riders in their scarlet jackets, the aristocratic ladies in close-fitting habits and the excited hounds. Flora obviously sympathised with the fate of the fox, and was more interested in watching the people on the Green, as it gave her the opportunity of seeing a wide variety of the local populace:

> The whole neighbourhood turned out to see the meet. Both roadways were lined with little basketwork pony-carriages with elderly ladies in furs, governess-cars with nurses and children, farm carts with forks stuck up in loads of manure, and butcher's and grocer's carts and baker's white tilted vans, and donkey-barrows in which red-faced, hoarse-shouting hawkers stood up for a better view ...
>
> On the Green itself school-teachers, curates, men in breeches and gaiters with ash sticks, men in ragged coats and mufflers, smartly dressed girls from Candleford town and local women in white aprons with babies in their arms pressed forward to see all there was to be seen, while older children rushed hither and thither shouting, 'Tally-ho! Tally-ho!' and only missed by a miracle being hit by the horses' hoofs.

Lark Rise to Candleford, p. 420

Fringford Feast, held annually on the Village Green, was another colourful occasion, although this time the clergy and aristocracy stayed away. It was a far grander occasion than the Cottisford Feast, with the trappings of a small fair — swing boats, roundabouts and hurdy-gurdies as well as a myriad of stalls and activities such as shooting galleries and coconut shies. All the young people dressed in their best and crowds came out from Bicester and nearby villages. Flora once again was an onlooker, preferring to watch the goings-on from her bedroom window at the forge, except for the feast to which 'Edmund' escorted her and from which he was banned from the coconut shy for knocking off too many coconuts!

It was occasions such as this which gave her the chance to appreciate some of the local colour of the area, later used as some of the raw material for her writing. As she grew in confidence she realised that she did not want to spend all her life in this one small area where she was unlikely to get advancement. So in 1897 she gave in her notice, probably went to Twyford for a while, took a series of temporary jobs and finally a permanent one at Grayshott in Surrey.

No.	NAME.	RESIDENCE.	Rate of Contribution per	Extra Annual Contribution.	Age last birthday.	Arrears forwarded from last sitting.		
						£	s.	d.
205	Isham George	Brackley	2/7		32			
206	Stockwell John	"	3/6		38			
207	Paxton John	Brackley	2/0		18			
208	Bockals Emmanuel	"	2/10		36			
209	Whitehead Harry	Westbury	2/0		18			
210	Williams C.W.	"	2/2		23			
211	Samuels Will.	Brackley	2/5		29			
212	Taylor Jos	"	2/9		34			
213	Morris W	"	2/0		19			
214	Shepherd G.	"	2/0		18			
215	Horton A	"	2/1		21			
216	Young W.	Evenley	2/1		22			
217	Prue S.	"	2/0		20			
218	Wynne C.	Brackley	2/0		20			
219	Rhoades Alfred	"	2/0		20			
220	Timms Albert	Cottisford	2/6		31			
221	Mansfield Fredk Geo	Brackley	2/1		21			
222	Edwards James	"	2/3		27			
223	Billings George		2/2		26			
224	Walker John		2/3		27			
225	Burgess Charles		2/3		27			
226	Jeffrey Frank		2/0		20			
227	Canning Will. Geo		2/0		18			

Rock of Hope LODGE for the Year 1885

Page from the Brackley Rock of Hope Branch of the Independent Order of Oddfellows. This page shows that Flora's father Albert Timms was assessed to pay a contribution of 2s 6d in 1885. He took sick pay from the Order on several occasions. (David Watts)

Brackley, Banbury, Bicester and Buckingham: Flora's Candleford

Candleford was but a small town and their cousins' home was on the outskirts ... To Laura it was both town and country and in that lay part of its charm. It was thrilling, after being used to walking miles to buy a reel of cotton or a packet of tea, to be able to dash out without a hat to fetch something from a shop for her aunt; and still more thrilling to spend whole sunny mornings gazing into shop windows with her cousins. There were such marvellous things in the Candleford shops, such as the wax lady dressed in the height of fashion, with one of the new bustles, at the leading draper's, and the jeweller's window, sparkling with gold and silver and gems, and the toy shops and the sweet shops, and, above all, the fishmonger's where a whole salmon reposed on a bed of green reeds with ice sprinkled over (ice in August! They would never believe it at home), and an aquarium with live goldfish swimming round and round stood round near the desk where they took your money.

Lark Rise to Candleford, p. 340

This is an amorphous description which could apply to many places and typifies why 'Candleford' is perhaps the most difficult place to tie down in detail, although Buckingham is where Flora's grandparents, Thomas and Martha Timms and her uncle, 'James Dowland' lived. Flora knew several towns which could have formed the basis for her 'Candleford'.

Brackley

As a child Flora would certainly have visited Brackley often. Her nearest town, situated just over the Northamptonshire border, this was where she and her family did their shopping, although there are surprisingly few direct references to it in *Lark Rise to Candleford*. Her father, Albert Timms, worked there, probably first for a builder by the name of William Hawkins in the High Street and latterly for James Coles, whose yard was on the Banbury Road. William Hawkins, his first employer, was the son of schoolmaster Thomas Hawkins. He was born in Brackley in 1826 and in 1841 was working as a painter. In 1851 he lived in the High Street with his wife Martha and brother, Edwin and described himself as a plumber, painter and glazier employing one man (presumably Edwin, who was a journeyman plumber and painter). By 1861 he had risen up the ladder and moved to St James. By this time he was employing five mechanics, one apprentice and three labourers. He now had four children: Charles Arthur (seven), William Hedges (six), Sarah Ann (four) and Thomas (one month). His sister Harriet (twenty-one) was living with them and they could afford one servant, Eliza Billing (eighteen). In 1871 the business had grown further and he employed twenty-seven men and four boys. His eldest son Charles, now seventeen was described as a builder.

The business continued to expand, so in 1881 William Hawkins, now a widower, was living in the Market Square with his sons Charles, William and Thomas and his sister Harriet was

Brackley market place with the town hall in the centre. (David Watts)

The Statuaries, the house belonging to James Coles, the monumental mason who employed Albert Timms, which is situated next to the site of his builders' yard (now a housing estate) on the Banbury road.

housekeeper and Leah Pettifer (twenty) from Helmdon was the servant. William by then employed fifty men and boys and his sons were all employed with him – Charles and William as builders and Thomas as a joiner. His eldest son Charles died in 1889 aged only thirty-five and William himself died in 1891, so his son William took over the business, describing himself as a builder and contractor. He was living in Chapel Lane with his wife Mary (thirty-seven) and children – Ethel (nine), Frank (seven), Alfred (four), Louisa (six months) – and his niece Martha (seven). They had no servant, so perhaps the business was less successful. In 1901 he was still running the business and his son Frank had become a builder's apprentice.

James Coles was born in Buckingham in 1853. He first appears in the Brackley census returns in 1881, described as a 'mantle mason, master employing two men.' He was living in the High Street with his wife Emily, sons, William (seven) and Ernest (two) and daughter Emily (six). In 1891 James was described as a 'stone and marble mason', living in the Banbury Road and William was working with him. James now had more children: Mary (nine), Benjamin (nine), Ellen (seven), Sidney (five), George (two) and Lawrence (three months). *Kelly's 1898 Directory of Beds, Hants and Northants* described his business as 'Coles, James, stone, marble, statuary, architectural and monumental masons, Banbury Road'. By 1901 the firm had become a real family business, employing James and three of his sons: William, Benjamin and Sidney, and presumably other masons. Their yard was to the rear of their house, (which had its name, The Statuaries, carved on a decorative stone), in the Banbury Road. In later life this building was used as the headquarters for the Conservative Club and the yard has been turned into a housing estate.

Brackley is a small, quiet town which reached the height of its prosperity in the early Middle Ages, when there was a castle just to the south along the Hinton road. Because the town has not developed greatly, there are still many traces of the medieval planned borough such as the large market place, which has not changed vastly since the nineteenth century. The town gradually declined from the late Middle Ages, and not even the opening of the LNWR Bletchley to Banbury railway with a station at Brackley made much impact on the town. Later another station was opened when the GWR built the Leicester to Marylebone line. Both railway lines have now closed. *Kelly's 1898 Directory* boasted that over £20,000 had been spent on sanitary works and that water was supplied free to every household.

Although Brackley was small, there was a wide range of occupations in the late nineteenth century. The main industry was brewing and there were lots of different shops from drapers and milliners, pillow-lace manufacturers, straw-hat maker, watchmaker and jewellers, tailors, boot and shoemaker, china and glass dealer, a fancy repository and Berlin wool depot, bookseller to fishmonger and poulterer, butcher, grocer and haberdasher, baker, confectioner, chemist and druggist and fruiterer. There were also occupations connected with farming such as woodman and farmer, corn miller, saddler, land surveyor, harness maker and shoeing and jobbing smith, plus, of course, builders. The market took place each Wednesday, specialising in cattle and corn on alternate weeks and a wool fair was held in June and a show of horses and agricultural produce in September with ordinary fairs in October and December. The population in 1881 was 2,504.

Although Flora makes few direct references to the town, another indication of the connection her family had with Brackley comes from the books of the Rock of Hope Lodge of the IAAF Manchester Unity Friendly Society in Brackley. Albert Timms belonged to this and the secretary was a local builder, Alan Wootton. Albert was contracted to pay in a regular sum each month, and would then receive sick benefits and funeral expenses. There are references to him drawing sick pay of 2s with 6d for incidentals on 16 March 1886. He received the same sum on 6 June 1887; 6s and 6d on 12 March 1888 and 2s and 6d on 17 December 1888 and notes of the amount of money he paid into the society. It is interesting that some months he did not pay his 2s 6d contribution, having to pay a larger sum later to make up for what he had missed – this echoes what Flora wrote about his attitude to money. A reference in *Still Glides the Stream* to Charity's father visiting the Oddfellows Benefit Club in 'Mixlow' could well refer to Albert Timms:

Above: Detail of The Statuaries showing the decorative carved nameplate.

Left: Part of Coles' builders' yard before it became a housing estate.

Calendar of the Independent Order of
Oddfellows, the friendly society to which
Albert Timms belonged. (David Watts)

The fourteenth of each month was her father's club night, when he walked into Mixlow to pay his subscription to the Oddfellows Benefit Club, and usually, as he said, made a night of it, meaning that he might not be home before eleven o'clock, a late hour at Restharrow. When he came home he would be gay and animated, not from what he had drunk, for he seldom took more than one pint of ale, but because the talk at the club had been stimulating. Members of other, more conventional fraternities used at that time to say that the Oddfellows were no better than a lot of old freemasons, and this idea was not discouraged by the Oddfellows themselves. Though their mysteries probably consisted of no more than a password to gain admittance to their clubroom, the addressing each other as 'Brother' while there, and the possession of an elected member known as 'our almoner', whose office it was to visit the sick and dispense benefits, they liked to think of their own as a secret society. In politics, the majority of the brethren were Liberals with a Radical tinge; many of them were less strict churchgoers than their neighbours – one man belonging to the Mixlow branch professed to be an atheist – and altogether, the Oddfellows were regarded as a daring lot; though, strange as it may have appeared to some people, their lives were generally exemplary.

Still Glides the Stream, pp. 159-60

Banbury

Banbury was a much larger town, the second largest in Oxfordshire, which is, unusually, mentioned several times by its real name in *Still Glides the Stream*. The first reference concerns 'Stella Pocock', who considers herself a cut above her neighbours and talks disparagingly about the pompadour aprons made for Charity and her cousins, largely because she did not have one herself:

The Betts' Banbury Cake Shop in the High Street, Banbury, *c.* 1878. (Oxfordshire Photographic Archive)

> They were getting common, she said; the last time she and her mother were in Banbury they had seen a gipsy selling clothes-pegs in an apron very like Bess's.

Still Glides the Stream, p. 90

Later in the book, 'Charity Finch', the heroine, has just been awarded the status of full pupil-teacher and wants to spend the precious sovereign she has been given as a reward in Banbury, with her cousin 'Bess', 'for she dearly loved a trip into Banbury in the carrier's cart to see the shops and to enjoy a cup of tea at Bett's' (p. 125). A few pages later she thinks of the trip she has not been able to take because she had undertaken an urgent secret errand for 'Bess'. She reflects that, 'if her mother were thinking of her at that moment, she would picture her with Bess, gazing into shop windows, or sipping tea and nibbling a Banbury cake in the Old Teashop' (p. 130).

Flora wrote to Leslie Castle several times about Banbury, which she remembered from her childhood as being a quiet country town:

> I had always thought of it in connection with the fighting in the Civil War and the Puritan hanging the cat on Monday for catching a mouse on Sunday and of Banbury Cross and, all the time, it has been growing into a large industrial town. I went there several times in the carrier's cart as a child and had that place partly in mind when creating my Candleford, though most of our relations lived in Buckingham.

Letter dated 24 February 1945

Banbury, famous for its cakes since the sixteenth century, was a much bigger market town than Brackley, with a population of 9,660 in 1881, although like Brackley it still retains much of its medieval plan. St Mary's church stands in Horsefair, up the road from the Victorian Banbury

Cross, with the High Street leading down to the market place on one side of it, and Parson's Street forming the other side of a triangle linking them. The Saxon settlement was turned into a planned town by Bishop Alexander of Lincoln in the twelfth century, and it became the second most important town in Oxfordshire, after Oxford itself. Its main industry at the beginning of the Victorian period was weaving plush – different types of which were used for purposes as diverse as liveries for the courts of the world, panning gold in South Africa, Japanese winter kimonos, friction gloves, photography, and embossed plush specially made for furnishings in the House of Commons, the House of Lords and the Reform Club as well as for private houses such as Broughton Castle.

Later in the century, plush came second to the industry of agricultural engineering. The foundations of this were laid in Banbury by James Gardner, who patented a turnip cutter in 1834. In 1848 his business was purchased by Bernhard Samuelson, whose engineering works in Tours had been closed down by the Revolution of 1848. He set up the Britannia Works on three sites near the railway station, and built a variety of machines, including the American McCormick reaping machines under licence. It may well have been Samuelson's machines that were beginning to appear in Flora's countryside:

> After the Jubilee nothing ever seemed quite the same. The old Rector died and the farmer, who had seemed immovable except by death, had to retire to make way for the heir of the landowning nobleman who intended to farm the family estates himself. He brought with him the new self-binding reaping machine and women were no longer required in the harvest field.

Lark Rise to Candleford, p. 246

Other occupations in Banbury included printing, basket making, straw plaiting, chair making, coopering, tailoring, cork burning, clay-pipe making, mop making, leather crafts, tanning and narrowboat-building.

It was the Banbury cakes that Flora remembered about the town – she made another reference to them in *Candleford Green* when she had her first tea at the Post Office:

> It seemed a pity to Laura that the first time she had been offered two eggs at one meal she could barely eat one and that the Banbury cake, hitherto to her a delicious rarity only seen in her home when purchased by visiting aunts, should flake and crumble almost untasted upon her plate because she felt too excited and anxious to eat.

Lark Rise to Candleford, p. 397

Banbury cakes now have a rich fruit filling in a pastry crust. The first reference to them came in Thomas Bright's *Treatise of Melancholie* in 1586:

> Sodden wheat is a grosse and melancholicke nourishment and bread especially of the fine flower [flour] unleavened. Of this sort are bag puddings made with flower, fritters, pancakes, such as we call Banberrie Cakes, and the great ones are confected with butter, eggs, etc., used at weddings, and however it be prepared rye and bread made thereof carried with it plenty of melancholie.

They had a dubious reputation in the seventeenth century too, when Ben Johnson, the playwright made his Puritan character Zeal-of-the-Land Busy, a baker, (who may have been based on the Banbury baker Richard Busby) give up his baking because his Banbury cakes were served at such pagan ceremonies as bride ales, May Day and Morris dances. 'The Original Cake Shop' was in Parson's Street from the seventeenth century, almost opposite the Reindeer Inn.

ORIGINAL CAKE-SHOP, PARSON'S STREET.

BETTY WHITE.

Above: Engraving of the Original Cake Shop run by the Brown family in Parson's Street, Banbury, from Alfred Beasley's *History of Banbury*, 1841.

Left: Silhouette of Betty White, renowned eighteenth-century maker of Banbury cakes, from Alfred Beasley's History of Banbury, 1841.

The owners in the eighteenth century included Betty and Jarvis White. Betty was said to be an excellent and careful baker who was jealous of her good reputation. 'My name is quiet Betty, I never meddles nor makes with anybody, no mealman never calls on me twice,' she would say. When people commented on the high price of her cakes she explained, 'only think, there's currants, they be twice the price th' used to be, and then there's butter an' sugar they be double the price th' was formerly'. Jarvis was rather fonder of leaning over the shop door and promoting her cakes than actually doing any work. He maintained that the cakes were so light that a sparrow could fly off with one in its beak. In the late nineteenth century Mrs Brown was running The Original Cake Shop, and Banbury cakes were also baked by William Betts in his half-timbered shop in the High Street and by Daniel Claridge in Parson's Street. The cakes had a worldwide reputation, being exported as far as America and Australia. The cake shop which Flora knew was demolished in 1969, but items relating to Banbury cakes can be seen in Banbury Museum.

Flora makes another reference to Banbury in relation to 'Queenie' the lacemaker, who made lace all the year ready to take it to sell at Banbury Fair:

'Them wer' the days!' she would sigh. 'Money to spend.' And she would tell of the bargains she had bought with her earnings. Good brown calico and linsey-woolsey, and a certain chocolate print sprigged with white, her favourite gown, of which she could still show a pattern in her big patchwork quilt. Then there was a fairing to be bought for those at home – pipes and packets of shag tobacco for the men, rag dolls and ginger-bread for the little 'uns', and snuff for the old grannies. And the home-coming, loaded with treasure, and money in the pocket besides. Tripe. They always bought tripe; it was the only time in the year they could get it, and it was soon heated up, with onions and a nice bit of thickening, and after supper there was hot, spiced elderberry wine, and so to bed, everybody happy.

Now, of course, things were different. She didn't know what the world was coming to. This nasty machine-made stuff had killed the lacemaking; the dealer had not been to the fair for the last ten years...

Lark Rise to Candleford, p. 84

Banbury Michaelmas Fair was quite an occasion in the nineteenth century, with people travelling long distances to visit it as there were few organised entertainments then, apart from those provided at fairs. As many agricultural labourers were employed on a yearly contract, which ended after the harvest, they would leave the farm, have a few days holiday and visit the local hiring fair to find a new job. There were many stalls selling items as diverse as ribbons, shawls, toys and dolls, gingerbread and Banbury cakes, plus entertainments such as a camera obscura, a Wild West show, swing boats, helter-skelter, Ferris wheel, haunted house and later, steam yachts and bioscopes. The town hummed with people and it was a happy time for the crowds.

Bicester

Flora would have visited Bicester when she lived at Fringford, and it bears much resemblance to the 'Mixlow' of *Still Glides the Stream*, although that also contains elements of Brackley. *Kelly's Directory of Berkshire, Buckinghamshire and Oxfordshire* published in 1887 described the town:

Bicester is an agricultural market and union town, head of a county court district, parish and polling place for the county … and includes the townships of Market End and King's End; the air is healthy and the town is well supplied with water of remarkable purity, to the use of which is attributed the celebrity the town has obtained for its excellent ale ...The London and North Western branch railway from Oxford to Bletchley ... has a station near to the town. Bicester, anciently called *Burinceastre* is supposed to have been founded in the seventh century. The etymology of its name is uncertain; by many it is conjectured to derive its name from *Birinus* (*Birini Castrum*); the Saxon canonized prelate and first Bishop of Dorchester, in whose time it had been a frontier garrison and may possibly have been built by his advice from the ruins of Alchester, which was a fortified city and a Roman station of considerable note under Aulus Plautius, the consul. Skinner (Etym., Ling. Angl.) conjectures the true derivation to be from the Anglo-Saxon *bern,* a granary, and *ceaster,* a town.

The town consists principally of one long street ... there is also a market place, with an outlet joining it to King's End, on the road to Wendlebury and Oxford, and two other streets branching from these called Chapel Street and Crockwell ... the church of St Eadburg is a spacious and handsome edifice of stone ...Three weekly newspapers are published here. There is a brewery and tannery. The chief business of the inhabitants arises from the market and cattle fairs ...

Bicester was formerly the seat of a priory, founded by Gilbert Bassett ... AD 1182, for a prior and eleven canons of the order of St Augustine and dedicated to the honour of St Mary and St Eadburg ... the site of the priory, in Place Yard, was excavated in 1819 ... Market End is a township and bailiwick, consisting of the lordship and the manor, leased for a term of 10,000 years by William (Stanley), 6th Earl of Derby, KG in 1596 ...

John Coker moved to Bicester in the 1580s, acquiring former monastic land. In 1634 grant of arms was made by heralds visiting Oxfordshire to Cadwallader Coker, an ancestor of the vicar of the same name whom Flora knew in Fringford, who came from Bicester.

Market End, which was called Bury End until about 1542, has the triangular market square at its centre. The charter granting a market was issued in 1239 to William de Longespee.

A third area grew up round the Saxon church, dedicated to the Virgin Mary and St Edburg, named after the daughter of Edward the Elder, and the Causeway, midway between King's End and Market End. Very little remains of Saxon work as the church was largely rebuilt in the twelfth century and enlarged over the next 300 years.

In 1881 the population of Bicester was 3,306. Well-established crafts in the nineteenth century included wool combing, straw plaiting, lace, rope, sackcloth and basket making, and leather slippers. *Kelly's Directory* for 1887 mentions John and Eliza Barrett making rope and twine, a tanner and currier, several boot and shoemakers and a basket maker. Bicester had the usual variety of shops and other trades included seedsmen, brewers and mineral-water manufacturers and a commercial traveller.

Flora would have known little of the early history of the town, but was aware of some aspects of life there from her childhood. She told the story of a retired bachelor, 'Mr Sharman', nicknamed 'the Major', who lived on his own, keeping his little house neat and tidy until he became old and weak. Emma Timms helped to care for him when he was ill; then he spent a few weeks in hospital in Oxford. When he returned he brought small presents for the children – a set of doll's dishes with food for Flora and a tin engine for Edwin, plus a silk handkerchief for Emma, a pipe for Albert and a rattle for the baby, which were received with delight. Emma carried on taking him food, and doing what she could, but eventually it was clear that he could no longer manage on his own, and the doctor had to call in the relieving officer and organise for him to be taken to the workhouse infirmary:

They were right in their decision. He was not able to look after himself; he had no relatives or friends able to undertake the responsibility; the workhouse was the best place for him. But they made one terrible mistake. They were dealing with a man of intelligence, and spirit, and they treated him as they might have done one in the extreme of senile decay. They did

Grimsley's fish shop in Sheep Street, Bicester, with the shop assistants (the one on the right is Flora's second cousin Jack Waine (1896-1962) proudly displaying a 203lb halibut. In one of her descriptions of Candleford, Flora marvelled over, 'The fishmonger's where a whole salmon reposed on a bed of green reeds with ice sprinkled over (ice in August! They would never believe it at home)' …
Lark Rise to Candleford, p. 340. (David Watts)

Bicester Union Workhouse, which opened in 1836, on the site of Orchard Way near George Street, built by James Long of Witney to cater for the poor of thirty-eight parishes. It was designed by John Plowman who charged a £50 fee and was built largely using pauper labour at a cost of £4,140. Most people only went to the workhouse when they were absolutely desperate, as conditions there were often degrading and families were separated. The building was demolished in 1966. (David Watts)

not consult him or tell him what they had decided; but ordered the carrier's cart to call at his house the next morning and wait at a short distance while they, in the doctor's gig, drove up to his door. When they entered, the Major had just dressed and dragged himself to his chair by the fire. 'It's a nice morning, and we've come to take you for a drive,' announced the doctor cheerfully, and in spite of his protests, they hustled on his coat and had him out and in the carrier's cart in a very few minutes.

Laura saw the carrier touch up his horse with the whip and the cart turn, and she always wished afterwards she had not, for, as soon as he realised where he was being taken, the old soldier, the independent old bachelor, the kind family friend, collapsed and cried like a child. He was beaten, but not for long. Before six weeks were over he was back in the parish and all his troubles were over, for he came in his coffin.

Lark Rise to Candleford, pp. 89-90

He would have been taken to the Bicester Union Workhouse, which was built on George Street, Highfield in Bicester in 1836 to accommodate 350 inmates. To be sent to the workhouse was a fate that elderly people dreaded; husbands and wives were separated, life was degradingly institutionalised and hard, and they would do anything they could to avoid it.

'Dr Henderson' is mentioned in *Candleford Green* as living on the green, but according to census returns there was no doctor in Fringford so he was probably based on the character of Dr Cecil Morgan Hendriks who lived in London Road, Bicester, near the junction with Market Hill, practising with Dr Cotterell from 1885 before buying the practice in 1890. Flora wrote that he lived in a long, low brown house with a red lamp outside. He had a loud bell, and people trying to contact him at night had to shout up to him through a speaking tube. Although he did not like being roused from his bed, and had a tendency to swear about it while harnessing his horse, he was noted for his excellent bedside manner.

When describing her first arrival in Candleford, Flora wrote a description that could well apply to Bicester, and Dr Hendriks' house:

Candleford seemed a very large and grand place to Laura, with its several large streets meeting in a square where there were many large shop windows, with the blinds drawn because it was Sunday, and a doctor's house with a red lamp over the gate, and a church with a tall spire ...

Lark Rise to Candleford, p. 305

Dr Cecil M. Hendriks was a dapper man with a pointed beard, sporting an eyeglass, who wore white spats and a light waistcoat and carried a silver-headed cane. He was born in Jamaica in the West Indies in 1856, and his wife Lydia also came from there. He came to England at the age of seventeen and had a successful career at University College, London before coming to Bicester. In the 1891 census he was described as 'Registered MB, MRCS Gen. Practitioner' and was living in London Road with his forty-one-year old wife and his children Esther (nine), Charles (seven) and Richard (six). His coachman, who took him out to visit patients, was Alfred Stone from Bicester, aged nineteen, and he had a cook, Caroline Cooper, aged twenty-one from Oxford and Mary A. Field, his housemaid (eighteen) came from Headington, Oxford. In 1901 he was described as a surgeon and was living with his wife and daughter Esther and an assistant surgeon, Harry Harley, aged twenty-eight from Ireland. His servants were cook Alice Gibbard aged twenty-eight and Edith Gibbard, housemaid, aged sixteen, both from Launton and probably sisters. He also served as medical officer and public vaccinator for the Stoke Lyne district, at the Hospital for Infectious Diseases and as assistant medical officer to the schools. He played the violin and his daughter Esther played the piano and his hobbies included shooting, golf and bowls. Dr Hendriks was one of the first people to

Dr Cecil Morgan Hendriks, the inspiration for Flora's 'Dr. Henderson', taken from his obituary in the *Bicester Advertiser*. (David Watts)

own a car in Bicester, and, most unusually, he had a sleigh for use in snowy weather. He died from septic poisoning and was cremated at Golders Green crematorium. His obituary in the *Bicester Advertiser* on 24 July 1925 showed a real sense of loss:

> During the war he gave his services to the Red Cross Hospital at Bicester Hall and to other hospitals in the neighbourhood. His geniality and fatherly care were greatly appreciated by his patients. For these services he was awarded the OBE.
>
> Dr Hendriks leaves a son and a daughter to mourn their loss. Mrs Hendriks died in 1903 and their younger son Richard in 1912 ...
>
> One could recount a host of stories of his kindness, which was proverbial.
>
> Wherever he could do good, he did it without ostentation. A life such as his will be sadly missed, for it may with truth be said of him that he lived and moved and gave his life and talents for others. He had either a kind word or a joke for everyone. His heart was so sympathetic that his patients' sorrows and troubles he made his own. He would give the last ounce of his strength if it would benefit the sufferer. Such were the characteristics of the gentleman – of the real type – whom Bicester and the neighbourhood now mourn. His death came as a profound shock to the inhabitants of Bicester, and the people of the countryside will miss the pleasant figure so frequently seen in and out amongst them helping and advising.

One of his public offices was that of medical officer for Bicester Post Office, and Flora may have met him in this context. According to local lore, he was a generous man who often neglected to present his bills to his patients when he knew that they would find them difficult to pay. However he meticulously noted down the fees in a notebook, which after his death

The King's Arms Hotel, Bicester.

Market Hill, Bicester, *c.* 1905. It is reminiscent of Flora's description of Candleford having several streets meeting in a square where the blinds were drawn over the shop windows as it was Sunday. Dr Hendriks, probably Flora's 'Dr Henderson', lived in the house on the left before the elm tree. (David Watts)

was found by his executors, who, to the horror of the local people, sent out all the bills. Dr Hendriks' generosity is mentioned in *Still Glides the Stream* (p. 96):

> The old doctor at Mixlow, who attended the country people for miles around that town and to quite half his patients sent in no bill because he knew that they were too poor to pay one, about the time when pompadour aprons first appeared instituted what was known as a Doctor's Club, the members of which paid twopence weekly and, for that, when ill, were entitled to free attendance. When this club had been long enough in existence for the members to claim benefits, there was such an outbreak of minor ailments that he had to engage ... an assistant ...

Another 'Candleford' institution Flora mentioned was a Mechanics' Institute where she was encouraged by Mrs Whitton to borrow books to read. There was a Mechanics' Institute in Banbury, founded by Sir Bernhard Samuelson, which now houses the public library in Marlborough Road. The equivalent in Bicester was a free reading room for labouring men, endowed by the Earl of Jersey, which opened in 1872, offering them newspapers and presumably books to read.

Flora's uncle, 'James Dowland' is very difficult to identify, and is unlikely to have lived in Bicester, but there was a builder there who may have been one of the inspirations for the character: Joseph Belsey Layton, a cabinet maker. He was born in 1849 in Clerkenwell, the son of Benjamin Layton, a joiner from Bicester, and his wife Sarah Anne (*née* Godden Wood). Benjamin died in 1857 and in 1861 Joseph, still a scholar at twelve, had moved back to Bicester to live with his uncle, George Layton, who was described as a cabinet maker in 1841 and an upholsterer in 1861, and his wife Frances. Living with them was Catherine E. Bricknell aged twenty-four from Kings Sutton, Northamptonshire, (who despite being twelve years older than Joseph was destined to become his wife) and thirteen-year-old Frances Bricknell from London was a visitor.

Ticket for Banbury Mechanics' Institute. Such organisations gave working people the opportunity to continue their education after leaving school, and ran lending libraries. Flora borrowed books from the free reading room in Bicester which had the same aims. (Oxfordshire Photographic Archive)

Joseph Belsay Layton (1849-1901) and his son George Layton (1878-1954) with some of their staff in the builders' yard behind Layton's shop on Market Hill, Bicester, in 1883. The staff from left to right: -?-, Joseph Grantham (staircase maker), Arthur Edward Waine (1863-1947 – stonemason and first cousin of Albert Timms), ? member of Symons family, James Small (foreman), George Layton Joseph Belsay Layton, -?-, -?-, Thomas Edward Waine (1846-1918 cousin of Albert Timms, who later became a wheelwright in Launton). (David Watts)

In the 1871 census Joseph (now a journeyman apprentice) and Catherine (now described as a china dealer) were both still living with George Layton and his wife Frances.

In 1872, at the age of twenty-three, Joseph married Catherine in Finsbury, London and took over her dealership in china, glass and earthenware in Market Square, Bicester, later extending the business to become a builders' merchant. He was listed in the 1887 *Kelly's Directory* as an upholsterer and china dealer in Market Hill, but he and his son George were actually the biggest builders in Bicester. They were never listed as builders in the Directories as they did not sell the houses, or build for other people, instead renting out their properties. In the early 1890s they started to build thirteen houses in Bath Terrace, eight houses in Manchester Terrace and a further eight in Newport Terrace, all in Victoria Road. Around 1900 they built seven large villa-style houses in London Road, some of which have black-and-white tiled paths like those described by Flora. Nineteen houses were also built in Field Street on the Fringford side of the town and Joseph himself moved into number seven which has since been divided into two houses.

The description of Laura's arrival in Candleford at her uncle's house could apply to the house with the hooded front door and a post-and-chain fence in Market Hill owned by Joseph Layton:

> But they were pulling up at a tall white house set back on a little green with a chestnut tree supporting scaffold poles and ladders and a sign which informed the public that James Dowland, Builder and Contractor, was ready and competent to undertake 'Constructions, Renovations and Sanitary Work. Estimates Free'.
>
> Readers have no doubt noticed how seldom builders live in houses of their own construction ... Uncle James Dowland's house was probably Georgian. The eight windows with their clinging wreaths of wisteria were beautifully spaced and the flight of steps which led up to the hooded front door was guarded by the low white posts and chains which enclosed the little green.

Lark Rise to Candleford, p. 305

Flora gave a detailed description of her 'Uncle James', an important looking man:

> Uncle James was so tall and stout and dark, with eyebrows so bushy and so thick a moustache, with so glossy a Sunday suit and so heavy a gold watch chain that, before him, the others present seemed to fade into the background.

Lark Rise to Candleford, pp. 305–6

This is similar to the photograph of Joseph Layton except that the latter has side whiskers and a beard.

Joseph's son George was also a highly respected man in Bicester. He lived in a mansion he built in London Road and in 1912 built Layton's Garage in London Road, from which he sold cars to the gentry. He became Chairman of Bicester Urban District Council in 1920 and was the first tradesman in Bicester to become a magistrate.

Bicester was almost certainly the post town referred to in *Still Glides the Stream* when trying to identify the writer of anonymous letters:

> Charity examined the postmark. It was that of Mixlow, their own post town. All the letters written at Restharrow and handed to the postman bore that postmark, as well as those posted in the town and in other villages for miles around.

Still Glides the Stream, p. 126

Market Hill, Bicester, *c.* 1900, showing Joseph Layton's house and the shop they ran from the 1870s until the 1950s. Flora describes 'Uncle James Dowland's' house as probably being Georgian, and in the centre of town. (David Watts)

London Road, Bicester. The houses were built by Joseph Belsay Layton. (David Watts)

Staff of Bicester Post Office, *c.* 1900. The postmaster Walter Joseph French (Flora's 'Mr Rushton') sits in the centre with Miss Wrapson on the left and Miss Tooley on the right. The women were described by Flora as the two daughters of a minister, quiet, refined women in their thirties. As they never married, there was no vacancy for Flora at Bicester Post Office. (David Watts)

Buckingham

Flora always maintained that Buckingham was the main influence for her depiction of 'Candleford'. It is the county town of Buckinghamshire, although now overtaken in prominence and size by the likes of Aylesbury and Milton Keynes, so that, like Brackley, the town retains its old-world character. It has its origins in the Anglo-Saxon period, the first mention of it being in AD 915 when Edward the Elder had it fortified for protection against the Danes. It grew in the Middle Ages because of the wool trade and received a royal charter in the sixteenth century. In the centre of the town is Castle Hill, which housed a Norman castle, where tradition says Hereward was imprisoned. The ruined castle was obliterated by the building of the parish church in the late eighteenth century, only the mound remaining. However by the sixteenth century Buckingham was in decline. Perhaps because of this, it retains some early elements such as St John the Baptist's chapel, a small stone building with a tiled roof, on Market Hill, which dates partly from the late twelfth century, with fifteenth-century alterations such as a traceried window and truss roof, made when it was converted into a Latin School by Edward VI. Not to be outdone, Queen Elizabeth founded Christ's Hospital for seven poor women. The High Street has some sixteenth and seventeenth-century houses. In the seventeenth century there were several craft guilds in the town, which indicate the principal manufactures: the Mercers, including apothecaries, chandlers, clothiers, goldsmiths, grocers, haberdashers, hat or cap makers, ironmongers, linen drapers, mercers, salters, silkmen and woollen drapers; the Cordwainers including collar makers, girdle makers, glovers, parchment makers, poynters and poynt makers, saddlers, shoemakers and tanners; the Tailors' Guild included brasiers, dyers, fletchers, furbishers, fullers, glaziers, painters, pewterers, tailors and weavers; the Butchers' Guild included bakers, brewers, butchers, cooks and millers.

Buckingham church collapsed in 1776 and the present church was built on Castle Hill and consecrated in 1781. It was transformed in the nineteenth century by George Gilbert Scott, who was born in Gawcott. (Tony Westbury)

Bridge Street, Buckingham. (Tony Westbury)

The Bull Ring, Buckingham. (Tony Westbury)

There was a disastrous fire in the town in 1725 so many Georgian houses built to replace earlier ones are found. Some earlier buildings survived including the seventeenth or early eighteenth-century town hall, Castle House and the Manor House. The Gaol, built in 1748, and now a museum, stands to the north east of the Market Square, decorated with turrets and embattled parapets.

Even in the nineteenth century it was a country town, with a population of 3,585 in 1881, closely linked with its agricultural hinterland (in 1881 *Kelly's Directory of Buckinghamshire* proudly boasted of the town's manufacture of artificial manure, its maltings and corn mills). Local crafts included lacemaking – Buckinghamshire lace was the finest made in the East Midlands – but the industry declined rapidly after lacemaking machines were developed in Nottingham, producing much cheaper lace from the 1850s. Apart from the usual range of shops and industries, the 1887 *Directory* mentions a manufacturer of waterproof oil sheets, a junior reporter, Bucks Direct Dairy Supply Company, a coach builder, a tin man, a livery stable keeper, a music warehouse and a hurdle maker.

Flora's grandfather, Thomas Timms and his wife Martha brought up their children Ann, Jane, Albert and Edwin in Gawcott Road (renamed Mitre Street in the 1881 census), Buckingham on the outskirts of the town, and Flora wrote to Leslie Castle that she visited them regularly as a child. In 1881, Martha, a widow described as 'formerly dressmaker, labourer's widow', was living alone at 15 Mitre Street. Flora also had cousins, the Waine family, who lived close by in Mitre Street, which would tally with the description Flora gave of her cousins living on the edge of town.

John Waine, who was born in 1842 in Launton, was a cousin of Albert's and another potential candidate for the role of 'James Dowland'. He was the eldest son of Clementina Wallington, Martha's younger sister and her husband John Waine who was born in North Leigh, but farmed in Launton from 1842-55, and after that became a labourer. He and Clementina had six other sons and a daughter. John Waine junior was a stonemason, who worked for Henry Harrison, monumental mason, who operated at different times from Cow Fair, High Street, Ford Street and Hunter Street in Buckingham. John was a superb craftsman who worked on churches throughout England, especially in the Oxford region, specialising in

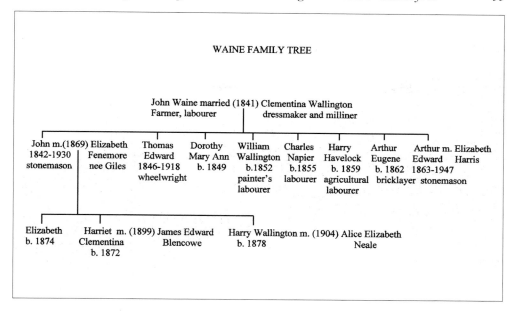

WAINE FAMILY TREE

John Waine married (1841) Clementina Wallington
Farmer, labourer   dressmaker and milliner

John m.(1869) Elizabeth	Thomas	Dorothy	William	Charles	Harry	Arthur	Arthur m. Elizabeth
1842-1930	Fenemore	Edward	Mary Ann	Wallington	Napier	Havelock	Eugene	Edward	Harris
stonemason	nee Giles	1846-1918	b. 1849	b.1852	b.1855	b. 1859	b. 1862	1863-1947
		wheelwright		painter's	labourer	agricultural	bricklayer	stonemason
				labourer		labourer		

Elizabeth   Harriet m. (1899) James Edward   Harry Wallington m. (1904) Alice Elizabeth
b. 1874   Clementina   Blencowe   b. 1878   Neale
                 b. 1872

Waine family tree.

flower and animal sculpture. The cemetery in Brackley Road, Buckingham has a number of gravestones carved between 1890 and 1930 with his trademark flowers, almost certainly carved by him. According to family tradition he carved the font in Buckingham church. He carried on working into his eighties and even carved his own gravestone, which is decorated with three-dimensional flowers including a rose, lily of the valley and fern leaves. He specialised in carving a Celtic-type cross, one of which can be seen on the top of St Bernadine's Convent, London Road, Buckingham, which was built from 1892-4. Perhaps there was a little of him in the stonemason Thomas Hearne of *Still Glides the Stream* (p. 26):

> Hearne had in his day been a first-class workman with experience, skill, and that something beyond skill which is a compound of taste and imagination. His firm had valued his services. When there had been a difficult or a delicate job to be done, it had been given to Hearne as a matter of course. Specimens of his workmanship stood, and some must still be standing, all over that countryside, in the renovated stonework of restored churches, the arches of bridges, stone piers at entrance gates, and on the façades of mansions.

On 8 July 1869 John Waine married Elizabeth Fenemore, a widow and the daughter of butcher John Giles, in Buckingham. John was first described as a butcher in 1861, living in Red House Lane. His wife Harriet was a lacemaker. In 1871 they lived in Gawcott Road. Elizabeth was recorded as working as a boot binder before and after marriage. John and Elizabeth had three children: Harriet Clementina, born in 1872, Elizabeth who was baptised in September 1874 and Harry Wallington Waine, baptised on 21 July 1878. The ages of the girls would fit in with the well-dressed cousins 'Ethel' and 'Alma' whose clothes were passed down to Flora, although admittedly there is no reference in the book to a brother, and the girls did not go up in the world as much as she suggested. Elizabeth became a domestic servant and was working in Streatham, London in 1901 for a builder, later having an illegitimate daughter and Harriet, who was living at home and described as a housekeeper in 1891, married James Edward Blencowe, a labourer of Mixbury in 1899:

Mitre Street, Buckingham looking west from the bottom of Bone Hill. The Timms family lived on the left at No. 15 or nearby, and their Waine cousins opposite at No. 6. (David Watts)

Font in Buckingham church believed to have been carved by stonemason John Waine. (David Watts)

Interior of Buckingham church. (David Watts)

Opposite below: Photograph taken at the wedding of Flora's second cousin Harriet Clementina Waine to James Edward Blencoe on 29 August 1899. Back row, left to right: Harry Wallington Waine (1878–1948), William Winter, Harriet Clementina Waine, (born 1872). Middle row: Elizabeth Waine, (born 1874), and James Edward Blencowe, labourer from Mixbury with his sister Emily Sophia Blencowe seated in front. (David Watts)

The hats were exactly alike and the feathers of the same fullness down to the last strand. The white embroidered muslin dresses they wore were also replicas of each other for it was the fashion then to dress sisters alike, regardless of type. But the girls had seen them and came running towards the spring cart with a twinkle of long, black-stockinged legs and shiny patent-leather best shoes ... Alma was twelve and Ethel thirteen, but their cool, grown-up manner might have belonged to twenty-five and thirty.

Lark Rise to Candleford, pp. 303-4

In the 1881 census the family lived in Mitre Street, Buckingham. In 1899 Harriet Clementina lived at 6 Mitre Street and her brother Harry at No. 13 . The Timms and Waine families must have known one another, both because of their close relationship, and the fact that both men were stonemasons. John's success, compared to Albert's decline in the trade could account for the evident antagonism between the two, and their differences of opinion. John was a morose character, and rather particular and fussy. He could well have had a dislike of alcohol, as did 'James Dowland', because his father was reputed to have drunk away his fortune. He was an active man who claimed to walk round Buckingham four times a day, even in old age, and walked to Launton every Sunday to visit his brother Thomas who was a wheelwright there. He died in 1930, and was buried in Buckingham.

Buckingham has a new link with Flora Thompson, as the Old Gaol Museum has a new display devoted to her which includes her actual typewriter, lent by Henry Westbury, and is building up a Flora Thompson study centre, acquiring her books and memorabilia about her and encouraging study of her work.

The search for the 'real' Candleford is a frustrating one, as the identification of 'Uncle Tom' as Thomas Whiting who lived in Twyford, not Buckingham, means that there are few references which can definitely be ascribed to Candleford itself, and it seems most likely that it was a mixture of places – Flora herself wrote that she had been far less specific in her writing after *Lark Rise*.

Grayshott: Flora's Heatherley

One hot September afternoon near the end of the last century a girl of about twenty walked
without knowing it over the border from Hampshire into one of its neighbouring counties.
She was dressed in a brown woollen frock with a waist-length cape of the same material and
a brown beaver hat decorated with two small ostrich tips, set upright in front, back to back,
like a couple of notes of interrogation. This outfit, which would no doubt appear hideous to
modern eyes, had given her great moral support on her train journey. The skirt, cut short just
to escape contact with the ground and so needing no holding up except in wet weather, was,
her dressmaker had assured her, the latest idea for country wear. The hat she had bought on
her way through London that morning. It had cost her nine and eleven-pence three farthings
of the pound she had saved to meet her expenses until her first month's salary was due in her
new post ... she had special reasons for wishing to make a good impression today, for she had
lately been somewhat unsettled through taking short holiday-relief engagements at the post
offices where she had worked and this new position, she hoped, would prove a permanency.
Her people at home were beginning to speak of her as a rolling stone, and rolling stones were
not in favour with country people of that day.

Heatherley, pp.13-14

Thus Flora began the continuation of her 'autobiography', which remained unpublished until
included in *The Country Calendar* in 1979. It has since been republished as a separate book.
Heatherley takes her away from Oxfordshire, to work in the Post Office for Walter Chapman
in the village of Grayshott, near Haslemere, on the Surrey-Hampshire border. She arrived as
a shy, uncertain girl in September 1898, facing the world miles from her home and family for
the first time. Ironically, although she stayed there only until 1900 or 1901, she came back to
the same area when her husband was appointed sub-postmaster at Liphook in 1916.

Grayshott was then a modern village, which at that time was still a hamlet of Headley. The
name *Gravesetta* occurs in a document of 1185 and *Graveschete* in a Bishop's Register of 1200,
signifying a clearing in a wood. The land was enclosed in 1859, and the site that became the
village had been sold in 1851 to defray the expenses of the Inclosure Commissioners. Part of this
land, the Grayshott Park Estate, was purchased by Edward I'Anson, who built Heather Lodge.
This house was later sold to Mr Vertue, becoming the centre for the local Catholic community
and eventually the Convent of the Centacle. The largest house in the village was Grayshott Hall
Farm, largely rebuilt in the 1890s of local stone dressed with red brick tiles, with its own lodge.
It was renamed Grayshott Hall and owned by Alexander Ingram Whitaker, JP, who had married
Bertha Catherine de Pury, granddaughter of Edward I'Anson in 1895. He was a public-spirited
man who contributed much to the development of Grayshott. Flora probably had him in
mind in describing 'Mr Doddington', who was informally thought of as 'squire'. He was a kind
employer and helped those who were sick or in trouble. The other houses in the area were those

of squatters and fugitives from justice – ironically similar to Juniper Hill at the time of enclosure, as they were considered a rough lot who would prevent Heather Lodge from being completed. The area was far from safe, as related in *Frensham Then and Now* (1938), where the author described how his father was returning home from Haslemere Fair after selling some cattle:

> It was now dusk. Immediately on entering Wagner's Wells Bottom I passed a drove of ponies lying down in the fern, and had only proceeded a few hundred yards when I heard a shrill whistle from my rear. Startled by the sound, the ponies I had just passed came galloping down on me. At once I realised that I had been marked down at the fair. As they overtook me I managed to grasp one of them by his mane and neck and ran beside him. Almost immediately I saw figures emerging from the high furze bushes which grew densely in the narrowest part of the valley. But with the ponies all round me I broke through them safely and reached Simmondstone sound in limb and pocket. I learnt afterwards that the gang who waylaid me were from Blackdown, over the Sussex border ... It was the custom of the Blackdown Gang to work Hindhead, while Hindhead went further afield.

The village was large enough to warrant a postal service in 1867, although all the post was delivered to Edward I'Anson's house for collection from there. The village shop opened in Henry Robinson's Mount Cottage in the 1870s. He sold this house to Edward I'Anson, moving into Crossways (then known as Hindhead Road). People used to collect their letters from his new shop there, and it became the Post Office in 1887.

The population of Grayshott increased rapidly in the later part of the nineteenth century, from 100 in 1872 to 666 in 1901, when there were 143 houses. As the Hindhead area was considered particularly healthy it attracted visitors in the summer. In *Kelly's Directory of Hampshire* for 1899 various shops and businesses are listed in Grayshott, revealing far more variety than Flora would have found in the villages she knew in Oxfordshire, including a fruiterer, beer retailer, draper, grocer and wine and spirit merchant, tobacconist, fishmonger, two butchers, greengrocer, baker and confectioner, draper and bookseller, ironmonger, dressmaker, launderer, saddler, two boot makers, physician, fly proprietor, cycle agent, builder and blacksmith.

It was to the Post Office where Walter Chapman operated as a carpenter, joiner, builder, cabinet maker and stationer that Flora came. This was situated in what is now Crossways Road (but the building was demolished in 1986 and replaced by a block of two shops). Many of the buildings Flora knew are still there, including the shops near the Post Office built in the late nineteenth century with red tile-hanging. The village was described in 1898 by Thomas Wright in *Hindhead*:

> ... Grayshott ... consists of a street of spruce-looking shops situated near a spot where five roads meet, and a number of handsome private residences and palatial lodging houses dotted about in the remains of a forest of glorious larches and Scotch pines ...
>
> Grayshott looks like a doll's village, not so much because of the size of the houses, but because of their quaintness. The upper storeys are covered with lozenge-shaped bright red tiles, made at Haslemere. It has a temporary look, and there is the feeling that one could upset it like a village built with a pack of cards. The tiles, which the damp south-west winds render necessary, are secured to walls built not of brick but of wood covered with felt. The houses are all new, having been erected during the last five or six years. Numbers of persons of distinction reside or have resided at or near Hind Head – famous poets, scientists, journalists, painters.

Most of the Grayshott people had moved from elsewhere – including distant places such as Birmingham and Shropshire – and had no local roots, which Flora felt affected their character and behaviour, as they tended to live 'for the passing moment' and were far more independent and casual in their attitudes than traditional village shopkeepers, and they took less pride in their work.

The Fox and Pelican refreshment house in Grayshott, where Flora sometimes bought her lunches while working at the post office.

One place Flora would have known was a curious 'refreshment house' set up in 1899 by the Grayshott and District Refreshment Association as an alternative to a public house, entitled the 'Fox and Pelican' after Bishop Fox of Winchester, founder of Corpus Christi College, Oxford, whose device was a 'pelican in her piety', feeding her young with the blood from her own breast. The signboard was painted by Walter Crane. The aim was to discourage drunkenness by providing food, tea and coffee, non-alcoholic drinks and light beers, keeping the stronger alcohol out of sight, to be dispensed on request. It was also a place for people to enjoy their leisure and George Bernard Shaw donated a collection of books for a library there.

Working in the Post Office of such a place was a fascinating if somewhat daunting adventure for Flora, because she came across a wide variety of people. She was awed and fascinated by the prominent authors who were among her customers, and she listened attentively to their conversation and longed to share in it:

> She would sometimes wish that one of those quick, clever remarks they tossed like coloured glass balls into the air could have come her way, for in her youthful vanity she persuaded herself that she could have caught and returned it more neatly than someone to whom it was addressed.

Heatherley, pp. 31–32

Among the renowned authors she met in this way were George Bernard Shaw, who had just had a cycling accident, 'a tall man on a crutch, with a forked red beard and quick, searching eyes, surrounded by a group of young men who appeared to be drinking in his every syllable' and Sir Arthur Conan Doyle, an enormously popular man, who in addition to his Sherlock Holmes novels wrote *Sir Nigel*, a medieval romance published in 1910, based on the local area, especially Frensham, Tilford and Waverley Abbey which Flora probably knew. Another author was Grant Allen who had written a scandalous novel, *The Woman Who Did*, which actually dared to mention sexual problems. Flora commented that it was in fact a serious and literary book, which attracted notoriety because 'of its supposed loose morals' and that the scandal made all the locals eager to read it.

Flora also mentions a poet, who 'raced about the parish ... on his bicycle with his halo of long fair hair uncovered and his almost feminine slightness and grace set off by a white silk shirt, big artist's bow tie and velvet knickerbockers', who was Richard le Galliene. The disadvantage of coming into contact with such famous literary figures was that she came to the conclusion that her own writings were so insignificant in comparison that she destroyed much of what she had done.

Flora became friendly with various local characters such as broom squires, who earned their living making besoms, and 'Mr Foreshaw', an elderly gentleman who had been a big-game hunter in Africa, who, John Owen Smith has postulated, may have been John Volckman, who died in 1900 aged sixty-three. John Owen Smith suggests that the brother and sister 'Richard and Mavis Brownlow', visitors to the area whom Flora became very attached to were William Burton Elwes, who was born in Essex in 1878, worked for most of his life for Cable and Wireless, much of his career being abroad, and his sister Lilian. They apparently encouraged Flora to try to take Civil Service exams, which she found too advanced for her and abandoned. The 'Brownlows' were bitterly disappointed at this as they had hoped she would come and work in London, where they lived when she passed them. Flora and 'Richard' grew close, but he confessed to her that he would never be able to afford to marry her.

She also took advantage of her leisure time to explore the countryside around her and the picturesque Waggoner's Wells on the edge of the village became a favourite haunt:

> These three lakes lie along the bottom of a narrow valley, acres of wild heath and woodland surround them on either side; immemorial forest trees line the banks and overhang the still green water, every leaf and twig reflected as in a mirror, so perfect is the image embosomed there that it reminds one irresistibly of the old fabulous drowned forests of legend.

Flora Thompson, *Guide to Liphook, Bramshott and Neighbourhood*

The ponds may have originated as hammer ponds or fishponds created in the seventeenth century by the Hooke family (who were clothiers until Henry Hooke built an iron mill) by damming a stream which formed part of the headwater of the river Wey. The site was purchased by the National Trust in 1919 as a memorial to Sir Robert Hunter, a founder member. They were originally known as Wakener's Wells.

The Post Office

The Post Office was, like the surrounding buildings, red tiled and Flora wrote that the shop window contained a display of attractive leather goods such as writing cases, purses and photograph frames, plus *Bibles* and prayer books. It also sold postcards of local views, which cunningly compared the area to the Swiss Alps to attract more visitors. Flora's responsibility was to look after the Post Office for Walter Chapman, in 'Heatherley' who was busy with his work as a cabinet maker, joiner and carpenter, running the Post Office and stationers as a sideline.

She worked with an eighteen-year-old girl, Sarah Annie Symonds, (called 'Alma Steadman' in *Heatherley*), who was known as Annie to her family, a cheerful girl who soon became a friend. Annie was the daughter of gardener John Symonds, and was born in Liscard, Cheshire in 1879. Her father had moved to Fir Cottage in Shottermill as gardener to Marshall Bulley, bringing his wife Elizabeth, Annie and her brother John, an electrical engineer with him.

The Grayshott Post Office run by Walter Chapman where Flora worked has been demolished, to be replaced by the hip-roofed shops.

Annie was still living there with her family in 1891 while employed as Post Office clerk. Flora dealt with postal matters and the telegraph machine, which she taught Annie to use, and prepared the accounts for Walter Chapman to sign.

In *Heatherley* Flora renamed the Chapman family as the 'Hertfords', perhaps because her employer Walter Gillman Chapman came from Barley in Hertfordshire. He was born in 1856, the son of James Chapman and his wife Mary Ann Dewberry, who married in 1850. James was a carpenter and joiner and publican of the Waggon and Horses in Barley. (Perhaps coincidentally, this is the same name Flora gave to the pub in Juniper Hill). The Chapman's children were George (born in 1851), Annie (born in 1855), Walter, Ernest (born in 1858) and Oliver (born in 1861). In 1861 Oliver was only a month old at the time of the census and a nurse was staying in the house, so Walter and Ernest were staying with their grandfather, Thomas Chapman, a farmer at Great Hormead in Hertfordshire.

Life was not altogether easy for Flora in Grayshott because she lived in the Chapmans' house and soon realised that they were very unhappily married. Walter Gillman Chapman was a dark, rather wild-eyed man who had apparently, according to Flora, fallen in love with a local girl but her parents had not approved of the match so he went to Australia to make his fortune. He planned to come back and marry her, but she died just before his return; he never recovered from his grief at her loss. He spent the next years drifting between England and Australia, and it was not until about twenty years later that he met his wife Emily, who was working as a governess to a family visiting the neighbourhood, and they began to go out together. Their behaviour occasioned gossip and she was sacked from her post, upon which he offered to marry her, although admitting that he did not love her. He certainly disappears from the English census returns after 1871, but otherwise it has not been not possible to verify the details.

When Flora came to Grayshott he was aged about forty-five. He clearly enjoyed his cabinet making, specialising in making up furniture to his customers' individual designs, and undertaking major commissions such as the woodwork for a private Catholic chapel.

His wife Emily, aged thirty-seven was a tall, thin and pale woman, with a love of music. She was born Emily Revelle in Hull in Yorkshire, the daughter of Henry Revelle and his wife Esther. The family was living in Walcot near Bath in 1881, where Henry was a haulier employing a man and a boy. Emily had no job at sixteen, although her fifteen-year-old brother Henry was an errand boy. Her sisters Eva, Ada, Agnes, Florence and Laura aged between twelve and two were also at home. In 1891 Emily was still in Walcot, staying in a boarding house with seventy-three-year-old widow, Oriana Fleming, who was living on her own means, accompanied by her lady's maid Mary Beavis and Laura Anderson from Glamorgan, aged thirty, who was also living on her own means, and Harold Anderson aged five. Emily was described as a nurse, presumably looking after Harold. Also in the lodging house at 29 Chapel Court were the lodging housekeeper, Elizabeth Walbridge, her niece Alice Watts and nephew Arthur Watts, a footman, housemaid Alice Carter, kitchen maid Kate Hurley and a visitor, Mary Toghill, who was a cook.

Perhaps Emily was still working for Mrs Anderson when she met Walter Chapman. The couple married in autumn 1892. Their children were Walter Gillman, born in 1895, Florence Louise, born in 1887, Thomas Gillman, born in 1889, Ethel, born in 1900 and Ernest James, born on 16 June 1901.

Flora soon noticed that the relationship between the couple was strained, with frequent rows. She wrote that she felt like a pig in the middle, particularly when they refused to talk to each other and communicated through her. Walter Chapman was deranged, believing there were intruders in the house at night:

> As far as Laura was concerned, things came to a climax one night after she had gone to bed and heard a loud bang which she thought at first was some kind of explosion. Rushing out on to the landing she found Mrs Hertford, in her nightdress, coaxing her husband back to bed. He held a small revolver in his hand and Mrs Hertford afterwards told Laura that he had thought he heard whispering beneath the landing window, and thinking it was burglars, he had fired his revolver to scare them away. Whether or not the shot scared anyone below, it certainly scared Laura, and she was not at all reassured when, thinking the proper time had come to tell Mrs Hertford about the footsteps she thought she had heard at night and of her impression that someone had been in her room, she was told that it was one of Mr Hertford's habits to prowl about the house at all hours of the night, opening and shutting doors and looking into dark corners with the idea of finding some unnamed enemy he believed was lying in wait for him. He had sometimes been in Laura's room for it was one of his ideas that Laura might be in league with the enemy. When he had this idea he would call his wife up from her sleep to play propriety, and while she stood at the door, he, with a shaded candle in his hand, would creep softly into the room to see if anyone beside Laura was there. Laura, of course, was always alone and in bed with her hair screwed up in Hind's curlers and her face thickly cold-creamed, and so obviously asleep that, for a time, he was pacified.

Heatherley, pp. 87-88

Flora was unnerved by the experience and decided in March 1899 that she must find a room in the village, but promised Mrs Chapman faithfully that she would say nothing of her husband's strange behaviour. Some months later a new telegraph office opened nearby, and there was far less work for Flora, and Walter Chapman could only afford the cheaper wages he paid Annie. In spring 1901 Flora went off to find work elsewhere and in the 1901 census, taken on 31 March, she was working as a Post Office clerk in Yately in Hampshire, living in

Headley Road, one of two principal roads in Grayshott. (John Owen Smith)

the household of William Betterwick (thirty-seven), grocer, baker and sub-postmaster, his wife Jessie and the housemaid Marion Harrison.

Emily Chapman, again pregnant, left home with her four children to stay with her brother-in-law Ernest Chapman, a builder, as she was frightened by her husband's accusations of infidelity and his violence. She and the children lived in rooms over the stables at Gorselands, the boarding house kept by Ernest and his wife Isabella in Bramshott. Just before the baby was due she was persuaded to go back home by Walter, but he soon resumed his accusations. Emily was terrified and confided her fears to the local doctor when the baby was born in June 1901, but he considered Walter not seriously deluded enough to be certifiable.

However on the morning of 29 July 1901 Annie Symonds and Edith Henrietta Smith, working in the Post Office and Gilbert Winchester, Walter's assistant in the workshop, heard screams from the house. Ernest Chapman's evidence at the inquest, reported in *The Herald*, revealed the tragedy that had occurred:

Witness was going to the office on Monday morning last, and was just getting off his bicycle when Gilbert Winchester beckoned to him, and told him something. The time was about a quarter to ten. Witness rushed into the sitting room of the deceased and there he saw the deceased lying by the corner of the table, huddled up. He saw no blood at first, but he went to her, knelt down on the floor, and took her up in his arms, and then he noticed a small pool of blood on the floor. The deceased was not dead then, for she groaned a few times. She was not able to speak, for witness spoke to her and she made no reply. He saw no knife or anything like that about then. Witness subsequently saw his brother, who was upstairs, when some little time later he was brought down by the constable ...

The doctor attested that Emily had been stabbed several times in the chest by a sharp instrument, the shank of which was found embedded four inches in the body.

The trial at the Assizes lasted less than two hours and Walter was adjudged guilty but not responsible for his behaviour due to insanity, and he was sentenced to be detained during His Majesty's pleasure. He was confined in Broadmoor Criminal Asylum and died on 15 September 1921.

Bournemouth: Married Life

Perhaps her unsettling experience with the Chapmans at Grayshott deterred Flora from getting another permanent job for a while, or perhaps such jobs were difficult to find. Whatever the reason, Flora's movements for the next two years, apart from her posting in Yateley in 1901 are uncertain. It was during that time that she met and fell in love with John Thompson, whom she may well have met while working at Yately, as he was working as Post Office clerk at Aldershot, not far away, lodging with Alfred Hoole, a tailor's assistant in St Michael's Road.

Flora and John were married at the church of St Mary the Virgin in Twickenham, London, presumably near where she was living at the time, on 7 January 1903. None of her family were present – Edwin was serving in the army in India, and it would have been a long and expensive journey from Juniper Hill for Albert and Emma Timms.

John Thompson, who was two years older than Flora, being born on 4 April 1874, came from a very different maritime background – Oxfordshire was a long way from the sea, so it was one with which Flora was unfamiliar. John's father Henry Thompson was born in Portsmouth in Hampshire in 1841. He joined the Royal Navy and in 1861 was serving as an Ordinary Seaman aboard the *District Ganges* in the North Atlantic fleet. He rose to the rank of Chief Petty Officer. In autumn 1871 he married Emily Stainer, who also came from a maritime background and he appears to have lived on the income from his naval pension after that.

Emily's father was Henry Stainer or Stayner, who was born at Ryde on the Isle of Wight in 1821. In 1831 he was living at Thanet St Lawrence in Kent, at the coastguard station, employed as a coastguard. He was married to Mary, from Littlehampton in Sussex and their children were: Mary, born in Walmer, Kent in 1845, Emily, born in 1846 at Ringwould, Kent, Mary Ann, born in Kingsdown, Kent in 1847, George and John, born in Thanet St Lawrence in 1849 and 1850. Their next children, Richard, born in 1857, Ellen Matilda, born in 1862, Charles James, born in 1864 and Catherine, born in 1866 were all born in Alverstoke. Curiously from 1871 Henry is renamed George, but all the other details tally, so he is almost certainly the same person. In 1861 the family were living in Alverstoke, Hampshire and Henry was a seaman and coastguard, living at 5 Government Cottages. Ten years later they were in Ryde on the Isle of Wight at 35 Arthur Street, when George was described as a Greenwich pensioner and dairyman. They were still there in 1881, and George was just described as a Greenwich pensioner. In 1991 he was a 'retired mariner', and his son John, who was living with him, was working as a postman. Could he have encouraged the Thompson boys to work in the Post Office? In 1901 George was widowed and living with his daughter Catherine and his son Charles, now a seaman, and his wife Harriett and their five children.

After their marriage Henry and Emily Thompson set up home in Green Street in Ryde. Their first son Henry William was born on 6 October 1872 but died young on 11 February 1899. John William, who later married Flora, was born on 5 April 1874; Emily Matilda was born on 26 November 1875 but died on 28 August 1877; Florence Elizabeth was born on 6

March 1877. In the 1901 census she was living in Westfield Broadway, Sandown on the Isle of Wight, working as a 'cook's general' in the household of retired architect Walter Baker. George was born on 5 February 1879, Mary Annie on 27 August 1881, Rosa Emma on 23 August 1883, Alfred Earnest on 4 January 1886 and Wilfred Albert on 28 November 1887. Amy May, who was born on 5 January 1890, died on 24 March. The last daughter was Amy Gertrude, born on 3 April 1892.

In the 1901 census George was the eldest child living at home, at the age of twenty-two. He had followed John into the Post Office was working as a telegraphist. Annie was a nursemaid, Rose was a dressmaker and Alfred was an errand boy. A grand-daughter, Emily Thompson, aged three, was also living with them.

After their marriage Flora and John Thompson moved into rented accommodation at No. 4 Sedgley Road in Winton, (they later moved to No. 6), a village in the parish of Moordown then on the outskirts of Bournemouth, which has since become a suburb. John was a sorting clerk and telegraphist at the main Post Office in Bournemouth in Beckford Road. Flora, as a married woman, was not permitted to work.

Fortunately she again lived near the countryside, as Winton, like Juniper Hill, had been established on open heathland which was enclosed in 1802. The name was taken from the surname of Winton (a contraction of the Latin name for Winchester) assumed by the Bishop of Winchester, as the area was said to be particularly popular with the bishops. In 1875 Winton was considered big enough to have its own Post Office which opened on the corner of Post Office Road (Castle Road) and Wimborne Road, in the front room of a brick cottage, which was later enlarged to make a double-fronted shop for George Troke's bakery and grocer's shop and Post Office, and a wall letter-box was installed. In the 1880s Winton had a population of over 1,400, and it was growing rapidly when Flora and John arrived there in 1903.

In 1890, thirteen years before Flora and John came to live there, Winton was thus described in the parish magazine:

Perhaps there is no other such place in the world as Winton, in all events it would be difficult to find one. Some of its characteristics it may no longer retain. We mean the beauty of its golden flowers in May and its purple heather in August. Much of this wild natural beauty has already succumbed. But picturesque as are the gorse and the heather and beautiful as are the glimpses of the Stour Valley, with St Catherine's Hill in the distance and grateful is the shade of the Winton Pines in the summer and their shelter in winter, it must be confessed that Winton's unique attraction consists not in these natural beauties which have their counterparts elsewhere, but in the affable style, disposition and arrangements of the working people's houses, such as in the newer parts of the settlement. It would be difficult to find any other place where so much care has been taken to study from a business point of view the precise wants and wishes of our working people as regards their homes. The houses of the great majority of our working people are not usually very attractive ...

Winton is neither country nor town but seems to take practical hints from both. Trees are not favourable to the growth of vegetables and so far the picturesque is a sacrifice to the useful, but the houses themselves are certainly not without their attractiveness, nor is the general view of Peters Hill looking south otherwise than picturesque. In the way of improvement there is of course a great deal to be done. The high road requires to be levelled, there is no public form of any kind of entertainment, no proper cricket ground, the supply of drinking water terminates as though Peters Hill was too much for it. The drainage is still primitive, the lighting though admirable depends on voluntary enterprise – a local committee supplies oil lamps etc. The fire engine like the water cart is conspicuous by its absence. Lastly we are, it is supposed, so orderly that we only require, or at least only get, the services of one resident policeman.

Quoted in S.J. Lands, *The Growth of Winton*, 1970

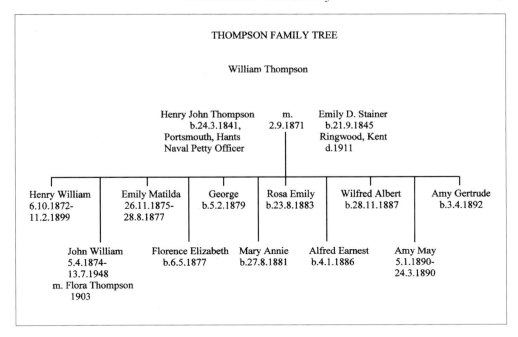

THOMPSON FAMILY TREE

William Thompson

Henry John Thompson	m.	Emily D. Stainer
b.24.3.1841,	2.9.1871	b.21.9.1845
Portsmouth, Hants		Ringwood, Kent
Naval Petty Officer		d.1911

Henry William	Emily Matilda	George	Rosa Emily	Wilfred Albert	Amy Gertrude
6.10.1872-	26.11.1875-	b.5.2.1879	b.23.8.1883	b.28.11.1887	b.3.4.1892
11.2.1899	28.8.1877				

John William	Florence Elizabeth	Mary Annie	Alfred Earnest	Amy May
5.4.1874-	b.6.5.1877	b.27.8.1881	b.4.1.1886	5.1.1890-
13.7.1948				24.3.1890
m. Flora Thompson				
1903				

Thompson family tree.

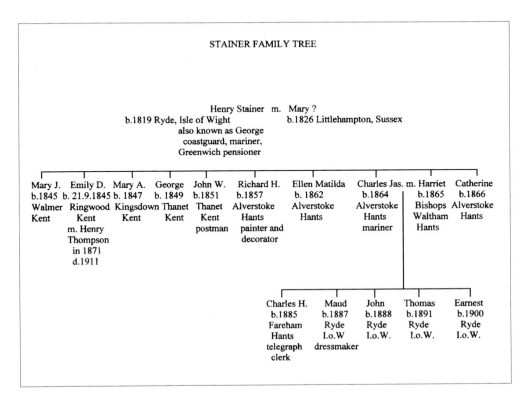

STAINER FAMILY TREE

Henry Stainer	m.	Mary ?
b.1819 Ryde, Isle of Wight		b.1826 Littlehampton, Sussex
also known as George		
coastguard, mariner,		
Greenwich pensioner		

Mary J.	Emily D.	Mary A.	George	John W.	Richard H.	Ellen Matilda	Charles Jas.	m. Harriet	Catherine
b.1845	b. 21.9.1845	b.1847	b. 1849	b.1851	b.1857	b. 1862	b.1864	b.1865	b.1866
Walmer	Ringwood	Kingsdown	Thanet	Thanet	Alverstoke	Alverstoke	Alverstoke	Bishops	Alverstoke
Kent	Kent	Kent	Kent	Kent	Hants	Hants	Hants	Waltham	Hants
	m. Henry			postman	painter and		mariner	Hants	
	Thompson				decorator				
	in 1871								
	d.1911								

Charles H.	Maud	John	Thomas	Earnest
b.1885	b.1887	b.1888	b.1891	b.1900
Fareham	Ryde	Ryde	Ryde	Ryde
Hants	I.o.W	I.o.W.	I.o.W.	I.o.W.
telegraph	dressmaker			
clerk				

Stainer family tree.

Wimborne Road, close to the various houses where the Thompsons lived during their time in Winton, had many purpose-built shops, and they had other shops nearby in Talbot Village Road. There was such a wealth of choice that it must have been like living in a small town.

For the first few months Flora delighted in taking long walks to explore the area around her new home. She lived on the edge of Winton, so it did not take long to get to the countryside. One of her favourite walks was to Talbot Village, a model village established in the mid-nineteenth century not far from Winton by Miss Georgina Talbot who is described on her memorial cross in St Mark's church in the village:

> She came of an ancient race, and possessed in herself that nobility of mind which delighted in the happiness of her fellow creatures ... In the neighbourhood of the village she passed twenty-five years of a blameless life, giving up time and fortune to bettering the condition of the poorer classes, seeking to minister to their temporal and spiritual welfare, and erecting habitations suitable to their position in life, herself enjoying a peaceful and happy existence in doing good, awaiting the end.

Quoted in Chas. H. Mate and Chas. Riddle, *Bournemouth 1810-1910* (1910)

Talbot Village had nineteen Gothic cottages each with an acre of garden, even a church and school. The inhabitants had to conform to strict rules of behaviour, the compensation being better accommodation than normally available.

Flora was always interested in literary associations, and another walk she took was to Skerryvore, where Robert Louis Stevenson lived from April 1885 until 1887. The house was given to Mrs Stevenson by her father-in-law and renamed after the lighthouse the family firm had built off the Argyll coast. Despite his illness, Stevenson continued to work, and several of his most famous books were written there. He left Bournemouth to holiday abroad in August 1887, never to return. However his house was remembered. Flora wrote of it years later:

> Skerryvore stands just as he left it. Memorial tablets to his pet dogs bear witness to his love for all living creatures. In their season rhododendron blooms make vivid splashes of colour against the dark pines that once delighted his artist soul. From the upper windows may still be seen the glimpse of the sea that he delighted to point out to his guests. Only he, the life and soul of it all, has gone.

The Catholic Fireside, 5 June 1920, vol. XVIII, no. 1594

Skerryvore was damaged in an air raid in 1940 and subsequently demolished and replaced by a memorial garden.

Flora and John's first child, Winifred Grace, was born in the autumn of 1903. She was christened on 7 August 1904 in St John's church in Moordown. Later in life Winifred preferred to be called Diana. Although Flora could no longer take long solitary walks, with a small baby in tow, and her life must have changed drastically, she continued to read as much as she possibly could, buying cheap second-hand books when she could afford them. She must have been delighted when a new public lending library opened in Winton in 1907. At this time she was not actively writing, but must have been storing up ideas and memories for future use.

Henry Basil Thompson was born on 6 October 1909. That year the family, still in rented accommodation, moved a couple of streets away to 2 Edgehill Road, calling their new home Grayshott Cottage. They had a convenient and comfortable house with a garden, but in some ways Flora seems to have missed the cottage of her childhood with its rag rugs. She still considered herself an onlooker in society, not making many close friends.

It was in 1910 that Flora felt ready to begin writing. She began buying *The Ladies Companion*, attracted by its book club which encouraged readers to read both the classics and

Flora with her son Basil. (Henry Westbury)

good modern English literature. She was fascinated by the literary competitions they ran, and resolved to try her hand at them. The first one Flora entered was in February 1911, on Jane Austen, one of her favourite authors. She must have been astounded when she won the prize – any book of her choice up to the cost of five shillings, and the joy of seeing most of her essay in print:

> Before Jane Austen began to write, the novelists of her day had depended on involved plots, sensational incident, and the long arm of coincidence; therefore when these quiet, gentle stories appeared, dealing with everyday people and events, the public did not immediately recognise her genius or appreciate the gentle sarcasm that plays around her characters. It is true that her genius was at once recognised by a few of the greatest men and women of her time. Sir Walter Scott admired her work exceedingly, so did Sydney Smith, the Countess of Morley and, strange to say, the Prince Regent. She found herself, indeed, her own public of devoted admirers, but was then as now 'caviar to the general' ... Jane Austen compared herself to a painter on ivory, and the enjoyment of her work is something like the possession of an exquisite miniature. Those who appreciate her art consider no praise too high. Those who do not, simply wonder how anyone can wade through the dull, tame pages, for no one loves Jane Austen moderately.

The Ladies Companion, February 1911

Flora's writing career had begun gloriously, winning her first competition. Her essay shows that she had done her research thoroughly and methodically, reading as much around the subject as she could. She carried on entering the competitions, winning joint second prize in April for an essay on Emily Brontë and had a mention for her writing on Catherine of Aragon at the end of April, winning again in July on the topic of Shakespeare's Juliet, and her successes continued.

That spring she took her two children for a trip on the train to the New Forest, while John was away at a conference of the United Kingdom Postal Clerks' Association. She loved the area, and when she came to write her nature essays for *The Catholic Fireside*, the first twelve were set in the New Forest, with her usual perceptive comment, such as the importance of forest rights to the commoner who relied on such ancestral rights as digging turf and collecting fallen branches to augment his meagre income.

Flora must have made many visits to the New Forest while she lived at Bournemouth to acquire the material for these articles. She also used the New Forest setting for the first short story she had published, *The Toft Cup*, about the discovery of a valuable cup which saved an old lady from poverty, which appeared in *The Ladies Companion* in January 1912, and in an unpublished novel, *Gates of Eden*. Flora was delighted to be earning money for her work, and determined to earn as much as she could to help pay for her children's education.

One competition she entered in 1912 had a pivotal influence on her future life. She commented on an ode written by the poet Dr Ronald Campbell Macfie on the sinking of the *Titanic*. Dr Macfie not only wrote to Flora to say how much he appreciated what she had written, but came to see her in Bournemouth. He was a medical doctor who specialised in the treatment of tuberculosis, and he told Flora he had decided not to marry so that he would be able to concentrate on his writing. He greatly encouraged Flora for many years in her writing of poetry, becoming a very close friend; she did not find it easy to make close friendships and valued his very deeply. It was through his influence that she later began the Peverel Society.

The Thompsons moved again in 1915 to 42 Frederica Road in Winton, two streets away from their original home in Sedgley Road, a detached suburban house, built close to its neighbours on either side, with a gabled roof, and decorative tile-hanging between the upper and lower bay windows, reminiscent of Grayshott. Flora later wrote of this house:

> Some years ago I was living in a house on the outskirts of Bournemouth, one room of which had a French window opening on to a small lawn with a grassy bank running round it. On this bank I planted dozens of clumps of snowdrops, having them brought specially by gipsies from the New Forest, and adding to them year by year. I left the neighbourhood rather hurriedly at midsummer and the snowdrops were forgotten, but mixed with my regrets for my snowdrops the next winter was a certain pleasure in imagining the new tenants' surprise when they found their grassy banks snowed over with the flowers.

Flora Thompson, *The Peverel Papers*, p. 35

In 1915 too, *The Ladies Companion* ceased publication, because of the First World War. Flora did not want to lose the money she had been earning, so she wrote articles for newspapers, more short stories and poems.

A little while after Flora heard that her beloved brother Edwin had been killed in action in Belgium, John Thompson decided to apply for a new job as sub-postmaster in Liphook, not far from where Flora had worked at Grayshott. Perhaps he was influenced in his choice by Flora's grief, feeling that the change would help her, and by the knowledge of how much she loved the area. He was given the job, and in August 1916 they moved to Liphook, hence the reference above to having to leave her newly planted snowdrops.

Liphook and Griggs Green:
The Peverel Papers

John Thompson was promoted to sub-postmaster when he and Flora moved to Liphook in August 1916. Their Post Office was in the main street in the building now used by the Midland Bank. They were provided with a small house which Flora called Ruskin House next to the Post Office which was refurbished for them, with new grates in the sitting rooms and a Kitchener range in the kitchen. The Thompson family lived there for about ten years until 1926 when they bought their own house at nearby Griggs Green.

Flora grew to know and love Liphook well, and as her writing developed became well-known enough locally to be asked to write a guidebook which was published in about 1925. This gives a fascinating glimpse of the village as Flora knew it:

> The Hampshire village of Liphook stands upon the London to Portsmouth road at the junction of three counties, Hampshire, Surrey, and Sussex; forty-four miles from London on the one hand and twenty-five from Portsmouth on the other ...
>
> Lying upon the borders of three of the most beautiful counties in the South of England the district around Liphook combines within itself the attractions of the whole three. The moorland pine and heather of Hampshire; the leafy vales, deep lanes and sparkling watercourses of Surrey; the turf and thyme-scented chalk downs of Sussex, all are within easy reach by foot, cycle or car ...
>
> In the heart of this lovely country, the white walls of its principal buildings tree-embowered, its roads wide and clean, its gardens bright with flowers and pleasant with healthy faces, at a point where six roads meet and form the 'loop' from which it was probably named, stands the village of Liphook.
>
> Technically speaking, it is not a village at all, but a hamlet of the neighbouring, but much smaller village of Bramshott.

> Flora Thompson, *Guide to Liphook, Bramshott and Neighbourhood*

Flora went on to describe the village square dominated by the Anchor Inn, an old coaching house with a Georgian façade, where such illustrious people as Samuel Pepys and Smollet had stayed. It could even boast of receiving royalty, as in 1815 the Prince Regent entertained the allied sovereigns there to celebrate victory at the Battle of Waterloo, and later the young Princess Victoria had bowed to the crowds from an upper window.

Perhaps she was reminded of distant Fringford when she wrote of the old smithy on the opposite side of the square:

> The smithy is very ancient, as the outside appearance testifies, but, even so, it must have been built to replace an even earlier one, for antique documents mention a forge of some kind upon the site as early as the beginning of the fifteenth century.

Liphook Post Office. (Henry Westbury)

Probably the days of the present one are numbered, for, after being in the occupation of one family for two centuries the ashes are cold, the anvil silent. A large and prosperous motor garage a few yards farther on provides for the different needs of the twentieth-century traveller by the Portsmouth road.

Flora Thompson, *Guide to Liphook, Bramshott and Neighbourhood*

She goes on to describe the other parts of the hamlet, including the elms and beeches of Chitley Park and the ancient Ship Inn which made up the old part, and the newer villas of Headley Road, the Newtown area of shops and houses, even a golf course, adding to the amenities:

The social life of the place is very pleasant. Between twenty and thirty large country houses and estates, many of them of great beauty and interest, lie within the postal delivery ... For the village there is a tennis club with well-appointed courts, cricket and football clubs, the latter of more than local repute: a Village Hall where dances are held and concert and theatrical companies give constantly changing performances: the Boy Scout and Girl Guide movements are especially flourishing, while the Women's Institute, there as elsewhere, has worked wonders in brightening village life.

Enough it is hoped, has been said to prove that at Liphook may be found fine air and natural beauty in fullest measure without the least sacrifice of personal comfort; peace and quiet without stagnation; and that it is no mushroom pleasure place sprung up in a few months to batten upon the health or pleasure seeker, but an old English village, a centre, small but exquisite, where the art of entertaining is hereditary.

Flora Thompson, *A Guide to Liphook, Bramshott and Neighbourhood*

It is evident from her guidebook how much she loved the area, and how well she grew to know all the best walks, finding her own favourite spots such as Weaver's Down:

> Gilbert White describes Weaver's Down as 'a vast hill on the eastern side of Woolmer' and although the 'vastness' of it fails to impress modern eyes, its wild and rugged beauty is unaltered. It is a land of warm sands, of pine and heather and low-lying bog lands; a stretching moor through which the spur of the South Downs, terminating in the little rounded hill, rising like a miniature mountain upon the Liphook side, runs like a back-bone.
>
> From the summit upon a clear day a magnificent view rewards the climber: heath and woodland, green field and glinting stream lie stretched at his feet, a perfect panorama of beauty. Forestmere Lake lies like a mirror in the woods directly beneath; to the south is the blue ridge of the South Downs; to the north the heathery heights of Hindhead.'

Flora Thompson, *A Guide to Liphook, Bramshott and Neighbourhood*

The guide is full of advertisements which indicate the varied commercial aspect of Liphook, such as hotels, (the Railway Hotel offered: 'good accommodation for golfing, cyclists, touring and char-a-banc parties. Moderate terms on application to the proprietor, E.W. Bosley. Within easy distance of the fine Liphook golf links. Motors and Carriages at most Moderate Charges...'), builders, surveyors and undertakers, a garage, blacksmith and printers. There was a wide variety of shops including two clock and watch makers and jewellers, a boot and shoemaker and an upholsterer. Stationery and ironmongery were available from The People's Stores in the square, while H. Budd who sold beekeepers' supplies was also a carpenter, painter and house decorator.

Many shops sold food: including various 'provision merchants' and even department stores including the General Supply Stores who claimed to be 'the leading dry goods store in the district, departments include ladies' and children's outfitting, millinery, hosiery and boots, furniture (new and second-hand and antique), beds and bedding, hardware, china, soaps and polishes'.

Plaque on the wall of Liphook Post Office commemorating Flora Thompson.

Miss A.B. Skevington was head teacher of the Day School for Girls and Preparatory School for Boys in Liphook where she offered: 'sound education on modern lines. Pupils prepared for public examination if desired. The curriculum includes all ordinary subjects, and Latin, French, drawing, nature study, class singing, handwork and needlework. Visiting mistresses for games, music and dancing. Private lessons in literature, French and Latin by arrangement.'

Despite being described as a hamlet, it was a far cry from Juniper Hill which could only boast the little shop in the back room of the inn.

The Thompsons moved to Liphook at a difficult time, as Flora was grieving after the death of her beloved brother Edwin and war brought extra duties for both John and herself in the Post Office. It was fortunate that they lived next door so that the post could be brought in to Flora at 4 a.m. each morning for sorting, while Winifred and Basil were still asleep, and for Clara Louise Woods to collect at 5.45 a.m., ready to cycle the twenty-mile delivery round which she did twice a day. Clara, the daughter of a gardener, was born in Bramshott in 1897 so she knew the local area well. Perhaps she decided to be a postman because in 1901 the family had a boarder, Mark Collins, aged thirty-five, who described himself as a rural postman.

John had to spend many nights sleeping on an uncomfortable camp bed in the Post Office in case telegrams came through. He had a rather military manner, perhaps inherited from his naval father, and was a strict but fair man. In his spare time he relaxed by going fishing.

It is ironic that much of the wartime mail was for Canadian soldiers stationed at nearby Bramshott, which must have reminded Flora constantly of the death of Edwin, who had been in the Canadian army.

Rather to her surprise and perhaps initial dismay, she found herself pregnant again at forty, and once her beloved son Peter Redmond was born money was tight; they had not anticipated any more children so all the baby equipment had to be bought again. Time, too, was at a

Canadian graves at Bramshott near Liphook. The presence of Canadian soldiers near Liphook must have reminded Flora constantly of her brother Edwin's death. (John Owen Smith)

Flora's son Peter Redmond with her sister
Elizabeth, *c.* 1926. (Henry Westbury)

premium with three children. Despite the arduous Post Office work, the household chores
and task of bringing up her family, Flora managed to snatch time to write in her own haven
– a little room, sparsely furnished with her desk, chair and waste-paper basket, where she could
read and write in peace.

After the war Flora was released from the chore of sorting the mail and Winifred and Basil
were at school so she was able to continue her personal development, improving her writing
by becoming a student on a postal course run by the Practical Correspondence College in
London. It was probably through this that Flora began writing for *The Catholic Fireside*, which
was to be influential in her career, giving her the scope to write about the nature she loved
so much; she gradually began to incorporate into her articles the memories of her childhood
which were to develop into *Lark Rise to Candleford.* The first writing she had published in *The
Catholic Fireside*, in 1920, was a rewritten romantic story with a medieval theme entitled *The
Leper*, (which had previously appeared in 1913 in *The Literary Monthly*), then she began her
series of nature articles in 1921.

Flora gave herself a new persona as author of these pieces, explaining to her readers that she
was a doctor's daughter who lived in a little cottage in the New Forest, perhaps because she
felt her real background would make her seem inferior to her middle-class readers.

Flora at this time achieved local fame in Liphook when her slim volume of poetry, *Bog
Myrtle and Peat*, was published in 1921. The *Daily Chronicle* of 2 March 1921 described her in
a headline as 'Woman of Letters. Village Postmistress Poetess – Her First Volume', going on
to say:

> The people of Liphook have always believed that with the pleasant situation of their village,
> and the natural beauties of their countryside, they had enough for proper local pride. Now
> they find that they possess a hitherto undiscovered and unsuspected poetess.

One can imagine Flora's embarrassment at reading this, as she was still a very shy, private person, but it caused great amusement in the family. In her heart of hearts, Flora longed to be a good poet, but although *Bog Myrtle and Peat* was well reviewed it did not sell very well, and the quality of her poetry did not match that of her prose.

In 1922 the character of her writing for the *Catholic Fireside* changed, to concentrate on nature, and her middle-class persona was no longer used. Her essays were retitled *The Peverel Papers* – no one has definitively explained how she chose the name. She continued the series for six years. Most of her writing was based on the walks she enjoyed around Weaver's Down, Waggoner's Well and Wheatsheaf Common. Flora liked to incorporate historical anecdotes into her writing, such as this one, about Woolmer Forest, close to where she later lived:

> At noon I rested upon a smooth mound, still known as Queen's Bank, though few remember it as the spot where Queen Anne, turning aside from the main road on her way seaward, condescended to rest and behold the magnificent herd of five hundred red deer, which were rounded up and driven through the valley for the pleasure of their royal owner.
>
> The forest was old in Queen Anne's day. Along the valley she overlooked from her bank the young Black Prince must often have passed with his hawk and hounds in the days when his parents had a hunting lodge close by. And even that older Woolmer was but a section cut from the still older forest of Andredswold, which stretched, a great wold-infested wilderness, from the borders of Kent to the Hampshire Downs.
>
> There are no red deer in Woolmer today. The fine herd of five hundred had dwindled to fifty by the middle of the eighteenth century, and these were eventually captured and carried in carts to Windsor.

The Peverel Papers, p. 175

Flora's deep love for and sensitive observation of the area is shown in this description of one of her favourite haunts, the Hermit's Pool:

> In the woods by the Hermit's Pool this glamorous quiet is especially noticeable. Scarce a leaf stirs or a wavelet ripples; the air is warm and heavy with the dank colours of tree-bark, moss and waterweeds. Over the long vistas of the narrow pathways a light fleece of greyish-purple mist floats until midday, even when the sky above the tree-tops is gold-shot with sunshine and the heath outside crackling dry with heat. The beeches upon the shore of the lake are already in their full October glory of gold and russet and amber, every leaf and twig so faithfully reflected in the still waters that it seems that a second beechwood is submerged there, like one of the old drowned forests of legend.

The Peverel Papers, p. 180

Peverel had another significance for Flora. Once Peter started school in 1923 she found she had some additional time, and suggested to *The Catholic Fireside* that she start the Fireside Reading Circle, for which she wrote well-researched literary essays, and organised writing competitions. Through this she became friendly with Mildred Humble-Smith, who entered the competitions. Mildred was the daughter of a ship's chandler and nautical instrument maker from Newcastle upon Tyne, and like Flora was married, and had two sons. She had studied English in Oxford, although as Oxford did not confer degrees on women at that time her degrees were nominally from Edinburgh and Durham. Her husband had left the Brazilian Navy and the family settled in Wimborne, Dorset, so she and Flora were able to meet, and as they became close friends they formed the Peverel Society together and she ended the Fireside Reading Circle in November 1925.

Flora's daughter Winifred. (Henry Westbury)

The annual subscription of their new circle, the Peverel Society, which catered for poets and prose writers, was 7s 6d. A brochure for the society, written later when she was living in Dartmouth, described how it operated: saying that it was formed 'for the mutual pleasure and advantage of writers, and those learning to write for the press'. The members would each submit a story, article or poem to the secretary by the beginning of each month. The secretary divided these into groups according to individual requirements and made up a portfolio for each group. These were circulated from one member of the group to the next, each one writing comments on the work before sending it on. The aim was for each member to get a variety of sympathetic comments on the work sent in. A 'Chats Book' was included with the portfolio, giving ideas on how to find the right markets for the work, discussing literary topics and answering queries. Flora hoped that in this way the writers would form friendships.

Membership built up to over 100 people from all over Britain, some being established writers, others novices. The brochure ended: 'a hearty welcome and the helping hand of friendly criticism awaits you!'

It was while she was at Liphook that Flora found another avenue for her talents, answering an advertisement in a literary journal for a ghost writer to a big-game hunter, and writing articles for him which appeared in *Chamber's Journal*, the *Scottish Field* and various African papers. The influence of this can be seen in some of her writing in *Lark Rise*, particularly the pig-killing scene:

> The killing was a noisy, bloody business, in the course of which the animal was hoisted to a rough bench that it might bleed thoroughly and so preserve the quality of the meat. The job was often bungled, the pig sometimes getting away and having to be chased; but country people of that day had little sympathy for the suffering of animals, and men, women and children would gather round to see the sight.
>
> After the carcass had been singed, the pig-sticker would pull off the detachable, gristly, outer coverings of the toes, known locally as 'the shoes', and fling them among the children, who scrambled for, then sucked and gnawed them, straight from the filth of the sty and blackened by fire as they were.
>
> The whole scene, with its mud and blood, flaring lights and dark shadows, was a savage as anything to be seen in an African jungle...
>
> But, hidden from the children, there was another aspect of the pig-killing. Months of hard work and self-denial were brought on that night to a successful conclusion. It was a time to rejoice, and rejoice they did, with beer flowing freely and the first delicious dish of pig's fry sizzling in the frying-pan.

Lark Rise to Candleford, p. 26

As well as the reference to the African jungle, this quotation illustrates another important aspect of Flora's work – it would have been easy to have seen the late Victorian era, as many writers have done, in a rosy glow, but all the way through *Lark Rise to Candleford* are little asides like the one above, which show Flora's clear understanding of the arduous aspects of life endured by the villagers.

Flora is commemorated in Liphook by a charming memorial sculpture, created by Philip Jackson, and presented by the Bramshott and Liphook Preservation Society. It is taken from the wistful photograph of Flora as a young woman, and evocatively portrays her shy, rather diffident character. It is now housed in the library as it was sadly vandalised when left outside. The original statue was unveiled in 1981 and a renovated version put in the library in 1995.

Griggs Green

In 1926 a night time switchboard operator was appointed by the Post Office to help John, which made it easier for him to live further away from work. The Thompsons decided to buy a house of their own for the first time, instead of living in Post Office accommodation. Through Flora's influence they found a house at Griggs Green, a place she already knew well and had grown to love from her walks:

The sculpture of Flora Thompson by
Philip Jackson, commissioned by the
Bramshott and Liphook Preservation
Society, housed in Liphook Library.

The older portion of the hamlet of Griggs Green, (one mile from the square) consists chiefly
of a smithy, an inn, and a row of whitewashed cottages standing back from the road upon a
tree-shaded green. The inn, The Deer's Hut, was, as its name implies, one of the old forest
ale-houses, nor has its function altered much, for neighbours from the scattered houses upon
the heath still meet there upon summer evenings to take their glass and discuss things upon
the Green before the door, just as their forebears must have done for centuries.

To reach Weaver's Down, leave the Longmoor Road at The Deer's Hut, and take the
footpath which passes its doorway. Just a fringe is left there of the old primeval forest oak and
holly and immemorial yew, but very soon this is left behind and the open heath of which
Woolmer at this day chiefly consists lies spread before the wayfarer ... the geologist, naturalist
or beauty-lover will each find a happy hunting ground there, and one that has scarcely been
touched since Gilbert White wrote of it.

Flora Thompson, *Guide to Liphook, Bramshott and Neighbourhood*

John Thompson had to take out a mortgage of £675 to buy the three-bedroomed house in
Longmoor Road called Woolmer Gate. It was a comfortable little red-tiled cottage, rural in feel,
with pine trees behind. She delighted in the peaceful surroundings and easy access along the sandy
paths to her beloved Weaver's Down, where she was often accompanied by her now grown-up
daughter Winifred. She was working split shifts from nine in the morning until one and again
from four thirty in the afternoon until eight, operating the Post Office telephone exchange.

The Thompsons were fortunate in their neighbours, the Leggett family, who lived at Grove House. They often let Peter visit them at the farm, which he loved, and which gave Flora peace and quiet to write. Eileen Leggett, who was sixteen when the Thompsons moved to Griggs Green, was offered a job as part-time operator of the telephone exchange through Flora's influence.

At this time one of Flora's sisters, Betty, who was also a writer, often came to stay. She had a book published long before Flora, a story about gnomes on Dartmoor, written for children and entitled *The Little Grey Men of the Moor*. Flora must have been enormously proud of her sister's achievements, and perhaps it encouraged her to think more of writing books herself.

Having settled so comfortably in their own home, in such perfect surroundings, it was a cruel shock for Flora when John announced that he had been offered the job of postmaster in Dartmouth in Devon; which he had applied for secretly, without consulting her. It was a good career move for him, offering a greatly improved salary and promotion, perhaps his last chance of it, as he was then fifty-three, but for Flora it was a bitter blow. John was presented with a cheque for £40 when he left, and described fulsomely in the *Haslemere Herald* on 12 November 1927. 'All wished to show their appreciation of Mr Thompson's work as postmaster during his eleven years stay among them,' wrote a reporter for the *Herald*, adding that people had 'always found him courteous, obliging and willing to help whenever possible' (quoted in John Owen Smith, *On the Trail of Flora Thompson*).

Fortunately Flora had a stay of execution before she had to uproot herself, as it took time for them to sell the house and John was unable to find anywhere suitable for them to live straightaway, so she, Winifred and Peter were able to stay at Woolmer Cottage for almost a year longer.

The move saw the end of her *Peverel Papers* series, the last one being published in December 1927. Eventually the move was organised and the day that Flora left there was torrential rain all day, echoing her sadness at leaving. The rain gave the house and grounds a desolate feel, with the rain dripping from the trees, and there was scarcely even time to visit the grave of a beloved dog in the garden because the taxi was waiting to take them to the railway station for their long journey down to Devon and their new life.

Dartmouth and Brixham:
Lark Rise is Born

Flora was devastated to leave the house in Griggs Green that she had loved so much to come to Devon, where she spent the rest of her life, but she gradually grew to enjoy the area. John, having been brought up on the Isle of Wight, was delighted to be near the sea again, and soon bought himself a little motor boat, the *Sea Mew*, in which he and Peter went fishing.

Their new house, called The Outlook, was on the hillside above the main part of the town in an area called Above Town. A blue plaque now marks the fact that Flora lived there. It was so steep that the house had to be reached by some steps, making furniture removal hard work. The area was criss-crossed with little alleys and from the house there were wonderful views towards Kingswear, the town of Dartmouth itself, and the estuary leading down to the sea. John built Flora a special room where she could write in the garden.

The Dartmouth area has been settled since Saxon times and has a rich legacy of history, greatly influenced by its natural harbour. The Normans used it as their main base in the area; William Rufus, hearing that his town of Le Mans was under siege while he was hunting on Dartmoor, sailed to the rescue from Dartmouth in 1099, and seven ships set off to the Third Crusade from here in 1190. Geoffrey Chaucer visited the town, and his character, the Shipman in the Prologue of *The Canterbury Tales* is said to have been based upon the local merchant John Hawley.

The town was protected by a castle and Edward IV decreed that the haven should be protected by a chain across it. In the sixteenth century the *Crescent* from Dartmouth engaged Spanish ships off Start Point during the campaign against the Spanish Armada.

Trade was also important; fish, wine and tin being major commodities. It was from here that the explorer Sir Humphrey Gilbert set out on voyages of discovery in 1578 and again in 1583, with Sir Walter Raleigh. It was from here too that the first journey of the East India Company set out in 1601.

As it had such a close association with the sea it is hardly surprising that ship building flourished here at Sandquay from the early nineteenth century. It was at Sandquay that Philip and Son, the ship builders who later employed Flora's son Peter, set up in 1858. A further indication of the town's important links with the sea was the opening in 1905 of the Britannia Royal Naval College in Dartmouth.

Flora's interest was more in the countryside around her than the history of the town, and she soon began to explore her surroundings. She was very fond of the coastal area round St Petrox church and Castle Cove. St Petrox began life as a small monastery at the mouth of the river Dart, first mentioned in 1192, which seems to have maintained a beacon to guide shipping away from the rocks. The church was rebuilt in 1641, and used to house provisions for the castle during the Civil War. By Flora's time it was only used for occasional services during the summer. The tiny church has dramatic impact, with water coming right up to the walls of the churchyard, which are crenellated like the castle. The cove is named after Dartmouth Castle, which, when it was built between 1481 and 1495 to replace an earlier one built in the late

Left: Site of the post office in Dartmouth where John Thompson worked.

Below: The Outlook, Flora and John's house in Dartmouth, which overlooked the harbour.

Opposite: Plaque on The Outlook put there to commemorate Flora Thompson and to celebrate the millennium.

fourteenth century, was highly advanced in style, being the first English castle designed for use with firearms, with rectangular 'gunports' (through which the weapons could be fired) similar to those on contemporary warships covering the area of the Dart estuary. It consists of one cylindrical and one square tower adjacent to each other, set on the rocky riverbank, facing Kingswear Castle, which is now a private house, on the opposite bank.

Flora and John discovered the delights of Dartmoor together, walking in Wistman's Woods, near Two Bridges, with its ancient wizened oak trees, covered in lichen, now a nature reserve, which must have enchanted her.

Flora continued with her writing, concentrating on short stories and books, most of which were never published, and running the Peverel Society. She was yet to find her real niche. She suffered a great personal blow when her mentor and sympathetic friend Dr Macfie died in 1931, as she had benefited greatly from his encouragement of her writing. He was one of the few people she could talk to about her writing and he was sorely missed for the rest of her life. In 1944 she wrote to Leslie Castle:

> I am sorry to hear you have lost your friend for I know well what a blank such losses mean; although you may find others afterwards that you like as well it is never in quite the same way. The chief friend of my life was a Scotsman, Doctor Ronald Macfie, and I lost him by death ten years ago, a loss never to be replaced.

It was not until 1935, two years after her mother Emma's death, when she herself was nearly 59, that she began to consider seriously writing about her childhood, making a start by noting down details of some of the rhymes connected with the children's games. Possibly the fact that she had been removed from her 'comfort zone' writing about the natural history of the Liphook area focused her mind on her own past.

Perhaps stimulated by these thoughts of her childhood, Flora sent off a story entitled *The Tail-less Fox*, which she had written at Liphook, about a poor woman with six children, to *The Lady*, perhaps to test the waters to see whether there was a market for such work. She

This photograph is believed by members of the Thompson family to be Flora and John Thompson. (The Old Gaol Museum, Buckingham)

must have been delighted when it was published in 1936, and capitalised on it by sending off an article on Queenie, the lacemaker she had known in Juniper Hill, which was published in April 1937.

She wrote fourteen more essays about her childhood, narrated by her alter ego Laura, and then she plucked up the courage to send them to Oxford University Press, perhaps a strange choice as they had a policy of not publishing fiction. However, Sir Humphrey Milford, the publisher, was immediately aware of the value of her work, and encouraged her to amplify what she had written into a book, and agreed to publish it as an autobiography. Flora was such an unassuming person that she would never have written an autobiography in the strict sense, to draw attention to herself, but by making herself the onlooker on the local scene, depicted the places and life around her, using her creative talents to embellish them, and disguise personalities. Geoffrey Cumberlege was her editor, and he became a friend over the years. They collaborated over her work. Lynton Lamb was commissioned to visit the Juniper Hill area and make ten pen and ink drawings to illustrate the book.

The Press published *Lark Rise* in March 1939, and Flora must have been delighted to find it favourably reviewed in such prestigious publications as *Country Life*, *The Yorkshire Post*, *The Sunday Times*, *The Times Literary Supplement* and *Time and Tide*. The accolades give great credit to a woman who, despite her background, achieved evocative writing about her own experience which is still popular half a century after her death.

Flora carried on writing, continuing the tale of her childhood with *Over to Candleford*, which expanded on her visits to her relatives in Twyford and Buckingham. However, she could not be unaffected by events in the outside world, as Britain drifted inexorably towards war

Above: Leslie Castle with Flora Thompson's typewriter, which he inherited. It is now displayed in The Old Gaol Museum, Buckingham. (Henry Westbury)

Right: Winifred Thompson, Flora and John's daughter, who became Flora's literary executor. (Henry Westbury)

with Germany, which was finally declared in September. The Thompsons were painfully aware of the dangers of their situation in Dartmouth and were fearful for the safety of the children. Winifred was on holiday in Switzerland when war was declared but accomplished the journey home without any problems, and was amazed when she got home to read in the newspapers that other travellers had encountered insults and hindrances. Basil was in Australia with his family, but Peter was drawn into the war, at first working long hours in Philip's shipyard, then joining the Merchant Navy.

Dartmouth was drastically affected by the Second World War. Philip's yard had to be guarded by the army and during the war converted many boats for naval use. This obviously made the town a prime target for bombs, and the shipyard and the Naval College were both hit in 1942. The naval students were removed to Cheshire. Two years later the college buildings became the headquarters for American forces.

Flora had to abandon her writing for days to make black-out curtains for the house, and both she and John felt vulnerable living in Dartmouth. John had retired from the Post Office in 1935, but was running his own business renting and buying property and became an ARP warden at the beginning of the war.

In March 1940, John and Flora left the town to live a few miles away in Brixham. Their new house, Lauriston, was a cottage positioned end on to the road, again on a hillside, away from the town centre. The house was big enough to let Flora have her own study in a spare room, and a cellar was converted into a Morrison air-raid shelter, which she had to retreat to often, armed with her precious manuscripts, over the next few years. As John was now buying antiques on commission for a local shop, she was able to collect some small pieces to decorate the house. Flora soon started work again and the proofs for *Over to Candleford* were completed by February 1941, although she said that she did not consider it as good as *Lark Rise*. Geoffrey Cumberlege immediately encouraged her to begin the next book.

Life hit her a hard blow that September, however; Peter was lost at sea when his ship, the *Jedmoor*, was torpedoed in the Atlantic. She must have kept a photograph of him displayed in the house because she wrote to Leslie Castle on 27 January 1946:

> I cut one lovely red rose (garden not greenhouse) on Christmas Day to stand beside Peter's photograph, so that shows how mild the weather has been, really, though to me it has often seemed cold.

Perhaps throwing herself into writing helped to ease the overwhelming grief. This time she abandoned the theme of *Lark Rise* to write *Dashpers*, the story of a house and its various owners, some of which does seem to take her back to her Oxfordshire roots. However Flora became ill, developing pneumonia and was not able to write for a while. When she felt well enough to start again, she deferred further writing on *Dashpers* and started work on *Candleford Green*, the third volume of the trilogy, which described her life once she had moved to Fringford to work in the Post Office.

Despite the privations of the war, Flora was able to have *Candleford Green* ready for publication in January 1943, again receiving wonderful reviews. She was too tired to begin anything new, and had a lukewarm response to her suggestion that she finish *Dashpers* for Oxford University Press. Geoffrey Cumberlege liked the idea of doing something with *The Peverel Papers*, but for some reason nothing came of that then, or for another thirty years.

She was encouraged to hear of plans to publish her three books as a trilogy, *Lark Rise to Candleford*, illustrated with wood engravings by Julie Neild, and introduced by H.J. Massingham, a noted writer on rural topics. He skilfully stressed the importance of the social-historical element in her work:

> It is clear, then, that Flora Thompson's simple-seeming chronicles of life in hamlet, village and market town are, when regarded as an index to social change, of great complexity and

heavy with revolutionary meaning. But this you do not notice until you look below the surface. The surface is the family lives and characters of Laura and her neighbours at Lark Rise, inhabited by ex-peasants, and the two Candlefords, where society is more mixed and occupations more varied. But the surface is transparent, and there are threatening depths of dislocation and frustration below it. Flora Thompson's method of revealing them is a literary one, as was George Eliot's; that is to day, by the selective representation of domestic interiors in which living personages pass their daily lives. The social document is a by-product of people's normal activities and by intercourse intensely localised, just as beauty is a by-product of the craftsman's utility-work for his neighbours.

The first edition of the trilogy was sold out even before it was published on 12 April 1945, again to great praise. Flora did not rest on her laurels, starting a new book she entitled *These Too Were Victorians*, (later re-titled *Still Glides the Stream*) which was again written about Oxfordshire, with her main character Charity, a schoolteacher. In the typescripts she has sometimes muddled the names 'Laura' and 'Charity', even on the same page, and it is evident from the book that many of Charity's characteristics are those of Flora herself. Charity is, like Laura, the pivot of the story, which is written in very much the same style as *Lark Rise to Candleford*. Fascinatingly, Flora wrote of Charity that she relished skipping, a characteristic she herself was remembered for in Juniper Hill:

She herself had trodden it [the footpath] daily, often with her skipping rope, her white pinafore billowing, her long hair streaming, her feet scarcely touching the ground.

Still Glides the Stream, p. 9

Could there also be an echo of her relationship with her students in the Peverel Society, for whom she acted as teacher in her description of Charity and her pupils:

Years of hard work and many disappointments: a typical schoolmarm's life. But there had been compensations. One here and there of her pupils had shown the sudden gleam of comprehension, the mental and spiritual response to her teaching which sometimes in her lighter moments she had referred to when talking to her colleagues as 'plugging in', or 'taking the bait', but which in her secret thoughts she had treasured as her most precious experience. That, and the privilege of fostering such promise, had been the chief joy of her life; but there had also been material advantages, personal independence, a home of her own, books, friends and holiday travel.

Still Glides the Stream, p.10

The village of Restharrow in which the book is set is thought to be based on Stoke Lyne or Hethe, both in the same area as Lark Rise, but they are less specifically described than Juniper Hill and Cottisford, and few characters are readily identifiable. However a few pieces of the jigsaw can be put together. For example the bungalow mentioned on the first page, which housed the retired village policeman, may have been one of a row of bungalows in Fringford, one of which housed PC Manning, who had been the village policeman in Hethe and had also worked for the Metropolitan Police as specified in the book.

It was a much more of a struggle writing this book, because Flora's health was declining, and she suffered from angina, which often confined her to bed, and prevented her from enjoying her walks. However, she finished the book in August 1946. The new title was derived from Wordsworth's 'River Dudden': 'Still glides the stream and shall forever glide.'

Flora managed to travel to Dartmouth on Armistice Day in November 1946 to lay a wreath of poppies for Peter, and was delighted that her nephew Leslie Castle laid one for Edwin at

The tombstone commemorating Flora Thompson and her son Peter in Longcross cemetery in Dartmouth, appropriately in the shape of a book. (William Hunwick)

Cottisford war memorial. Through the cold winter she corrected the proofs of *Still Glides the Stream*. However, in May, when she seemed so much better that John had dared to leave her for a day while he went off on business, Flora had another angina attack, and he came home to find her back in bed. She died peacefully later that evening, before seeing *Still Glides the Stream* in print.

After the funeral service at St Barnabas' church in Dartmouth, she was cremated and her ashes are buried in Longcross Cemetery, Dartmouth. Her gravestone is in the shape of an open book, with 'to the dear memory of Flora Thompson May 21st 1947' on the left-hand page, and 'and of her beloved younger son Peter Redmond Thompson, MN lost at sea Sept. 16th 1941' on the right-hand page. It is typically unpretentious, giving away little about a very private woman, who yet managed to reveal much of herself and much of the world of her childhood in the pages of her books.

Flora Thompson's Timeline

29.7.1875	Albert Timms, stonemason, and Emma Dibber married and rented a cottage in Juniper Hill.
13.11.1875	Their first daughter, Martha was born, but died two weeks later.
5.12.1876	Flora Jane Timms, ('Laura' of *Lark Rise*) was born at Juniper Hill. She was baptised in Cottisford church on 4 March 1877.
12.9.1879	Edwin Timms ('Edmund' of *Lark Rise*) was born.
1882	Flora started school in Cottisford.
4.4.1882	Albert Timms was born – he lived only one day.
3.2.1884	May Timms was baptised.
1.8.1886	Ethel Elizabeth Timms was baptised.
30.3.1887	Emma Timms' father John Dibber was buried at Cottisford church.
1887	Queen Victoria's Golden Jubilee celebrations were held in Shelswell Park.
1888	Probably the year Flora and Edwin first walked to 'Candleford' (Twyford) on their own to stay with Uncle Tom.
7.10.1888	Frank Wallington Timms was born.
1888	Flora Timms won the Diocesan Prize at school, having been commended in 1886 and 1887.
2.11.1890	Annie Gertrude Timms was baptised.
1891	Flora went to work at Fringford Post Office for Mrs Whitton.
7.5.1893	Ellen Mary Timms was baptised. She was buried on 26.5.1895.
1897	Flora left Fringford and took a series of temporary post office jobs, in various places, probably at Twyford, Bucks and including Essex before going to work for Walter Chapman at Grayshott Post Office, Hampshire.
6.3.1898	Cecil Barrie Timms was baptised. He lived to the age of two-and-a-half and was buried on 7.4.1900.
September 1898	Flora began work in Grayshott at Walter Chapman's post office.
1899	Edwin fought in the Boer War in South Africa. He was captured by the Boers and abandoned in the Veldt, narrowly escaping dying of thirst. His regiment went straight from South Africa to India after the war, where he stayed for about five years.
1900	Flora left Grayshott and did more temporary jobs.
March 1901	Flora was working in the Post Office at Yately, Hampshire. John Thompson was working in the post office in Aldershot, Hampshire.
29.7.1901	Walter Chapman murdered his wife Emily.
7.1.1903	Flora Jane Timms married John Thompson at the church of St Mary the Virgin, Twickenham. None of Flora's family were at the ceremony. John was the son of Emily and Henry Thompson, a Chief Petty Officer in the Royal Navy. The couple went to live in Winton, Bournemouth where John was a sorting clerk and telegraphist at the main post office.
24.10.1903	Flora and John's daughter Winifred Grace was born. Although busy as a housewife and mother, Flora continued to educate herself by borrowing books from the local library.
1907	Edwin Timms came back from India on leaving the army. He worked on an Oxfordshire farm for two years but, depressed at the low wages, decided to emigrate to Canada.
1909	Flora and Winifred travelled by train to Aynho and pony and trap to Juniper Hill to stay with her family and see Edwin before he left England.

6.10.1909	Flora and John's son Henry Basil was born.
1909	The family moved to 2 Edgehill Road, Winton, which they renamed Grayshott Cottage (they had previously moved from No. 4 to No. 6 Sedgley Road, Winton).
1910	Flora began to buy *The Ladies Companion* and was about to enter their literary competitions when John succumbed to appendicitis and had to be nursed at home for two weeks.
	Frank Wallington Timms emigrated to Australia, aged twenty-one.
February 1911	Flora entered a competition in *The Ladies Companion* to write a 300-word essay about Jane Austen, and won the 5s prize and had most of the essay published.
April 1911	Flora was mentioned in *The Ladies Companion* for her essay on Catherine of Aragon.
Summer 1911	John Thompson's mother died on the Isle of Wight.
January 1912	Flora's first story *The Toft Cup* was published in *The Ladies Companion* and Flora began to realise that she could earn money from her writing. Several more of her stories were published in the magazine over the next couple of years.
1912	Flora first came into contact with Dr Ronald Campbell Macfie, a Scottish physician and writer, after entering a competition to comment on his ode on the sinking of the *Titanic*. He greatly encouraged her writing, particularly her poetry over the next few years.
1913	Flora sold *The Leper* to *The Literary Monthly*.
1914	Flora and John took their family to visit John's widowed father on the Isle of Wight.
	Edwin Timms joined the 32nd Battalion of the Canadian Expeditionary Force in Winnipeg.
1915	*The Ladies Companion* stopped publication. The Thompsons moved to 42 Frederica Road, Winton, which they renamed Grayshott Cottage.
	Edwin was transferred to the 2nd Eastern Ontario Battalion and sent to France. He was given home leave in March, but Flora was unable to visit him because the children had whooping cough, and there was snow.
1916	Edwin was posted to France and killed in action on 26 April. He was buried in Woods Cemetery, Zillebeke, Belgium.
	John Thompson was promoted to sub-postmaster and in August the family moved to Liphook to live in the house adjoining the post office (now the Midland Bank). Flora spent four hours from four o'clock each morning sorting the post from home and John spent many nights sleeping on a camp bed in the post office in case of telegrams.
1918	Flora and John's son Peter Redmond was born on 18 October.
	In December Albert Timms died and was buried in Cottisford church on 17 December.
1919	Flora answered an advertisement in *The Daily News* about a writing course offered by the Practical Correspondence College in London. As a result of taking the course she began submitting her work to *The Catholic Fireside* and her subsequent earnings helped pay for Winifred and Basil's schooling in Haslemere and Petersfield.
1920	Flora rewrote *The Leper* and the story became her first contribution to *The Catholic Fireside*.
Early 1921	Flora began to write a series of nature articles for *The Catholic Fireside*.
	The first of a series of twelve articles set in the New Forest was published on 1 January.
1921	*Bog Myrtle and Peat*, Flora's slim paperback of her poetry, was published and dedicated to Dr Ronald Macfie. It was not very successful and Flora became depressed.
1922	The style of the nature articles in *The Catholic Fireside* changed to become less fictional and more focused on nature. The series was renamed *The Peverel Papers*, probably after her nickname for Weaver's Down, Liphook. Over the next six years seventy-two *Peverel Papers* were written. Flora received letters praising her work, especially her sketches of country life, which gradually encouraged her to write about her childhood.
1923	Peter began school, giving Flora more time to write. Flora initiated 'The Fireside Reading Circle' for *The Catholic Fireside*. She wrote literary essays for the magazine on authors such as Dickens, George Eliot and the Brontës and more general studies on short stories, novels etc. She judged writing competitions for the 'Circle' and through that became friendly with one competitor, Mildred Humble-Smith.
c. 1924	Flora's younger sister Ethel Elizabeth Timms (known as Betty), who also worked in the post office, won literary competitions.
c. 1925	Flora joined the Antiquarian and Field Society attached to Haslemere Museum.
1925	Flora wrote a guidebook to Liphook.

Around this time her *Peverel Papers* began to include features on some of the characters she had known in her childhood such as 'Queenie' and 'Old Sally'.

Flora ended the 'Fireside Reading Circle' in *The Catholic Fireside*. She and Mildred Humble-Smith instead founded the Peverel Society, with Lady Mary Sackville as their patron. The society was advertised in *The Catholic Fireside*, offering writing courses.

Flora answered an advertisement in *The Literary Journal* to ghost-write for a big-game hunter, and her work was published in *The Scottish Field*, *Chamber's Journal* and various African papers.

1926	The Thompsons bought a house at Griggs Green on the outskirts of Liphook.

Basil went to Australia, accompanied by Winifred's fiancé, initially to visit Flora's brother Frank who had emigrated to Queensland. Winifred's engagement did not survive.

Winifred worked at the Liphook Post Office telephone exchange.

Flora's sister Betty often came to stay at Liphook. She had a book of children's stories published, *The Little Grey Men of the Moor*.

Mildred Humble-Smith also had a children's book published, *Girls of Chiltern Towers*.

1927	John Thompson was given the job of postmaster in Dartmouth, Devon in August, to Flora's dismay, as she was reluctant to leave Hampshire.

In December the last of *The Peverel Papers* was published.

1928	Flora, Winifred and Peter were able to stay at Woolmer Cottage while John house-hunted in Dartmouth. They did not move until the autumn.

Their new home, The Outlook, was in the Above Town area, approached by steep steps, with wonderful views.

John bought a small motor boat, *Sea Mew*, which he and Peter often took out to sea.

Basil had abandoned sheep farming in Australia and returned to try engineering.

Flora had no further connection with *The Catholic Fireside* and instead wrote more short stories, which do not appear to have been published.

She continued to spend much time on the Peverel Society.

1931	Flora's friend Dr Ronald Macfie, who had given her so much encouragement, died aged sixty-six. Flora was very sad, writing his name on the flyleaf of a book with the quotation from Shakespeare's *Antony and Cleopatra*: 'The bright day is done and we are for the dark'.
1933	Flora's mother Emma Timms died aged eighty at Hethe, where she was living with one of Flora's sisters.
1935	John Thompson retired on 12 April. He now appreciated Flora's writing and had built a writing room for her in their garden.

Flora began collecting together her memories about her childhood, writing verses of singing games in an empty diary.

Basil was working as an engineer on ships sailing between North and South America. Winifred became a nurse.

Peter was apprenticed as a ship's engineer at Phillips' shipyard.

1936	Flora sent a story, *The Tail-less Fox*, written in Liphook and set in a poor cottage, to *The Lady*, and it was published in December. Flora realised that there was scope for more writing about her childhood.
1937	In April Flora's essay on 'Old Queenie', the lacemaker from Juniper Hill, was published in *The Lady*.

In August another essay entitled 'An Oxfordshire Hamlet in the Eighties' was published in *The National Review*.

Flora began work in earnest on *Lark Rise*.

Henry Basil, an engineer with the Prince Line between New York and Buenos Aires, married Dora Wallace in America.

1938	Basil brought Dora to visit his family.

'May Day in the Eighties' was published in the spring issue of *The National Review*.

Flora sent the completed text of *Lark Rise* to Oxford University Press. She was encouraged to extend the essays into a full-length book by Sir Humphrey Milford, publisher to the university. His deputy Geoffrey Cumberlege became her editor, and gave her continuing encouragement. The book had to be published as autobiography as the Press did not publish fiction.

In September illustrator Lynton Lamb stayed in Brackley and did ten pen and ink illustrations for *Lark Rise*.

1939 In March *Lark Rise* was published, widely reviewed in such magazines as *Country Life*, *The Sunday Times* and *The Times Literary Supplement*.

Flora's fame reached Oxfordshire, and she was delighted and amused when her family told her that Lady Bicester of Tusmore Park liked the book.

Flora worked on *Over to Candleford*.

In September war was declared. Winifred only just managed to get home from Switzerland before hostilities commenced.

Henry Basil and his family had settled in Australia.

Peter worked till late each evening in the shipyard and then joined the Merchant Navy.

Flora was distracted from her work by making black-out curtains from old camping blankets.

John's war contribution was to become an ARP air-raid warden. Flora had to take telephone messages when he was out. He spent his spare time fishing.

Flora and Mildred Humble-Smith discussed disbanding the Peverel Society for the duration of the war, but let it continue a little longer.

Flora continued working on *Over to Candleford*, but found it a great struggle. She even offered to return her advance to Oxford University Press, but Geoffrey Cumberlege urged her to continue.

1940 In March the Thompsons decided they were too vulnerable to bombing in Dartmouth, made a target by its Royal Naval College, harbour and shipyards. They found a cottage built on a hillside in Brixham called Lauriston, similar to one she describes in *Dashpers*. It was large enough for them to turn the spare room into a study for Flora.

John began to sell antiques on commission.

In June France fell to the Germans and the French coast was occupied which led to air attacks along the Devon coast.

1941 The proofs of *Over to Candleford* were completed.

On 16 September the Thompsons received a telegram to say that Peter's ship, the *Jedmoor*, had been torpedoed, leaving only six survivors. Peter had died.

Flora, who was devastated by her son's death, wrote to Geoffrey Cumberlege, 'He was our youngest, a latecomer and tenderly loved. That there are thousands of mothers and wives suffering as I am only seems to make it harder to bear'. (Harry Ransom).

Mildred Humble-Smith had also lost a son at sea, and neither of them had the heart to continue the Peverel Society, which was disbanded.

Despite her grief, Flora continued to work on her novel *Dashpers*, about a house and its inhabitants.

She contracted pneumonia during the winter and had to spend several weeks in bed.

1942 Flora had renewed strength to begin writing in the spring, but *Dashpers* was left to one side and she began *Candleford Green*. Writing was far from easy because of wartime conditions - there were many raids on Dartmouth and Brixham and Flora often had to retreat into her Morrison air-raid shelter with her typescript.

1943 *Candleford Green* was published and was well received.

Geoffrey Cumberlege asked what she would like to offer for publication next. When she sent what she had written of *Dashpers* however, his comment was, 'I like everything you write, but I do not think this shows you at your happiest'.

Flora instead sent him *The Peverel Papers* she had written for *The Catholic Fireside*, which were much more favourably received, '*The Peverel Papers* are full of good things. I can tell you here and now that we shall be delighted to publish it'. (Harry Ransom).

However, *The Peverel Papers* were not to be published until long after Flora's death.

Flora began a lengthy correspondence with her nephew Leslie, son of her sister Annie, who had written to say how much he appreciated the book.

Flora was still not well.

1944 Oxford University Press were planning to publish Flora's three books as a trilogy, *Lark Rise to Candleford*. The wood engraver Julie Neild was asked to do the illustrations, although wartime conditions prevented her from visiting Juniper Hill, she asked for much information from Flora to make her drawings as accurate as possible.

The introduction to the trilogy was written by the noted country writer H.J. Massingham who had already written appreciatively of Flora's work.

Flora was working on *Heatherley*, about her life at Grayshott, but it was never submitted for publication.

1945

In February Flora was ill with heart problems and depressed not to be able to go for walks when spring brought better weather. She commented wryly, 'what a bore it is to get old and ill'. (Letter in private collection, quoted by Gillian Lindsay).

In March Flora received her advance copies of *Lark Rise to Candleford*, immediately signing the first one and returning it to Geoffrey Cumberlege.

The trilogy was published on 12 April. The edition of 5,000 copies was sold out in advance.

The Second World War ended in Europe in May, making travel easier. Flora's nephew Leslie came to stay and was taken fishing by John. Flora's sister Betty often visited.

Basil and his wife, settled in Australia, now had three children.

Flora began to write another book, entitled *These Too Were Victorians*, which was to be published as *Still Glides the Stream*.

A Guild edition of *Lark Rise* was published, one third of which was sold to Australia and the Commonwealth.

1946

Flora was ill in the spring, suffering from angina. She was cheered and honoured on reading in *The Periodical*, produced by Oxford University Press, that the publisher Sir Humphrey Milford considered that the two most important books he had published during his twenty-two years at the Press were A.J. Toynbee's *Study on History* and Flora Thompson's *Lark Rise to Candleford*.

In the summer John sold his boat *Sea Mew*, feeling he was too old to go out in it on his own.

Winifred came to stay for two weeks, enabling John to take a short holiday while she looked after Flora.

In August Flora completed *These Too Were Victorians*, re-titled *Still Glides the Stream* before publication, which was probably based on Stoke Lyne or Hethe, or a mixture of the two. It was illustrated by Lynton Lamb.

In November the Reprint Society decided to publish 15,000 copies of *Lark Rise to Candleford*, offering royalties of about £1,800 for Flora.

John was earning extra money buying and renting property and Flora bought 32 Bolton Street, Brixham, a double-fronted house once used as a hotel.

Leslie Castle bought a ticket for the Irish Sweepstake on Flora's behalf – she drew the favourite and sold part of the ticket for £250 so that she made a profit even when the horse only came in fourth. She sent £100 to Leslie.

On Armistice Day in November Flora laid a poppy wreath in memory of Peter at the Dartmouth war memorial. Leslie laid one for Edwin at Cottisford.

Flora was ill again over Christmas.

1947

Throughout the winter she worked on correcting the proofs of *Still Glides the Stream* and wrote an article about herself for *Reader's News* as the Readers' Union were publishing an edition of *Lark Rise*.

In May Flora seemed better and on 21 May John felt able to leave her for a day while he went out on business. She had an angina attack while he was out, followed by a heart attack that evening and died aged seventy.

Flora's funeral service was held at St Barnabas' church in Dartmouth, followed by a cremation. Her ashes were buried at Longcross Cemetery, Dartmouth, with a gravestone in the shape of an open book which she shares with Peter.

John Thompson was devastated by Flora's death. He stayed with friends in Bournemouth and then on the Isle of Wight. He sold their house Lauriston, moving to a smaller house in Brixham.

1948

Still Glides the Stream was published.

John Thompson died on 13 July aged seventy-four.

Winifred became Flora's literary executor. She suggested the publication of *The Peverel Papers*, but although Geoffrey Cumberlege liked it, the project was not pursued. He was not interested in publishing *Gates of Eden*, her novel about a stonemason's daughter who runs away and falls in love with a married doctor-poet.

Around this time the biographer Margaret Lane travelled to Oxfordshire to research material for an article on Flora.

1949

Winifred was forced by ill health to give up the nursing home in Cheltenham she had been running with two friends. The three of them retired to Bath.

1957

Margaret Lane published her essay about Flora Thompson in *The Cornhill Magazine* in January.

1966   Winifred Thompson died aged sixty-three. Flora's papers went to the University of Texas.

The ninetieth anniversary of Flora's birth was marked by a performance of parts of *Lark Rise* in the grounds of Cottisford House.

Evensong was held in Cottisford church.

Lord David Cecil, Goldsmith's Professor of English at Oxford gave a lecture on *Lark Rise to Candleford* to an audience of 200 in the Rectory Barn, Cottisford.

1976   A small commemorative plaque was put on the wall of The End House, Juniper Hill, where Flora was brought up.

A literary lunch was held at The Anchor, Liphook with the guests of honour, Geoffrey Cumberlege, Sir Hugh Casson and Margaret Lane. Anne Mallinson organised an exhibition about Flora's life and times at her Selborne Bookshop.

Sir Hugh Casson presented a short programme about Flora on BBC2.

A *Lark Rise* festival was held at Shelswell Park.

1978   Keith Dewhurst's play *Lark Rise*, based on a day during the harvest, was performed at the National Theatre, London.

1979   Keith Dewhurst's *Candleford* was first performed at the National Theatre.

A Country Calendar was published by Oxford University Press with an essay by Margaret Lane on Flora's life, extracts from *The Peverel Papers*, some of Flora's poems and *Heatherley*.

1986   *The Peverel Papers*, edited by Julian Shuckburgh, was published by Century Hutchinson, featuring further extracts from Flora's nature writing.

1990   *Flora Thompson: The Story of the 'Lark Rise' Writer*, the first full biography of Flora, written by Gillian Lindsay, was published by Robert Hale.

1997   A commemorative plaque was put in Cottisford church to commemorate Flora Thompson.

John Owen Thompson published *On the Trail of Flora Thompson* about Flora's life in Grayshott and Liphook.

John Owen Smith's play *Flora's Peverel*, about her life in Liphook, was first performed.

1998   *Heatherley* was republished with an introduction and historical notes.

John Owen Smith's play *Flora's Heatherley* was performed in Surrey and East Hampshire.

2000   A blue plaque was put on The Outlook, Flora's home in Dartmouth.

2005   Exhibition about Flora Thompson opened at Buckingham Museum, where a Flora Thompson study centre is opened.

2007   New permanent exhibition about Flora Thompson opens at Buckingham Museum.

Appendix One: Money Owed by the Wallington Children to Local Tradesmen

Elizabeth Call, shopkeeper of Piddington, for provisions	£18	0s	6 ¾d
Samuel Claridge, haberdasher of Bicester for linen and hosiery	£14	0s	8d
Thomas Wood, butcher of Ludgershall for butcher's meat	£11	0s	1 ½d
Thomas Wallington, butcher of Piddington, for butcher's meat	£2	1s	11d
Aaron Foskett, shoemaker of Grendon for shoes	£8	12s	2d
John George, Bicester for mercery and drapery	£7	6s	7d
William Jeacock, maltster of Marsh Gibbon for malt and beer	£12	0s	1d
John Scott, maltser of Marsh Gibbon for malt and beer	£1	7s	6d
William Golder, mealman of Blackthorn for flour and other goods	£9	1s	1d
John Jenkins, coal merchant of Lower Heyford for coals	£7	8s	9d
William Parre, carpenter of Piddington for carpenter's work	£2	14s	5 ½d
John Jordan, shopkeeper of Piddington for provisions and clothing	£63	0s	0d
William Hawkins, the balance of an account for barley and a cow	£14	15s	6d
– which, together with other items, taxed came to	£171	19s	10 ¾d

Money was also owed to Hannah Smith, schoolmistress of Islip, for board and education for the girls: £14 0s 6d for Clements (also known as Clementina), £3 7s 10d for Elizabeth and £29 17s 8d for Martha. Leonard owed £22 14s 6d to Abraham Chapman, schoolmaster of Islip and a further £8 11s for clothes to William Wharton, tailor and draper from Bicester.

The pub sign of the Fox Inn, Flora's 'Waggon and Horses'. (David Watts)

Appendix Two: Inventory of the Fox Inn, Juniper Hill

Made in 1875 on the death of Thomas Harris

Taproom
Deal table, 1 elbow Windsor chair, 11 other ditto, 23 tumblers, butter cooler, steelyards and ball, 2 toasting forks, 15 champagne glasses, 5 smoothing irons, teapot, set of tea things, tea kettle, beer warmer, set of fire irons, two dozen plates, 12 meat dishes, 2 yellow ditto, 5 vegetable dishes, 2 basons, 6 cups and saucers, 3 corner cupboards, fender, 15 spittoons.

Shop
About one quarter cut of bacon, about 10lb beef suet, deal counter, beam scales and 8 weights, part of a tin of lard, oak table with drawers, quantity of sweets, quarter of a gross of matches, 1 pair of candlesticks, pestle and mortar, 2 lamps, sugar nippers, nightshade, pair of spurs, elbow and 5 chairs, mahogany table, writing desk, tea tray, 3 pewter measures, 1 funnel and 3 spirit measures.

Bakehouse
2 washing trays and 1 tub, 2 flour bins, salting lead, 24 pint cups, 9 quart ditto, 9 quart jugs, 12 pint ditto, beam and flour scales and 2 weights, meat saw, spring balance and scale, 2 field bottles, 2 clothes baskets, 3 wooden water buckets, 2 galvanised ditto.

Spirits, beer etc.
1 gallon of rum, 35 gallons of 9 per cent beer, 18 gallons of mild.

Hovel
About 21 bushels of potatoes, about 21 bushels of seed potatoes, 3 bushels of peas, 9 empty bags, 50 slates, ¼ bushel of pig potatoes, 2 wheelbarrows, iron pig trough, chaff box and knife, bench, gate and sundry wood, 3 socket pipes, 2 stocks of bees, water butt and tap, about 120 bushels of potatoes, 2 shovels, washing bowl, 2 boilers, 4 iron saucepans, 1 tin ditto, 2 baking tins, strainer and Dutch oven, ½ bushel of flour, 3 beer cans, 2 hand saws, stone pig trough and 7 sacks.

Bedroom No. 1
A four-post bedstead and furniture, feather bed, flock mattress, feather bolster and 5 pillows, 3 blankets, counterpane, oak table, set of drawers, 4 volumes of books (*The Tablet*), 2 chairs, night commode, washstand and ware, large oak chest, 2 pieces of carpet, small lamp.

Bedroom No. 2
French bedstead, flock mattress, straw ditto, feather bolster and pillow, 3 blankets, counterpane, round table and glass, large chest, clock in oak frame, broom, 3 chairs.

Bedroom No. 3
2 stump bedsteads, feather bed, bolster and 2 pillows, 2 flock mattresses, 3 blankets and counterpane, feather bed, straw mattress, 1 flock bolster, 1 feather ditto, counterpane, 2 blankets, dough kiver, 2 chairs.

Bedroom No. 4

Four-post bedstead and furniture, feather bed, flock mattress, 3 blankets, counterpane, feather bolster and pillow, shut-up bedstead, painted chest of drawers, looking glass, clock, clothes line, 2 chairs, oak table, oak bureau, 5 pairs of sheets, 6 chamber towels, 6 tea cloths, 4 table cloths, 7 electro tea spoons, 3 metal spoons, three dozen black knives and forks, carver and fork, steel, 10 pillow cases.

The Loft

2 deal tables, 4 trestles, 4 skittles and ball, potato fork, 2 dung forks, 3 two-tined forks, spade and pickaxe, 2 iron bars, 12 besoms, cross-cut saw, 9 stools.

Coal House

Beam and scales, 3 x 56lb weights, 2 gates, pick and stone axe heads, about 10cwt of coal.

Sow and 6 pigs. Iron pig trough

Value £96 10s 3d

Appendix Three: Inventory of the Rectory, Cottisford

Sale Catalogue of the Rectory, Cottisford in 1896

The Rectory Cottisford
Four miles from Brackley and six from Bicester
The capital household furniture: carpets, feather beds, bedding, linen, china, glass, plated goods
Pianoforte by Broadwood
Kitchen Utensils, Poultry
Brown Nag Horse, Rick and Stump of Meadow Hay (to go off)
Spring trap, capital pony trap, dung cart, harness, garden
A few lots of Agricultural Implements and Miscellaneous Effects
The property of the late Rev. C.S. Harrison
To be sold by Auction by Messrs Paxton and Holiday on the Premises on Tuesday, August 25th, 1896 at ten
    for eleven o'clock punctually
By direction of the Executors

Catalogue

Store Room
1. Coffee urn, 3 moderator lamps and 3 water cans
2. Small iron stove
3. Side-saddle
4. Plaster bust, a print in oak frame and a map
5. Part of an iron bedstead and sundries
6.

Bedroom No. 1
7. A Seinde rug, stool, box and a cane-seated chair
8. 4ft 6in. wooden French bedstead
9. A fibre and wool mattress
10. Feather bed, flock bolster and feather pillow
11. One double and two single blankets and a coverlid
12. Painted washstand and towel airer
13. Mahogany chest of 5 drawers
14. Painted chest of 5 ditto
15. Two pairs of repp window curtains
16. One pair of linen chintz ditto
17. Hip bath
18. Six and 2 elbow mahogany-framed chairs, with cabriole legs and hair-stuffed seats and backs
19.

Bedroom No. 2
20. Piece of linoleum, part of a rosewood pole fire-screen and a pair of dumbbells
21. Painted chest of 4 drawers

22. 2 and 1 elbow cane seated chairs
23. Three blankets
24. Feather bolster and 2 feather pillows
25. Double straw palliasse
26. Ditto
27. Sofa bedstead, straw mattress and hair ditto
28. Feather bed and a white knotted quilt
29. 4ft 6in. iron bedstead
30. Two wooden boxes and a foot tin
31.

Bedroom No. 3

32. Sundry pieces of carpet and oilcloth
33. 4ft 6in. iron stump bed
34. Double straw palliasse
35. Flock bed, bolster and two feather pillows
36. One double and 3 single blankets and a coverlid
37. Two cane-seated chairs and a mahogany-framed swing-glass, 11½in. x 8in.
38. Painted chest of drawers
39. Ditto
40. Mahogany corner washstand and a towel airer
41. Painted washstand and a three-rail towel airer
42. Mahogany one-leaf table and cover
43. Mahogany-frames swing-glass, plate 13in. x 9in., American clock and a hand-bell
44. Sponge bath
45.

Study

46. Tapestry carpet, about ten yards run, piece of matting and a mat
47. 4ft-stained open bookcase, fitted with 8 shelves
48. Pole fire-screen, cash box and japanned bonnet box
49. Walnut and inlaid chess table with drawer
50. An elbow smoking chair with cushions
51. Mahogany loo table and cover
52. 4ft-stained bookcase with cupboard and 4 shelves over
54. Four shelves, iron curtain rod and damask curtain
55. 2 tin boxes, 2 book rests etc.
56. 5ft-wooden French bedstead
57.

Bedroom No. 4

58. Three pieces of Kidderminster carpet, hearthrug and piece of linoleum
59. Iron fender and poker
60. 4ft 6in. iron bedstead
61. Double straw palliasse
62. Wool mattress
63. Bordered feather bed, bolster and pillow
64. Three blankets and a white Marseilles counterpane
65. Four crown-back cane-seated chairs
66. Sponge bath
67. Painted double washstand and a four-rail towel airer
68. An oak-grained linen cupboard, fitted with 2 sliding shelves and a large drawer 5ft 9in. x 5ft 4in. x 15½in.
69. An oval mahogany Pembroke table
70. Swing-glass in maple painted frame, plate 19½in. x 15½in.
71. Pair of lace window curtains and iron rod
72. A maple painted chest of 5 drawers
73. Wicker clothes basket and a small mahogany stand table
74.

Dressing Room No. 5

75. Three pieces of oilcloth and hearthrug
76. Deal washstand and two-fold mahogany towel horse
77. Shaving glass in mahogany frame and a clothes basket
78. An oak chest of drawers with mahogany front
79. A painted dressing table with 3 drawers and blue and muslin hangings.
80. Mahogany-framed swing-glass with 3 jewel drawers, plate 24in. x 18in.
81. An antique oak chest of 4 drawers
82.

Bedroom No. 6

83. High wire fender and a painted sponge bath
84. Three pieces of tapestry carpet and a piece of floor cloth
85. 5ft-mahogany Arabian bedstead
86. Two fibre mattresses
87. Feather bed, bolster and pillow
88. One double and two single blankets and a white Marseilles quilt
89. Mahogany washstand with marble top and a 5-rail mahogany swivel airer
90. Oak chest of 5 drawers with mahogany front
91. Mahogany boot rack
92. Stained cornice pole, rings and pair of lined chintz window curtains
93. Painted dressing table with blue and muslin hangings, and a mahogany-framed swing glass, plate 24in. x 18in.
94. Set of dress pegs and a mahogany bidet
95. An easy chair in chintz and extra Holland cover
96. Box ottoman in chintz
97. Wicker basket and a ditto clothes basket
98. Pair of oleographs in gilt frames and glazed
99. Coloured print in maple frame, 'one at a time'; a print 'Woodman's daughter'; a photograph in gilt frame and a coloured print in oak frame
100.

Bedroom No. 7

101. Pierced fender, set of fire irons, japanned coal vase and a hearth brush
102. Large Scinde rug and a piece of oilcloth
103. Three-ft 6 in iron stump bedstead and a double straw palliasse
104. Wool mattress
105. Small wool bed, 3 feather and 1 flock pillow
106. Mahogany enclosed washstand with 2 drawers under
107. Rosewood and inlaid work table
108. Mahogany-framed swing-glass, plate 18in. x 13in.
109. Mahogany loo table on pillar and block, and cover
110. Two iron curtain rods and a pair of lace window curtains
111. Thermometer, 2 flower glasses and a colza lamp
112. A double-barrelled breech-loading gun and a spear
113. A maple painted hanging press, fitted with pegs and drawers under, 6ft 9in. x 4ft 3in.
114. Sundries
115. Mahogany-framed couch with squab and bolster in cretonne
116. Carved oak coffer
117. Mahogany enclosed washstand with cupboard and drawer under
118. Painted night commode
119. Three pictures, framed and glazed
120.

Linen

121. Two pairs of linen sheets
122. One ditto and three twill sheets
123. Six linen pillow cases and 12 huckaback towels
124. Five pillow cases and 12 chamber towels
125. A damask table cloth and 6 serviettes

126. A similar lot
127. Two damask table cloths and 6 serviettes
128. Two ditto and 5 fish napkins
129. Three ditto and 4 ditto
130. Three ditto and 4 doyleys
131. Nine toilet covers and 3 large bath towels
132. Fourteen tea cloths and 3 knife cloths
133. One large and one small counterpane
134. A similar lot
135. A set of dimity bed furniture and a pair of curtains
136. Four round towels, 3 cloths, 12 dusters, 2 ham and 2 bacon bags
137.

Landing and Staircase

138. Piece of tapestry carpet, 23ft long
139. Ditto of floor cloth, 28ft long and 3 cocoa-fibre mats
140. Tin candlesticks and sundries
141. An oak coffer
142. Two carriage rugs
143. Odd curtains, carpet etc.
144. An oleograph in gilt frame
145. Tapestry stair carpet, 47ft long and 22 brass stair rods
146.

Entrance Hall

147. Thirty feet of linoleum as laid
148. Six slip mats
149. An 8-day clock in oak case by R. Flower, Retford
150. Two mahogany hall chairs
151. Oak hall table with drawer and turned legs
152. Butler's mahogany tray and stand
153. Driving whip
154. Tool chest and tools
155.

Outer Hall

156. Piece of cocoa matting, 2 cocoa mats, door porter and scrape
157. A tortoise stove and piping
158. Iron hat and umbrella stand
159. Weather glass by Carpenter
160.

Library

161. Timepiece and chimney ornaments
162. Moulded fender and fire irons
163. Indian rug and a skin rug
164. The Brussels carpet as laid, 10ft 3in. x 9ft
165. Birch elbow chair with stuffed back and cushion in cretonne, 1 cane and 1 wicker-seated chairs
166. [blank]
167. Mahogany whatnot
168. Stained cornice pole, rings and pair of figured muslin curtains
169. Mahogany Sutherland table and cover
170. Walnut-framed inkstand
171. Walnut-framed couch with stuffed spring seat in green cloth and extra cretonne cover
172. A rosewood nest of 7 drawers
173. A stained 4-tier bookshelf
174. A painted semi-circular side table
175. A rosewood prie-dieu chair with stuffed seat and back
176. Mahogany 4-tier whatnot on castors

177. Walnut stationery case and oak and brass letter scales and 5 brass weights
178. Two engravings in walnut frames
179. Wicker flower stand and piece of oilcloth
180.

Drawing Room

181. Scroll fender with steel top and standards and a set of spiral fire implements
182. Brussels carpet as laid, 16ft 6in. x 11ft 9in.
183. A crimson and black Kidderminster square 9ft x 9ft
184. An all ball easy chair on castors, with stuffed seat and back in cretonne and a cushion in needlework
185. Walnut-framed Chesterfield couch with hair-stuffed spring seat in figured damask and satin cretonne cover
186. Five and 1 elbow mahogany-framed chairs with hair-stuffed seats and 4 plush covers
187. A carved Elizabethan chair with stuffed seat and back in plush
188. Wicker elbow chair and a stool
189. Walnut-framed easy chair with spring-stuffed seats
190. An oak Glastonbury chair
191. Mahogany music canterbury
192. A cottage pianoforte in mahogany case by Broadwood
193. 9ft-mahogany cornice pole, rings and pair of muslin curtains
194. Large sheep-skin mat and small hair rug
195. Two engravings in oak frames, 'Marriage of St Catherine' and 'The Annunciation'
196. Two ditto 'Village Festival' and 'Evening'
197. Engraving in gilt frame 'Dying Douglas'
198.

Dining Room

199. Fender and set of fire irons
200. Japanned coal vase and small folding chair
201. Bordered Turkey carpet, 11ft 6in. x 10ft
202. Kidderminster square and Wilton rug
203. Set of mahogany dining tables with three extra leaves, 11ft 4in. x 4ft 7in.
204. Two tapestry table covers and chimney ornaments
205. Mahogany library table with fluted legs on castors, 4 drawers and morocco-leather top
206. Inkstand, stationery case and blotting pad
207. Six mahogany-framed dining chairs in American cloth
208. Mahogany-framed easy chair, spring-stuffed seat in American cloth
209. Oak chair commode with covered back
210. Mahogany chiffonier
211. Mahogany 3-tier dinner wagon
212. An oak dumb-waiter and 8 table mats
213. Water bottle, table bell and writing desk
214. Pair of paraffin lamps with opal shades
215. 13ft 6in. mahogany cornice pole and rings, pair of muslin and pair of striped window curtains
216. A 5-fold screen
217. Two photographs, rosewood tea stand and cosy
218.

Pantry

219. Quantity of jam pots and stone jars
220. Two bread pans, sundry ware etc.
221. Set of 4 steps
222. Wire meat safe
223. Deal table, wire meat cover, and 4 baking tins
224.

Servants' Hall

225. Copper tea kettle and heater
226. Suspension lamp and 1 benzoline ditto

227. Paraffin lamp, bracket ditto and a hand lamp
228. Two plated chamber and 2 brass candlesticks, pewter cup and 1 small circular tray
229. A deal flap table with drawer
230. Butler's tray, tea tray and 2 waiters
231. A deal clock by Kemp
232. Patent mangle
233. Copper warming pans
234. Two water cans and tin-lined plate basket
235. One large and two small water cans
236. Six large and 6 small white-handled knives
237. Two carvers and forks, steel and bread knife
238. Twenty-one ivory-handled knives, bread knife, 2 carvers and forks and mahogany knife box
239. Housemaid's box, dust pan, brushes etc.
240. Four oil cans, fire guard and sundries
241. Sundry oil lamps, wire basket etc.
242.

Plated Goods

243. Two butter knives, a swan salt cellar, and 2 sauce ladles
244. Ten tea spoons and a pair of sugar tongs
245. Four table and 5 dessert spoons and 2 tub salt cellars
246. Eleven large and six small forks
247. One large waiter, 2 pickle jar stands, 2 steels and candle snuffers
248. Twelve dessert knives and forks
249.

China and Glass

250. Four decanters
251. Five ditto
252. Four ditto, 1 lamp globe, 5 finger bowls and 2 glass dishes
253. Eleven finger bowls
254. Five water bottles and two tumblers
255. Butter dish, sugar basin, mustard pot and salt cellar
256. Nine tumblers and 5 liqueur glasses
257. Eighteen wine glasses and 6 ditto
258. Fourteen ditto and 4 ditto
259. Two large dishes, 4 custards and 2 salt cellars
260. Four pickle jars and 5 tumblers
261. Two small dishes, 10 ice plates and sundry glass
262. Two small muffin dishes, two teapot stands, milk ewer and sugar basin
263. Two bread and butter plates, 2 plates, 7 cups, 12 saucers and butter dish
264. Three willow pattern cups and saucers, three teapots and 3 breakfast cups and saucers
265. Nine pudding basins, large yellow dish and 9 pie dishes
266. Earthenware colander, cheese pan, 3 stew jars and 5 large jars
267. Pestle and mortar, 2 cake tins, 2 cans and a collard-head tin
268. Sundry ware
269. Ditto
270. Ditto
271.

Kitchen

272. Quantity of cocoa-fibre matting and 5 mats
273. Iron tea kettle and a large iron boiler
274. Sundry tin wares
275. A deal dresser with 2 drawers
276. Oak paper case
277. Ten black-handled knives
278. Four ditto, 4 forks, oyster knife, 2 screw drivers and 2 corkscrews
279. Three wooden spoons, paste pin, suet chopper and skewers

280. Fish kettle and brass kettle
281. Two copper preserving pans
282. Painted flour bin
283. Set of scales and 8 weights
284. Deal kitchen table with drawer
285. Two rush-seated chairs
286. Two Windsor chairs and 1 elbow ditto
287. Set of five dish covers
288. Six smoothing irons and 1 box iron
289. Fender, 2 coal shutes, tongs and fire shovel
290. Two block-tin kettles, 1 tin funnel and a gallon can
291.

Scullery

292. Four iron saucepans, 1 steamer and frying pan
293. Three ditto, enamelled stew pan and frying pan
294. Pair of galvanised buckets
295. Ditto, ditto and tray
296. Small churn and a filter
297. Wire sieve, colander and bowl
298. Dough kiver and two paste boards
299. Tin ware and 3 baking tins
300. Plate rack
301. Water can, form and washing-up tub
302. One hair broom, 1 broom and sundries
303. Single-barrelled gun
304. Double-barrelled gun
305.

Cellar

306. Two beer barrels and a barrel stell
307. Two ditto and ditto
308. Two wine casks, sundry boxes etc.
309. Quantity of boxes

Laundry

310. Ironing board and 2 clothes horses
311. Two clothes horses
312. Stove and piping
313. Two washing trays, boxes and sundries
314. Two hearth rugs and a bird cage
315. Two ditto and two ditto
316.

Dairy and Hovel

317. Three milk tins, strainer, skimmer, butter kiver, cream pan and prints
318. Cinder sieve and washing dolly

Live Stock

319. Brown Nag Horse, very fast and with good action
320. Five hens and 1 tom
321. Six ditto and 1 ditto
322. Ten young fowls
323.

Outdoor Effects

324. Rick of meadow hay, containing about 2½ tons (to go off)
325. Stump of ditto (ditto)
326. Iron-armed dung cart with shambles

327. Spring trap (in good condition)
328. Pony trap with lamps and cushions (nearly new)
329. Set of pony harness
330. Set of gig harness
331. Ditto
332. Set of light-cart harness
333. Saddle, leathers and irons
334. Horse rug and roller
335. Pair of carriage lamps and an iron grease jack
336. Odd collars and sundries
337. A double corn bin
338. Corn bin
339. Hand saw, stable tools and brushes
340. Lawnmower by Fellows and Bates
341. Iron garden roll
342. Garden engine
343. Three watering pots and a garden chair
344. One-horse plough by Ransome
345. Pair of light harrows by Page and Whipps
346. Drag by ditto
347. Iron horse hoe
348. Turnip drill and small turnip roll
349. Root pulper by Warren
350. Winnowing machine
351. Chaff machine by Benthall
352. Wheelbarrow and half-bushel scuttle
353. Dung drag, hay knife and 2 sieves
354. Two iron poultry troughs and a 2ft-iron pig trough
355. Hen coop
356. Two ditto
357. Twenty-four-round ladder
358. Hay tub and wooden pig trough
359. Two ditto and a bucket
360. Steelyards and ball
361. Sundry tools
362. Ditto
363. Yoke and 2 buckets
364. Short ladder, sundry boxes etc.
365. Tub, sawing horse and firewood
366. Firewood
367. Heap of manure
368. Three rain water butts
369. Three ditto
370. Three ditto
371. Sundries
372. Ditto

Catalogues may be had at the Crown Hotel, Brackley, White Hart Hotel, Buckingham, Inns in the district; or off F.D. Holiday, Auctioneer, Valuer and Estate Agent, Bicester and Banbury and Chipping Norton.

T.W. Pankhurst, printer, Bicester

The original advertisement for the sale may be found in the Oxfordshire Studies Centre in the Central Library, Oxford.

Appendix Four: Inventory of Fringford Post Office and Forge, 1898

Blacksmith's Shop

Pair of blacksmith's bellows, Tuyere iron, iron water trough, 9 pairs of tongs, 1 pair of pincers, poker, shovel, 3 copper bits, quantity of iron various, pair of old steelyards, 3 new nudget chains, new chains, drilling machine. Quantity of staples and shut links, pair of scales, pair of compasses, sundries in window, iron vice, 2 old rasps, 2 old files, quantity of iron various, quantity of old bits, 8 spanners, quantity of old spanners, quantity of old horse shoes, 2 strings of washers, 11 door latches, quantity of hooks, nail tools, old castings, shoe iron, about 10cwt of old shoes. 1 square rule, 2 old ditto, and 2 straight ditto, docking irons bull ringing irons 3 shoeing boxes and tools, anvil and block, quantity of screws 3 spanners, 9 pritchells, 9 hammers, 2 sledge hammers, quantity of scrap iron, anvil and wedge block.

Second Forge

12 pairs of tongs, shovel, poker, brush, pair of circular bellows, and tuyere iron, odd shoes, 2 screw hammers, 2 spanners, 2 braces and saw, 4 cold chisels, hand vice, 2 pairs of punches, pipe tongue, 2 rasps, 184 horse shoes, iron vice, small ditto, quantity of grate screens and taps, sundries in window, quantity of washers, tin man's tools, 12 files, 2 bull's feet parers, docking iron, tooth file, 3,600 horse nails, various sizes, quantity of nuts, scrap iron, 6 nail passers, small chisel, screw driver, spoke shaver, 1 drawing knife, mandrill and bulsters.

Store Room

10 wooden rakes, quantity of wood for stales, sundries, patterns etc., old ropes and old wire, scrap iron, 150 screws and bolts, old copper boiler, quantity of nails, nail box, 32lbs of clout nails, 3 gross of frost nails, 23lbs of screw bolts, quantity of common bolts, quantity of screw bolts various, 4 dozen rubbers, 1 bundle fork stales, 26 fork stales, broom paddle and mop stales, 2 ½cwt of hoop iron, 6 new scythes, 2 sheets of tin, nest of drawers and contents, quantity of tow, 12 mowing machine knives, quantity of snap heads, sundry old nails and box, 15,000 horse nails, 2 shelves. About 2 tons of iron various, 5 galvanised sheets, 6 shovel handles, about 1¼ tons of coal, 6 spreaders, 12 x 4 ½ ft-stales, sundries.

Outside

A bay cob rising 4 years old, strong spring cart, lamps and rug, old boxes, quantity of straw, set of harness, stable tools, pig trough, hog tub and buckets, 60-gallon copper, quantity of blacksmith's coal, pig, pig trough, portable forge, sundries, old iron, ladder and 2 short ditto, 4 Scotch fir poles, 20 score of fir fagots, heap of manure, hard wood, 4 stocks of bees and patent hive, wheelbarrow, sack barrow, water tank and wheels, firewood, 2 boxes and contents, iron grease jack, 19 stamps and punches, old iron, quantity of bar and flat iron, 2 gross of roughing studs, tube expander, mandrill, 15 spring hooks, 18 galvanised ditto, 2 planes, padlock and key, 12 saw files, 5 hammer handles, 4 curry combs, 8 hoes, 7 wheat hoes, shoeing knife, engine jack, 5 iron bars, 2 cramps, hand saw, 2 bick irons, small mandrill, claw, 2 half-pound files, 8 round files, 2 square files, quantities of files, 2 shoeing rasps, grindstone and frame, 5 stales. 6 shovel stales, 4 ash whippers, iron-tooth draught rake, scythe and snathe and iron vices, 12 pairs of harness, drilling machine, 2 ratchet drills, quantity of screw bolts, 2 plough wheels, quantity of hame flats, quantity of handles, shoeing box and nails, 33 pair bits, sundries behind shoeing house door, 7ft-bar of steel, slat steel bar, sundry stocks and dies, garden tools, 4 augers, shoeing stove and piping, iron mop box, drum firewood.

The Lane Shop

Tyreing platform, quantity of coal, bellows and tuyere iron, wooden troughs and tools, anvil, bench and vice, cupboard, 3 tyreing dogs and hammer, 1 rake, stack of thorn faggots.

House Garden
2 sacks of potatoes, garden produce.

The Close
Part of a rick of meadow hay, the continuous iron fencing.

Stable
Iron hay rack.

Shoeing House
Iron manger.

Household Furniture

Bedroom No. 1
A 4ft 6in. stump bedstead, 2 cushions, flock bed, 3 flock pillows, feather bed and bolster, 4 blankets, coloured quilt, pair of sheets, 2 pieces of carpet and hearthrug, Windsor elbow chair, quantity of bed oakking, oak round table, 2 towel airers, dressing table, hair brush, carpet broom, rush seat, chair, clothes basket, blind roller, curtain rod and curtain.

No. 2
A 4ft 3in. wooden bedstead, double straw palliasse, feather bed bolster and pillow, 3 blankets and a coloured quilt, mahogany chest of drawers, painted washstand ware, towel airer, painted dressing table, swing-glass, 3 pieces of carpet, mahogany night commode, 2 rush seated chairs, roller and muslin blinds.

No. 3
Wooden bedstead, flock bed, feather bed, 2 pillows, flock bolster, 3 blankets, quilt, 2 rush-seated chairs, 3 pieces of carpet, corner washstand and ware, galvanised pan and glazed night pan, swing-glass, roller blind.

No. 4
Wooden bedstead, flock bed, 2 feather bolsters, 2 pillow, 3 blankets, 4 pieces of carpet, hearth rug, painted night commode. painted dressing table, swing-glass, French bedstead, flock bed, 4 blankets, under blanket, pair of sheets, coloured quilt, 3 cane-seated chairs, dressing table, painted chest of 5 drawers, painted washstand, mahogany swing-glass, clock, roller blind.

Linen
Pair of twill sheets, 6 pairs of linen sheets, 7 pillow cases, 8 kitchen table cloths, 14 tea cloths, 10 table cloths, 8 old tea cloths, 11 round towels, 12 chamber towels, 6 towels, 6 knife cloths, 2 small table cloths.

Passage
Piece of Brussels carpet, 2 door mats, oak coffer. In cupboard: 4 dishes and 2 vegetable dishes. Chamber ware, high wire guard.

Parlour
Tapestry carpet, mahogany pembroke table, a two-leaf oak table, pair decanters, fender and fire irons, coal hod, hassock, a two-leaf oak table and cover, quantity of books, work table, 5 old trays, 2 coloured fruits, sundry ornaments, weather glass by Ortelli, 2 roller blinds, 3 cretonne curtains, mahogany easy chair, mahogany elbow chair, 6 Windsor chairs, clock, 2 benzoline lamps, 6 stem glasses, 14 tumblers, 4 ale glasses, glass jug and dish 6 ports, 3 nip glasses, 1 stem glass, cruet stand, breakfast cruet, preserve dish, 2 glass salt cellars, 10 table, 2 dessert, 5 tea and 4 salt spoons. Set of 3 jugs, teapot, jug, glass sugar basin, glass butter dish.

Passage
Cocoa-fibre mat, a two-leaf oak table and stool, a two-leaf oak table with drawer, timepiece, a 3-tier hanging shelf, paraffin lamp, hurricane lantern.

Kitchen

Dust pan, brush, shovel, 2 brushes, hair broom, fender, fire irons, iron saucepan, iron kettle, pieces of cocoa matting, 2 elbow wheel back Windsor chairs, oak stand table, a two-leaf deal table with drawer, 5 and 1 elbow Windsor chairs, painted corner cupboard, a 30-hour clock in oak case, mahogany and oak bureau, paraffin lamp, roller blind, 2 iron curtain rods and green curtains. Iron curtain rod and pair of damask curtains, 7 old irons, 50 pieces of Cashmere soap, meat saw, wood spoon etc., 5 small lamps, quantity of knives, forks and spoons, 2 block-tin teapots, blue and white tea ware, sundry ware, 15 tea spoons, 6 spoons, shaving glass, boot jack, brass jack.

Pantry

39 packets of Cashmere soap, wine cask, 2 brown ware jars, 3 jars, jar of ketchup, 4 jars, 2 beer cans, perforated safe, 2 tins of lard, 2 baking tins, sundry ware etc., copper boiler, redware pan, three pewter plates, 2 oil tins and contents 2 barrel stills, wire egg basket.

Wash House

Salting lead and stand, copper kettle, hand bowl, wooden bowl, dinner ware, 2 pewter plates, tin bowl, deal table, clothes basket, coal hod, fish kettle, 3 iron saucepans, 2 copper boilers, 2 stools, 1½ sacks of white oats, Bradford's mangle, boot brushes etc. 4 wet hams, quantity of wet bacon.

£163 2s 9d
Add half share of stamp
  5s 0d
_____

£163 7s 9d

Valued by the undersigned at the sum of one hundred and sixty-three pounds seven shillings and ninepence inclusive of half share of stamp
F.D. Holiday
Valuer, Bicester

Bibliography

Barrington, Peter *The Changing Faces of Bicester, Book One*, 1998

Barrington, Peter and Watts, David *The Changing Faces of Bicester, Book Two*, 1999

Blomfield, J.C. *History of the Present Deanery of Bicester*, published in 8 volumes between 1882 and 1894

English, Barbara *Lark Rise and Juniper Hill: A Victorian Community in Literature and History, Victorian Studies*, Vol. 29, autumn 1985

Flaxman, Ted and Joan *Cottisford Revisited*, 1999

Greenwood, Martin *Fringford Through the Ages*, 2000

Greenwood, Martin *Villages of Banburyshire: Including Lark Rise to Candleford*, 2006

Hemery, Eric *Historic Dart, David & Charles*, 1982

Hedges, S.G. *Bicester Wuz a Little Town*, Bicester Advertiser, 1968

Horn, Pamela *North Oxfordshire Village Life: Flora Thompson and Lark Rise to Candleford*, Oxfordshire Local History, Vol. 2, No. 8, spring 1986

The Juniper Hill Mob, Limited Edition of the *Oxford Times*, July 1991, No. 57

Lands, S.J. *The Growth of Winton*, Dorset County Council, 1970

Lane, Margaret *Flora Thompson*, 1976

Lindsay, Gillian *Flora Thompson: The Story of the 'Lark Rise' Writer*, Robert Hale, 1990

Liphook Community Magazine, summer 1981, summer 1985, autumn 1986, autumn 1995

Mate, Chas. H. and Riddle, Chas. *Bournemouth 1810-1910*, Bournemouth 1910

Reed, Michael *The Buckinghamshire Landscape*, Hodder & Stoughton, 1979

Smith, J.H. *Grayshott, the Story of a Hampshire Village*, Westwood, 1978

Smith, John Owen *On the Trail of Flora Thompson Beyond Candleford Green*, 1997

Steane, John M. *The Northamptonshire Landscape*, Hodder & Stoughton, 1974

Thompson, Flora *Lark Rise to Candleford*, Penguin, 1973

Thompson, Flora *Still Glides the Stream*, Oxford University Press, 1948

Thompson, Flora *Heatherley*, published by John Owen Smith, 1998

Thompson, Flora (ed. Margaret Lane) *The Country Calendar*, Oxford University Press, 1979

Thompson, Flora *The Peverel Papers*, Century Hutchinson, 1986

Thompson, Flora *Guide to Liphook, Bramshott and Neighbourhood*, c. 1925

Trotter, W.R. *The Hilltop Writers*, Book Guild, 1996

Tudor Jones, J.S. *Headley 1066-1966: The Story of a Hampshire Parish*, 1966

Warson, Gillian R. *Fact and Fiction: Flora Thompson and the Fewcott Part Book*, 2003

Young, David S. *The Story of Bournemouth*, Hale, 1970

ed. William Page *Victoria History of the County of Buckingham*, Vol. 4, London, 1927

ed. Mary D. Lobel *Victoria History of the County of Oxfordshire, Volume VI, Ploughley Hundred*, Oxford University Press, 1959

Watts, David and Barrington, Peter *The Changing Faces of Bicester, Book Three*, 2000

Watts, David and Barrington, Peter *The Changing Faces of Bicester, Book Four*, 2001

Watts, David and Barrington, Peter *The Changing Faces of Bicester, Book Five*, 2003

Wing, William *Brief Annals of the Bicester Poor Law Union and its Component Parishes in the Counties of Oxford and Buckingham, Bicester*, 1879